Contemporary Approaches to the Study of Religion

Religion and Reason 28

Method and Theory

in the Study and Interpretation of Religion

Mouton Publishers

Berlin • New York • Amsterdam

Contemporary Approaches to the Study of Religion in 2 Volumes

edited by
Frank Whaling
University of Edinburgh

Volume II: The Social Sciences

Mouton Publishers
Berlin • New York • Amsterdam

Library of Congress Cataloging in Publication Data

Main entry under title:
Contemporary approaches to the study of religion.
(Religion and reason ; 27; 28)
Contents: v. 1. The humanities – v. 2. The social sciences.
1. Religion–Study and teaching–History–20th century
–Addresses, essays, lectures. I. Whaling, Frank, 1934–
II. Series.
BL41.C59 1983 291'.07 84–14807
ISBN 3-11-009834-2 (v. 1)
ISBN 3-11-009836-9 (v. 2)

CIP-Kurztitelaufnahme der Deutschen Bibliothek

Contemporary approaches to the study of religion :
in 2 vol. / ed. by Frank Whaling. – Berlin ; New York ;
Amsterdam : Mouton
NE: Whaling, Frank [Hrsg.]
Vol. 2. The social sciences. – 1985.
(Religion and reason ; 27; 28)
ISBN 3-11-009836-9
NE: GT

 Typesetting: Permanent Typesetting, Hong Kong. – Printing: Druckerei Hildebrand, Berlin – Binding: Lüderitz & Bauer Buchgewerbe GmbH, Berlin. Printed in Germany.

Contents

Preface

The two volumes of CONTEMPORARY APPROACHES TO THE STUDY OF RELIGION were conceived as a sequel to Jacques Waardenburg's CLASSICAL APPROACHES TO THE STUDY OF RELIGION published in 1973. Waardenburg had told the story of the development of the study of religion as an academic enterprise from its beginnings in the nineteenth century until the time of the Second World War. The aim of the present volumes is to bring the story up to date from 1945 to the present day.

It became evident that this was a mammoth task that called for the energies and abilities of more than one person and the space of more than one book. A team evolved to write two books, and these two volumes are essentially the product of a team. The team is excitingly international including as it does two scholars from Germany, one from New Zealand, three from Great Britain, two from the United States, two from Holland, and for good measure one who divides his time between Britain and the United States. Although lacking the presence of a non-western scholar, with this qualification the team is cosmopolitan and representative.

After it had been decided that this project was to be a team effort, the question remained of how recent developments in the study of religion were to be described and analysed. One possibility was to proceed historically: to begin at 1945 and to show year by year how methods and ideas had evolved. Although not impossible, this approach would have been difficult even for one person to attempt. It would, of necessity, have involved a good deal of repetition, and the likelihood of repetition would certainly have been increased through the presence of a team.

In place of a historical narrative, an alternative procedure has been adopted. Each member of the team has summarised the developments in the study of religion since 1945 in the area of his or her own expertise. In volume one, Ursula King analyses historical and phenomenological approaches, Frank Whaling looks at comparative approaches, Kees Bolle sums up studies of myths and other religious texts, Ninian Smart grapples with the scientific study of religion in its plurality, and Frank Whaling places the study of religion in its global context and looks at the relationship of the philosophy of science to the study of religion. In volume two, David Wulff investigates psychological approaches, Michael Hill, Günter Kehrer and Bert Hardin share the task of interpreting sociological approaches, Tony Jackson deals with social anthropological approaches, Jarich Oosten looks at cultural anthropological approaches, and Wouter van Beek reflects on cultural anthropology and the many functions of religion. In this way, a breadth and depth of expertise is brought to bear upon this important topic.

This does not mean that there is never any overlap of subject matter. Names such as Lévi-Strauss, Pettazzoni, Eliade, Dumézil, Wilfred Cantwell Smith, and so on, inevitably crop up in more places than one, and this is to the benefit of the whole. Our practice has been to include a bibliography after each chapter, even though some of the books appear more than once. The only exception applies to Ninian Smart's typically perspicacious small chapter. Insofar as the books on that bibliography are all found elsewhere, it has simply been left out.

Whether our age contains academic giants such as Müller, Weber, Durkheim, Jung, and the like, who loomed large in Waardenburg's work is debateable. The five modern scholars mentioned above supplemented by others such as Widengren, Zaehner, Parrinder, Berger, Smart, Panikkar, Wach, Brandon and Nasr, to name but a few, are hardly negligeable. However a feature of our age is the rapid development of varied currents in the study of religion, some of which are small yet not unimportant. It is to the credit of the members of our team that they have dealt with both the smaller and the larger streams within the wider river of their own approach, and that, while doing justice to their own area, they have not lost sight of the total field of religious studies.

I am grateful to my colleagues for their endeavour. They have brought to this project a plurality of nationalities, a plurality of methods, and a plurality of insights. This means that these two volumes are not wedded to the approach of any particular school in the study of religion, they take an overview of them all; it means that the scholars involved are flexible enough to enhance the work of a team.

The co-ordination of a team so talented and yet so scattered has inevitably led to delays, and I am grateful to my colleagues for their patience. Thanks are due also to Lamin Sanneh and John Carman of the Harvard Center for the Study of World Religions for advice and hospitality during the editing of this project. Above all I am happy to pay tribute to the unfailing help and encouragement of the General Editor of the RELIGION AND REASON series Professor Jacques Waardenburg, whose original book inspired this series of two volumes on CONTEMPORARY APPROACHES TO THE STUDY OF RELIGION, and whose advice has accompanied everything that has been done.

I

Introduction

FRANK WHALING

Edinburgh

This volume is the second in a series of two volumes that deal with contemporary approaches to the study of religion. The first dealt with contemporary approaches to the study of religion in the humanities, whereas the present work concentrates upon the social sciences. It was the original intention to include within one cover all the contemporary approaches to the study of religion. However for reasons of space this did not prove possible. This introduction therefore refers only to the contents of CONTEMPORARY APPROACHES TO THE STUDY OF RELIGION: THE SOCIAL SCIENCES. Readers are recommended to obtain the other volume which focuses on the study of religion in the humanities. Ideally these two works belong together and the introduction to volume one, while concentrating upon the humanities, gives an overview of the contents and issues in both volumes.

CONTEMPORARY APPROACHES TO THE STUDY OF RELIGION forms a sequel to Professor Jacques Waardenburg's CLASSICAL APPROACHES TO THE STUDY OF RELIGION. In that book Professor Waardenburg analysed the history of the study of religion from the time of Max Müller to the Second World War, and he also provided extracts from the writings of over forty leading scholars of the period to illustrate his analysis. That approach was possible in regard to the earlier period when the study of religion was emerging as an area of study in its own right. Lines of development were simpler and more clear-cut. By comparison the present period looks far more complicated.

Not only has the study of religion as a whole became more complex, the study of religion in each part of the whole has become more varied as well. Each particular approach to the study of religion has sown new seeds so that there is life and interest in individual methods of studying religion in their own right as well as in the contribution they make to the whole. In our first volume on the humanities we traced in depth contemporary approaches within the history and phenomenology of religion, the study of myths and texts, comparative religion, the scientific study of religion in its plurality, the philosophy of science in its relation to the study of religion, and the study of religion in its global context. In this present volume we turn our attention to the social sciences and to contemporary psychological, sociological and anthropological approaches to the study of religion.

This book is the work of a team of scholars. The days have passed when it was possible for one person alone to survey a gamut of different approaches. Seven scholars from three continents have combined their expertise to bring together the fruits of a wide range of knowledge in an integral effort. David Wulff from Massachusetts writes on the psychological approach to the study of religion, Michael Hill from Wellington New Zealand and two scholars from Tübingen in Germany Günter Kehrer and Bert Hardin write on the sociological approach to the study of religion, and two Dutch scholars Wouter van Beek of Utrecht and Jarich Oosten of Leiden team with a British scholar Tony Jackson of Edinburgh to write on the anthropological approach to the study of religion. It is appropriate that in a field of study that has become so inter-disciplinary, so international, and so inter-linked a global team of colleagues should have formed together to create this work. This international team-work may well be symbolic for the future study of religion. It will be noted that the five nations represented on this team do not include any from outside the West and, while there may be elements of regret in this circumstance, it is faithful to the so-far mainly western provenance of the social sciences and the social scientific study of religion.

Our definition of 'contemporary' is to some extent arbitrary. Our basic starting-point is 1945 which marks the end of the Second World War. There are two reasons for the choice of this date. It would be a reasonable date to choose anyway because it signifies an evident interruption in the evolution of world history, the start of the atomic age, and the signal for the onset of a new global age which holds out prospects, both horrendous and exciting, in all spheres of human endeavour. As well as being a 'watershed year' in its own right, 1945 represents the cut-off point in Waardenburg's CLASSICAL APPROACHES TO THE STUDY OF RELIGION, and this is all the more reason for starting our analysis at the end of the Second World War. In fact some of our chapters go back before 1945 in order to put contemporary developments onto a broader canvas. For example, David Wulff traces his account of contemporary approaches to the psychological study of religion with the founding fathers such as William James, and he makes the point that the two main trends within the psychological approach, the descriptive and explanatory ones, have continued from the beginning until now; likewise Kehrer and Hardin trace the main contemporary theoretical developments in the sociology of religion back to Pareto, Durkheim, Weber and Malinowski; moreover Jackson points out that social anthropological fieldwork is often begun anything up to twenty years before it is finally written up. It would be artificial to suppose that 1945 constituted a completely new departure in the study of religion or in anything else. Nevertheless for our purposes, and for good reasons, it ushers in the period of CONTEMPORARY APPROACHES TO THE STUDY OF RELIGION.

One aspect of this contemporary period is the increasing diversification of the discussion of religion within the social sciences. New movements have arisen, and debate within established movements has intensified, inside each discipline and between each discipline. Within separate nations or language groups as well as within each discipline new paths have been trod and new discussions have been begun. Even within such a relatively homogeneous group of disciplines as the social sciences there is often a wistful lack of knowledge about developments in the study of religion outside one's own discipline, and sometimes of the breadth of developments *within* one's own discipline. And if this observation is true of disciplines it is often even more true about language groups which are prone to follow directions and trends that are influenced by linguistic boundaries. Part of the contribution of this book is to bring together and put into some sort of framework and order the many and varied discussions about religion within the length and breadth of the social sciences.

This is done in two ways. Firstly, this book brings out clearly, in several places, the various strands within western scholarship. For example, Kehrer and Hardin examine American theories such as the structural-functionalism of Parsons, the sociology of knowledge of Berger, and the evolutionary model of Bellah, Dutch theories of phenomenological sociology, and German notions such as the systems theory of Luhmann, and the work of the Frankfurt School upon the sociology of religion; Jackson outlines the different approaches of the British, French and American schools within the social anthropology of religion; Wulff highlights the work of the varied elements of the American, German and French schools within the psychology of religion; Hill singles out the American, British and French contributions to the sociology of religion; Oosten indicates the ethnocentric presuppositions built into western cultural anthropology and then shows the richness and variety within the West of the 'process of confrontation, translation and communication' that constitutes the anthropological study of religion; and van Beek exhibits in a less systematic but equally effective way the inter-linking disciplinary and national cross-currents within the anthropology of religion. In the second place, the division of labour and the difference of nationalities within the team ensure that a broad coverage is given to different areas of knowledge and language groups. Thus, while ranging as widely as they wish, Kehrer and Hardin bring to bear upon their analysis a German perspective, van Beek and Oosten bring a Dutch perspective, Wulff brings an American perspective, Jackson a British perspective, and Hill a New Zealand perspective. Within the anthropology of religion, Jackson concentrates upon social anthropology, Oosten upon cultural anthropology, and van Beek upon the dialectic between society and the individual. Wulff impressively surveys the whole range of issues in the psychology of religion, while Kehrer and Hardin share with Jackson the task of summarising the wide span within sociology of religion. In this way the usual parochialism of nations and disciplines is surmounted. As we intimated earlier, the subtle parochialism of veiled western superiority is not transcended in that it assumes that western ethnocentricity will be overcome in a *western* way. However until there are more non-western social scientists of religion and more concentrated in-depth social scientific studies of non-western major religions (as opposed to primal religions) it is likely that this situation will continue and our volume reflects reasonably accurately the present academic context.

Throughout the work, in addition to the discussion of the major trends within the psychology, sociology and anthropology of religion, certain themes recur. We will review some of these themes briefly now. In the first place the question is raised of the relationship between the study of religion in general and the study of religion within the approach concerned. Are the psychology of religion, sociology of religion, and anthropology of religion part of the general study of religion, part of the disciplines of psychology, sociology, and anthropology, or equally involved in both particular disciplines and the general study of religion? In principle the latter alternative is the ideal situation wherein there is a dual involvement within the discipline concerned and the wider study of religion, and it is for this reason that we hope that readers of this volume will also read CONTEMPORARY APPROACHES TO THE STUDY OF RELIGION: THE HUMANITIES in order to locate the social scientific approaches to the study of religion within the total study of religion. At the same time it is true to say that there has been a concern to emphasise the role of the discipline concerned. This can be seen in two ways. On the one hand, a division has been made between religious psychology, sociology, and anthropology, and the psychology, sociology and anthropology of religion. In the first instance, although much useful work has been done, psychology, sociology and anthropology are placed at the service of particular religious groups. Thus 'sociologie religieuse' in France and certain elements within religious developmental psychology have, as part of their concern, the motive of helping the mission and nurture of the church in one or more of its branches. They belong therefore more properly to the orbit of Christian theology than to the social sciences. Although a number of Christian theologians have made useful contributions to the field—we may cite Troeltsche and Niebuhr as obvious examples—the social scientific study of religion cannot be subordinated to Christian theology. The wider question, on the other hand, is whether the study of religion within the social sciences is not subordinated to the concerns of the social sciences. This has been the implicit criticism of some of the phenomenologists of religion who have been at pains to emphasis the irreducible elements in religion such as the 'sense of the sacred' or the 'idea of the holy'. Is not religion subordinated to culture in cultural anthropology, to society in social anthropology and sociology of religion, and to the human psyche in psychology of religion? It would be easy to set up this discussion in terms of 'either-or', either the social sciences or religion, and as we shall see in a moment much depends upon how we define the word 'religion'. In this book careful consideration is given to social scientific theories that do attempt to explain religion, notably Marxist notions that religion is a product of the social environment and can be understood solely in socio-economic terms and Freudian notions that religion is the projection of man's psychological needs. At the other extreme, as Michael Hill points out, there are those scholars mainly within theology but occasionally within philosophy who would want to stress the transcendent elements within religion at the expense of those elements open to social scientific scrutiny. If the study of religion is conceived to be the investigation of transcendent reality conceived as God, Allah, Yahweh, Brahman, or Nirvāṇa in the major religious traditions, or the investigation of mediating foci within the major living religions such as Christ, the Qur'ān, the Torah, Ātman or Īśvara, and the Buddha or Śūnyatā, then such a study is not directly the concern of the social scientific approaches. They operate according to the principle of the 'exclusion of the transcendent,' not in the sense that the transcendent does not or need not exist but in the sense that it is not their business to investigate transcendent reality as such. As David Wulff points out the principle of the 'exclusion of the transcendent' is a negative rather than a positive injunction which leaves out of account the possible significance of the transcendent in the fundamental structure of religious consciousness, nevertheless the methodological tool of leaving aside all judgments about the existence of religion's transcendent objects, neither affirming nor denying their reality, is a useful working element in the social scientific approach. According to the principle of the division of labour a *via media* emerges whereby other disciplines within Religious Studies concern themselves with historical data, phenomenological structures, textual analysis, theological notions of transcendence, philosophical beliefs, aesthetic values, and so forth, and the social sciences are left free to make their own unique contribution to the study of religion. By being true to the techniques, methods and theories of their own disciplines, social scientists are enabled to make their maximum contribution to the study of religion in the light of their own interests. Lying behind this assumption is the notion that the social scientific approaches to religion complement one another and that together they complement the approaches toward the study of religion adapted by disciplines outside the social sciences. This notion of complementarity is implicit throughout most of this book.

In the second place the question is raised of the role played by definitions of religion. The task of defining religion is notoriously difficult, the definitions given are varied, and the types of definitions that are advanced bring other consequences in their wake. Although dealing only with the social scientific approaches to the study of religion, our contributors mention a number of definitions of religion that depart in different directions. One classical divide is that between nominal and real definitions of religion. The latter types of definition tend to reify hypothetical constructs into 'essences' that are taken to be universal, for example Spiro's definition of religion as 'belief in superhuman beings and in their power to assist or harm man'. This definition is real by contrast with Geertz's more symbolic and nominal definition of religion as 'a system of symbols which acts to establish powerful, pervasive, and long lasting moods and motivations in men by formulating conceptions of a general order of existing and clothing these conceptions with such an aura of factuality that the moods and motivations seem uniquely realistic'. In addition to the divide between nominal and real definitions, there is the further classical divide between inclusive and exclusive definitions. Inclusive definitions may define religion widely as a quantum of religiousness universally present in man *qua* man over against religion as membership of a religious community, or they may see religion in an inclusively Durkheimian manner as the need for individuals to be regulated by some shared commitment to a central set of beliefs and values (for example American civil religion), or they may comprehend traditions such as communism, humanism and nationalism as belonging to the same species as religion. By contrast exclusive definitions will attempt to sharpen the boundaries between 'religion' and 'non-religion', between conventional religious systems and central core value systems divorced from religious communities, between the capacity for self-transcendence built into man *qua* man and the practice of that self-transcendence within a religious fellowship. This debate is especially common within the sociology of religion, and it affects the way the process of secularisation is analysed. If religion is defined as belonging to a religious institution, when the institution grows or declines there is a corresponding growth or decline in religion. If religion is the religiousness that is part of man's human nature the situation is different for religion defined as religiousness cannot 'become secularised', it can only change form and expression. The chapters on sociology of religion complement each other because Hill inclines more to an exclusive definition and Kehrer and Hardin incline to a more inclusive definition of religion. Although inclusive and exclusive definitions of religion appear to be radically different, our contributors point out that scholars such as Berger and Luckmann, who diverge in this radical fashion in regard to definitions, are nevertheless able to collaborate satisfactorily, and the same applies to our contributors themselves.

Another divide within definitions of religion focuses upon definitions that relate to the individual rather than the social group. David Wulff points out that psychologists of religion tend to focus their definitions of religion upon the religiousness of the individual and especially upon the religious experiences of individuals. These in turn may be defined exclusively in terms of experience of the transcendent or divine, or more inclusively in terms of any deeply serious attitude towards the world of experience out of which emerges, however inchoately, a sense of life's meaning. Wouter van Beek, with his interest in psychological anthropology, defines religion in terms of the dialectic between the individual and the social group.

The debate about definitions of religion has significant ramifications in a number of directions. There is no one agreed definition of religion in the social sciences, but the variety of definitions serves to indicate the areas of interest and the breadth of treatment of religion in the social scientific field.

The third matter for comment relates to the scope and nature of the data involved in the social scientific approach to the study of religion. We have already touched upon this question in our reflection upon definitions. It usefully divides itself into two parts. In the first place there is the question of what kind of persons, societies and religious traditions are mainly investigated by social scientists. In the case of psychology of religion the main stress is upon the religious experience of the individual. The interest of different schools may be in the abnormal or the normal individual, abnormal piety or normal piety. In one way or another various expressions of personal religious experience and faith provide a rich mine of data to be explored by the psychologist of religion. In addition to having an interest in religious persons, the psychology of religion is also concerned to explore religious contents as found in the comparative study of religion and mythology. Thus Jungian psychology, for example, is interested in uncovering the symbols, myths and archetypes that point to the universal unconscious of mankind, and much of the psychoanalytic literature on religion focuses on religious contents (rituals, symbols, stories, movements, art, leaders, and so on) rather than individual case-studies as such. Nevertheless in most psychology of religion concern for the individual's religiousness, however defined, lies somewhere in the foreground or background, and the bulk of the sources used are to be found in the Judaeo-Christian tradition of the West although there is a small but growing interest in the other great world religions.

Social anthropology has a more obvious interest in the religion of small-scale societies, mainly those outside the industrial West. In this it is largely complementary to sociology which envinces a more obvious concern for religious communities and industrial society in the West. Traditionally the social anthropologist goes to live among the people he is investigating in order to gain field-work experience of the society in question. His basic raw material is therefore the social life and the oral tradition of particular small-scale societies. As Jarich Oosten points out, cultural anthropology too has a huge investment in the data of non-literate cultures but it is interested also in the data of literate cultures—in the major religions as well as the religions of more primal cultures. The desire of the cultural anthropologist to transcend the ethnocentricity of western culture in order to understand other religious and cultural world-views makes it more likely that he will use data from non-western cultures, both non-literate and literate. The data concerned will relate to the internal structure of religion as a cultural order and the structure of its relationships toward other cultural orders.

Sociology of religion, while having its roots in the investigation of non-western primal societies in the work of pioneers such as Durkheim, has gravitated to a greater involvement in the study of modern western religion and society. Although in principle the interests of sociology of religion are wider than the society and religion of the West, in practice much of its present research and theorising relates to the West. Whether it be the analysis of internal religious structures as in the debate on church/sect typology, the interpretation of secularisation, or even the apparently historical and multi-religious analysis by Bellah of religious evolution, the main focus of interest in much contemporary sociology of religion turns out to be the state of religion and society in the modern West.

The scope and nature of the data of religion used by social scientists therefore differ. However in one respect there is reasonable agreement. Most social scientists would focus their concern upon religious persons, groups and cultures that are contemporary in the sense that they are alive now. The primary emphasis is upon the present-day state of religion rather than the past history of religion; the main stress is upon the modern situation of religion in the West, in non-western primal religious societies, or in the other major living religions. There would appear to be a number of reasons for this preference to dwell upon the contemporary situation. One factor lies in the nature of the social sciences themselves as disciplines of recent development geared, by their proclivity for field-work and 'empirical' research, to focus upon contemporary rather than historical problems. Another factor is the rapid rise of modern communications which make it much easier for the contemporary scholar to actually visit the religious persons, groups, societies or cultures he is interested in. By getting on a plane in America or Europe (or elsewhere), by taking a train or car, scholars can visit small-scale societies, other cultures, new religious movements in the West, alternatively they can see them on television or video, and they can transfer the results of those visits onto computers. A third factor is the increasing pace of religious change in the contemporary world which tends to focus attention more upon the present situation. The entry of eastern religions into the West, the rise of new religious movements in the West and indigenous churches in Africa and new religions in Japan, the appearance of cargo cults and millenarian groups, the influence of religion upon independence movements in other cultures, worldwide mobility and emigration since the Second World War, the interacting dialectic of social, technological and religious change—these have all conspired to give greater prominence to the notion of religious change. And even when religion was viewed as a force strengthening social cohesion and integration as in American civil religion or in primal societies, the general background remained one of incipient or actual change. A fourth factor is the dynamic flux operating within western society itself and within religious life in the West. Although a western social scientist may be neutral, uncommitted and value-free in his attempt phenomenologically to get inside the world-view of a small-scale society, another culture, or another religious person, the process of confrontation, translation and communication involved in conveying that world-view has potential repercussions for present western society and religion which are part of a moving rather than a static picture.

The question of the scope and nature of the data involved in the social scientific study of religion can be seen within a second perspective. Within the social sciences, and especially within psychology and sociology, there is an increasing use of quantificatory data. This point is brought out particularly by Wulff and Hill. In surveys that are neither exclusivistic nor reductionistic, Wulff shows how, in relation to the psychological approach, self-observation, self-report, open-ended questionnaires, interviews, standard questionnaires, projective techniques, naturalistic observation, 'scientific' experimentation, and the analysis of historical and comparative materials are all viable, and Hill shows how, in relation to the sociological approach, the sample survey, standard questionnaires, interviews, census statistics, the statistics of religious communities, historical data, and content analysis are all helpful. In general the use of statistics and quantificatory data are becoming more important in social scientific investigations of religion. Two comments are apposite here. On the one hand it is already clear that computers and other electro-micronic devices are becoming increasingly relevant in scholarship especially in the sciences. The use of computers tends to orient research in more quantitative directions. How will their increasing use affect the social scientific study of religion? What kind of knowledge can they store? By what criteria should this knowledge be researched? What is the relationship between computer information and other kinds of information? This book points in the direction of complementarity. Just as there are different complementary approaches to the study of religion, so there are different and complementary kinds of data. Quantificatory data are not opposed to but complementary with other species of data. However it is important that increasing reflection should be given to the significance of ever-increasing card-indexes, standardised reporting systems, quantificatory analyses, data banks, computer research and the like. The significance of the information revolution for the study of religion should not go unrecognised, and mature judgment upon the advantages and disadvantages of that revolution for the study of religion should not be lost by default. This leads on to our second comment. The social sciences have traditionally provided a bridge between the natural sciences on the one hand and the humanities on the other hand. As well as utilising methods and data that are more scientific in nature, the social sciences share with the humane sciences the intuition that the study of religion has to do with man, and that the psychology, sociology and anthropology of religion involve the study of religious *man* in his psychological, social and cultural dimensions.

A fourth matter for comment is the relative lack of daring comparative models and theory formations in the contemporary social scientific study of religion. During the classical period of religious studies outlined by Waardenburg, social scientists, especially anthropologists, were fertile in the formation of theories about religion. Nowadays there is no one dominant theory of religion among the social scientists, nor is there, with one or two exceptions, the desire to generate general theories of religion. General theories of religion require wide powers of abstraction from particular contexts, and the social scientists have generally been more content to investigate the multiplicity of particular contexts than to venture out onto the waters of abstract conceptualisation. As Oosten points out, Inuit religion consists of the religion of western, central and eastern Inuit; the religion of the central Inuit in turn consists of the religion of the Netsilik Inuit, the Iglulik Inuit, and the Caribou Inuit; the religion of the Iglulik Inuit in turn consists of the religion of the Iglulingmiut, the Aivilingmiut, etc. The scope of the treatment and the theory can be narrowed or widened according to the interests of the researcher, and if it is widened enough it may, in the thought of a Lévi-Strauss, extend to cover mankind. Generally the stress has been upon the particular rather than the general, the concrete rather than the abstract. If comparisons were to be made in cultural anthropology, it was felt to be a more responsible and controlled procedure to compare groups that shared a common history or culture rather than to attempt comparisons of groups that were unrelated historically or culturally. The notable exception, of course, is Lévi-Strauss who is treated at different places in this book. He points out that it is the fundamental structures of the mind and linguistics that direct us back to particular comparative examples of actions, myths, words, or religious phenomena; theory leads to comparison; one deducts from the general to the particular; empirical phenomena are means rather than ends. Lévi-Strauss's main field work took place in South America but he attempts to show how the structural relationships built into the myths of South America extend to myth in a wider setting and refer back ultimately to the universal logical structure built into the human mind itself. By contrast the social anthropologists, like the majority of the cultural anthropologists, would be chary in making the leap from particular contexts to multiple contexts, from particular societies to wide groups of societies. Their concern for mainly non-urban tribal societies, for all the aspects not just the religious aspect of a society, for living societies, and for field-work in particular societies makes them cautious of broad theories and hermeneutical assumptions.

Sociology too has fought shy of broad comparative models during our period. Weber remains the great name in this regard but he was well before our time. Joachim Wach is the most obvious exception as a comparative sociologist but his interests were wider than those of sociology of religion and he would rank as a hermeneutist, a comparative religionist, and a phenomenologist as well. The comparative work done in church/sect typology is relatively limited in scope restricted as it is to Christian groups. The sociologists too have been cautious about advancing full-blown theories of religion.

Psychologists also have been more content with short-range than with long-range theories. Jungian psychology is an obvious exception to this with its theorising about dominant motifs such as the archetype, the universal unconscious, and the significance for the 'self' of religious myths and symbols. However it is significant that many of the leading figures in the Eranos Circle dominated by Jung, such as Buber, Scholem, Suzuki, Zimmer, James, Rhys Davids, Zaehner, Pettazzoni, Tucci, Eliade, Kerényi, Daniélou, Heiler, Neumann, van der Leeuw, van der Post, Campbell, Goodenough, Radin and Tillich were scholars of religion in a wider sense rather than psychologists of religion as such. Extensions of Jung's work, such as Zimmer's work on Indian religion, Campbell's *Masks of God* on mythology, and Neumann's work on *The Great Mother* would normally be situated outside the strict province of psychology of religion. It would be true to say also that there is some overlap between the concerns of Otto in his concept of the holy, Heiler in his work on prayer, and van der Leeuw in his work on the essence of religion and concerns of the psychology of religion. But again they would rank as phenomenologists, and also as theologians, rather than as psychologists of religion in the narrower sense. The wider theorising has been pursued by phenomenologists and comparative religionists more than by psychologists.

However, as we intimated earlier, this has left social scientists free to intensify the research and discussion within each specialisation, to throw up new "seeds" and themes for research, and to apply virtually any of their methods and short-range theories to the study of specific sets of religious data. Hence the increasingly complex involvement of the social sciences in the study of religion and the variety of trends that are outlined in this book. To list but the main ones: the psychology of religion has worked on measures of religiosity, Freudian and Jungian themes, the diversity of religious experience (Allport), peak experiences (Maslow), transpersonal mysticism, religious development, ego psychology (Erikson), object-relations theory, the 'new narcissism' (Kohut), soul-making psychology (Hillman), experimental introspection (Dorpat School), the piety of different age-groups, conversion, ecstatic religious phenomena, the physiology of mysticism, religious education, religious projection, and so on; social anthropology has worked on the nature of primal religious thought, totem and taboo, belief systems, primal cosmologies and cultures, rituals, symbols, myths, spirit mediums and possession, magic, purity and pollution, rites de passage, millenary cults, shamanism, and so on; cultural anthropology has worked on religion as a cultural order, how religious concepts, emotions and experiences are shaped by the cultural order, how religious beliefs, practices and institutions explain the origin of and preserve the cultural order, the role of myths, symbols and rituals, the relation of religion to other cultural orders, the contrast between literate and non-literate religions, the relationship between great traditions and little traditions, the role of language and religious concepts, the relationship between ritual and ethical practice, and so on; and sociology of religion has worked on religious demography, the relation between economic activity and religious profession, the study of sectarian movements, the process of secularisation, Marxist-Leninist theories of religion, church/sect typology, the different types of religious organisation, studies of religion as an integrating force in society, studies of religion as a force for social change, new religious movements, the relationship between the sociology of religion and the sociology of deviance, religious sociology, the problem of death and suffering, religious evolution, the work of the Frankfurt School, the system theory of Luhmann, sociology of religion and the sociology of knowledge, Mol's work on the relationship of religion to differentiation and identity, and so on. A catalogue of some of the main trends in the social scientific study of religion brings out clearly the great variety of work that is being done. It also highlights the need within the social scientific study of religion and the study of religion as a whole for a new integration. Part of the aim of our two volumes is not only to indicate the variety of research interest in the various areas of the study of religion but also to relate the different approaches to each other in a fresh integration. The notion of complementarity between varied approaches is a helpful one, but accompanying it is the need for an overview of the whole field. There is the need for a fresh integration and in our two books on CONTEMPORARY APPROACHES TO THE STUDY OF RELIGION we have attempted to bring out the multiplicity of approaches and to indicate ways in which they can be viewed as a whole.

A fifth matter for comment is the personal stance of the social scientist who studies religion and the notion of truth that he brings with him. It would be futile to suggest that the personal equation has no bearing upon the questions a scholar asks, the theories and methods that he employs to answer them, or the conclusions that he draws. After all, even interpreting a graph requires some personal input from the scholar. One's own religious position, whether it be strong, weak, or negative is not irrelevant; one's own temperament, ability, upbringing, motives, and personal vision have some influence upon one's academic work. The atheism of a Freud or a Marx is clearly a factor within the explanatory theories of religion they propound, and the Christian commitment of an Evans-Pritchard is not irrelevant in the sphere of scholarship. The whole question of 'truth' and 'truth claims' in religion is extremely intricate. It operates at a number of different levels. It is often superficially discussed. In this book it is brought out in a number of different ways. The point is made that much depends upon what we mean by 'truth claims'. Do they refer to the researcher himself, the discipline concerned, or the people being researched? Are they personal, methodological, or ontological? Are they general or specific, 'first-order' or 'second-order'? Personal religious truth for the researcher may involve commitment within a particular religious community, an ontological commitment outside any particular religious community, agnosticism, or atheism. Truth claims within a discipline may refer to descriptive truth relating to empirical research, or hermeneutical truth relating to the persuasiveness of a wider theory. Truth claims concerning religion range from the admission that religion is a present sociological or psychological reality which is destined to wither away when mankind reaches economic or psychological maturity (Marx and Freud), the notion that religion is a present sociological and psychological reality which is destined not to wither away because these realities are permanent, and the supposition that religion is a transcendent reality that the social scientist can only observe at a sociological or psychological level. The truth claims of others may be viewed as being relatively true for them, as being sociologically or psychologically true but philosophically mistaken, as being part of a wider genus of religious truth, or as being sociological or psychological projections. The permutations are endless. In general social scientists have tolerated but not enthusiastically welcomed two extremes: the interpolation of a positive religious commitment into research whereby religious sociology, psychology and anthropology became aids to mission, religious education, or institutional renewal, and the interpolation of a negative religious commitment into research whereby religion, however defined, was explained away. The mainstream tendency is to employ what the phenomenologists would call *epoché*, to put into brackets one's own religious convictions or lack of them in order to understand the sociological, psychological, or anthropological religious phenomena one is examining. Equally the social scientist will not normally view other religious communities or the religious experiences of others as true or false, superior or inferior. He or she will try to understand what the religion of the people being studied means to them. Increasingly, in order to overcome a western ethnocentric parochialism that is cultural as well as religious, the second phenomenological category of *Einfühlung* may come into play. This involves the attempt to empathise with those one is studying and to see the universe through their eyes. A stance of neutrality may be empathetic according to this viewpoint. By contrast with other disciplines within the study of religion, wherein *epoché* and *Einfühlung* may also be used, the process of translation and communication that inevitably follows is conveyed in sociological, psychological and anthropological rather than in historical, comparative, philological or other terms. It is difficult to generalise about personal stances and truth claims but there is evidence, brought out in different ways in the chapters of this book, that personal religious positions (those of the researcher and the researched) fit into this kind of framework, and that methodological positions emanating from religious commitment or religious alienation are departures from this framework rather than themselves the framework.

Finally, what of the future? Our contributors are naturally cautious in regard to future prognostications. The drama in which we are involved is a moving one rather than a static one. The social scientific disciplines are developing, western society and other societies are developing, the study of religion in general is developing. Prediction is hazardous. Nevertheless in the light of the perspectives of this book we hazard the following hopes. In the first place, close contacts will remain between the disciplines of social and cultural anthropology, psychology and sociology and the study of religion. Theories and modes of research in these disciplines will continue to be applied to religious phenomena, and new developments in these disciplines will open up new avenues of exploration in the study of religion. There is a sense in which the study of religion is one aspect among other studies within social and cultural anthropology rather than a separate speciality in its own right and therefore cross-fertilisation of research would happen in anthropology anyway. With sociology and psychology of religion the relationship with the parent disciplines is not quite so intimate, and a greater autonomy is possible. Nevertheless inter-relationship is likely to be the order of the day in these disciplines as well. Secondly it seems likely, partly as a result of books such as this, that a greater awareness will arise among social scientists of religion of the full sweep of research in their own particular area both in regard to the contributions from different language groups and in regard to the contributions from varied schools of thought. Also possible is a greater mutual awareness within the social sciences of religion in general of the mutual contribution that each particular discipline can make to the social scientific study of religion. Already there is a growing interest for example in social psychology and psychological anthropology, and the chapter in this book by van Beek is a portent of the potential mutual fecundation between the psychology of religion with its greater interest in the individual and the sociology and anthropology of religion with their greater interest in society. Thirdly, the time seems to be propitious, although this does not mean that it will necessarily happen, for more long-range and broader theories to emerge. The stress upon field-work or first-hand research has built up the amount of data available to social scientists of religion. The increasing use of computers will allow this to be marshalled more swiftly. The situation is arising where, with the principle exception of the work of

Lévi-Strauss, we have data in search of organising theorums. The time is ripe for more theory-formation to emerge. At the same time field-work and first-hand research will continue whether more imaginative hermeneutical patterns emerge or not. Fourthly there is a growing awareness that the study of religion in general forms a field of studies in which the social sciences have an important part to play. Although the rigours of academic specialisation raise obvious barriers to social scientists informing themselves in the wider history of religions, general studies of religion are paying more attention to contributions from the social sciences and there are signs that the interest is mutual. Our two volumes on CONTEMPORARY APPROACHES TO THE STUDY OF RELIGION are intended to feed into this wider concern for the broader study of religion. The principle of complementarity of approaches, and the potentially more universal application of the phenomenological devices of *epoché* and *Einfühlung*, offer useful connecting links by means of which the study of religion may proceed towards a wider integration.

The major aim of this volume is to offer to social scientists of religion an overview of their area both in general and in particular so that they may engage in comprehensive and critical reflection upon the various elements of their task from the setting up of goals to ultimate interpretations. The second aim of this volume is to supplement the first volume of this series CONTEMPORARY APPROACHES TO THE STUDY OF RELIGION: THE HUMANITIES to the end that social scientists of religion and other scholars of religion together may advance the study of religion as an inter-disciplinary, international, and inter-cultural enterprise of the highest importance in our emerging global world.

2

Psychological Approaches

DAVID M. WULFF

Wheaton College Norton, Mass.

The realm of religious experience and practice is indisputably one of fundamental psychological importance. Just as psychologists who would truly understand living human beings must take into account the religious dimension, so scholars of religion seeking to comprehend the extraordinary diversity of religious expression must recognize the pervasive influence of the psyche's structure and dynamics. The psychology of religion ought therefore to be a thriving enterprise, fostered by the interest and collaboration of a large number of variously trained scholars.

The situation is in fact quite otherwise. Throughout its erratic development, the field has been widely neglected if not also disparaged, and even today many psychologists and scholars of religion look upon it as a field unworthy of serious interest. Psychologists, the evidence suggests, tend to be indifferent or antagonistic toward religious faith and its expressions, and many apparently see no need to include in their investigations what to them is unimportant. Scholars of religion, on the other hand, fear that psychological analysis of religion will likely be insensitive and reductionistic; some even declare it to be irrelevant, regardless of its spirit or quality.

In this climate of indifference and distrust a small number of scholars have nonetheless specialized in the psychological study of religion. The field arose as a self-conscious endeavor late in the nineteenth century, the offspring chiefly of liberal Protestant theology and the aspiring, newly independent discipline of empirical psychology. In America, where the psychology of religion is said to have been founded, it has been pursued most often by psychologists, typically of Protestant background and largely sympathetic to the religious life. In the German-speaking world, a majority of the field's proponents have been Protestant theologians or historians of religion; Freud and Jung are, of course, important exceptions. In French-speaking countries, religiously uncommitted specialists in psychopathology early played a leading role, but today Catholic psychologists interested in the dynamics of normal religious faith are at center stage.

Although the American, German, and French literatures have to this day remained relatively discrete, they show notable parallels in their development. In each are found two fundamental trends: a *descriptive* one, which emphasizes sympathetic phenomenological analysis, commonly undertaken to aid religious education and pastoral care; and an *explanatory* one, which seeks to uncover the causal connections presumed to be responsible for the experience and conduct of religious persons, some of whom, at least, are thought to be deluded. Understandably, the descriptive approach has been preferred by religiously committed researchers, whereas the explanatory one has been advanced chiefly by outsiders.

These radically different agenda are undoubtedly a factor in the psychology of religion's precarious status: the descriptive trend suggests to some psychologists that the field is not a science but merely a branch of practical theology and apologetics; the explanatory trend, on the other hand, confirms for many scholars of religion that the psychologist is less interested in illuminating the religious life than in destroying it. These suspicions, in combination with the radically disruptive effects of the two world wars as well as certain intellectual developments hostile to the field, in both theology and psychology, eventually led to the field's decline on both sides of the ocean—in the 1920s in America and the 1930s in Europe.

Trends in Present-Day Psychology of Religion

Today, all three literatures are undergoing revival. On the one hand, reevaluation and even reprinting of some of the early works evinces growing recognition that there is much to be learned from the scholarship of the inaugural period. On the other hand, a considerable variety of new studies have appeared, employing a broad range of recently developed methods and insights. The literature in fact has burgeoned dramatically since World War II, especially in America.

The American Literature

Discerning trends in this literature is greatly complicated by the diversity of topics that have been subsumed under the rubric 'psychology of religion.' The outcome, as Capps, Ransohoff, and Rambo (1976) observe, is a field that appears hopelessly diffuse. Some scholars, such as Meissner (1961), prefer to label the literature as a whole 'psychology *and* religion,' reserving the *of* variant for those studies that employ psychological theories and methods to illumine specific religious phenomena. The remaining works would fall, then, under such topic areas as pastoral psychology, religious education, research on religious professionals, and dialogue between theology and psychology. The trend analysis that Capps and his associates carried out on the basis of their broadly comprehensive though somewhat idiosyncratic bibliography of chiefly American works reveals that six of the eight top-ranking subdimensions fall outside the more strictly defined psychology of religion. Moreover, for the period from 1950 to 1970, these subdimensions show a sharper increase than the less sectarian and applied ones.

The diffuseness of the literature on psychology and religion reflects the diversity of contributors who are drawn to it. Psychologists, psychiatrists, anthropologists, historians of religion, theologians, and religious educators, among others, bring with them widely varying backgrounds, assumptions, and interests. Furthermore, as Strommen

(1971) points out, the typical contributor makes but a single, incidental incursion into the field, commonly without a guiding theory or hypothesis. Rarely, observe Capps and his colleagues, do contributors demonstrate familiarity with more than a single area of research.

Within the psychology of religion proper, one may discern two outstanding trends in the work of American investigators. Among those trained in the research methods of contemporary social science, on the one hand, there is a strong tendency to emphasize quantitative research. The first task of such an approach is the development of a measure of religiosity, which most researchers today agree is multidimensional. One may then seek to establish piety's correlates by calculating the degree of relation between one's scales of religiosity and established measures of other variables, including various social attitudes, personality traits, and demographic factors (Argyle and Beit-Hallahmi 1975). Research of this type is featured in the *Journal for the Scientific Study of Religion*, a publication sponsored by the Society for the Scientific Study of Religion, an organization founded in 1949 by a group of sociologists and psychologists. It also appears regularly in the *Review of Religious Research* and sporadically in a wide range of specialized psychology and sociology journals.

To many scholars of religion, on the other hand, elaborate statistical analysis of questionnaire data seems both unnecessarily mystifying and inevitably trivial. Far more promising from their point of view are the depth psychologies of Freud, Jung, and their successors. The psychiatric approach to religion tends also to emphasize the dynamic viewpoints of these Europe-derived theories. Anthropologists occasionally draw on them as well. The resulting literature is widely scattered throughout journals of religion, psychiatry, and clinical psychology, among others. The viewpoint is represented, too, in a variety of books, many of them critical investigations or interpretations of Freud or Jung (e.g., Homans 1970, 1979; Philp 1956, 1958), but an occasional one using depth psychology as a tool of analysis (Campbell 1959–1968, Carstairs 1957; O'Flaherty 1980). Both the depth-psychological and the quantitative approaches, as the references here may suggest, are current in the British literature as well.

A third, somewhat less obvious trend in American scholarship also has roots, often unrecognized, in European thought. Prominent humanistic psychologists such as Gordon Allport (1950), Erich Fromm (1950), and Abraham Maslow (1964) not only have articulated an appealingly positive model of human nature that more or less accords with liberal theology but also have written small, widely read books on psychology and religion. Allport in particular has been influential. On the one hand he has restated and developed several of James's (1902) themes, emphasizing anew the diversity of religious experience, distinguishing mature from immature forms, and defending the value of mature religious faith. On the other hand Allport has contributed two widely used scales to the correlational literature: the Study of Values, based on Spranger's typology, and the Religious Orientation scale, which distinguishes intrinsic and extrinsic attitudes. Allport's approach to religion, like that of other humanistic psychologists, is essentially descriptive and typological rather than explanatory.

A significant outgrowth of Maslow's reflections on peak experiences is yet another trend, broadly labeled transpersonal psychology. Interested as they are in mystical experience, meditation, and other altered states of consciousness, the transpersonal psychologists have naturally turned to the various religious traditions, especially Eastern ones, for insight into transcendent, egoless experience. Related to the human potential movement, transpersonal psychology aspires not only to nurture exceptional individual development but also radically to transform society (Boucouvalas 1980). Seeming at times to be more a new religious movement than a disinterested scholarly discipline, transpersonal psychology has nonetheless inspired a corpus of research useful to a comprehensive psychology of religion (e.g., Tart 1969).

A final trend of note likewise lies on the boundaries of the psychology of religion, strictly defined. From the beginning, contributors to this field have actively sought to aid religious education by studying the course of religious development, noting especially the capacities and needs of each age group and making recommendations for successfully guiding individuals into a life of (usually Christian) faith. Today such research has grown far more sophisticated, drawing on advances in research methods and developmental theory. This voluminous literature is helpfully reviewed by various authors in Strommen's (1971) handbook on religious development. Among the studies they cite, British educator Ronald Goldman's (1964) investigation of the development of religious thinking deserves special mention for its careful design, rich findings, and the import of its author's recommendations for a child-centered religious education. A recent descriptive and normative study by James Fowler (1981) is likewise well grounded in empirical research and will doubtless be highly influential. Drawing on the seminal work on faith of Wilfred Smith (1963) and the developmental thinking of Piaget, Erikson, and Kohlberg, Fowler found evidence in his interview data for six sequential stages of faith, ranging from the intuitive-projective faith of the young child to the universalizing, self-transcending faith of the rare person of full maturity.

Excellent though some of the recent research on religious development is, its normative character may well trouble those who aspire to a strictly objective psychology of religion that is free of sectarian concerns. Yet such concerns are pervasive in the field as a whole. One sees them reflected, for example, in the prophetic spirit of the research on prejudice in the churches; in the articles of the *Journal of Psychology and Theology*, which are expected to be consistent with the Evangelical Christian point of view; and in the curious paucity of negative findings in the research reports of the practitioner-researchers of Transcendental Meditation. Evidence of various kinds demonstrates that in fact persons interested in the psychology of religion or fields allied with it are likely to describe themselves as religious, and indeed, many have had a theological education. It is apparent that, for many contributors, involvement in the psychology of religion is a direct expression of a personal religious commitment.

Occasionally, of course, the opposite situation holds true: the psychology of religion also serves as a forum for the religiously hostile to attack piety and its expressions. Perhaps best known is Freud's reduction of religion to infantile wish-fulfillment. British analyst Ernest Jones, one of Freud's most faithful disciples, channeled his own, violent atheism into a series of papers that blithely banalize some of the Christian tradition's most treasured symbols. American psychologist George Vetter (1958), after disdainfully documenting the sorry side of the Christian tradition, accounts for its beliefs and rituals through a simple associationist theory of learning. Less sweeping but no less incisive are some of the criticisms voiced by the humanistic psychologists.

No doubt Smith and Fowler would be right in pointing out that *every* psychology of religion—indeed, any scholarly effort whatsoever—is a statement of faith, an expression of the coherence and meaning that its author perceives in the world. It becomes a question, then, of the degree to which the dimensions of that faith set limits upon one's endeavor. The psychologist of religion must steer a course between two great dangers: the Scylla of apologetics and the Charybdis of psychologism. Where the psychology of religion has not simply become an instrument of a particular, often narrow theological outlook it has too often claimed the last word on religious truth. Even among those who successfully avoid these twin dangers, parochialism in psychological conception or religious perspective is so common as to be the rule.

Warning long ago against these and other dangers, Schaub (1926) observes that the diversity in viewpoint and method evident even then might be read equally as a sign of immaturity and promising vitality. That diversity remains to this day, as illustrated by Vande Kemp's (1976) survey of American college courses on or related to the psychology of religion. Given the paucity of introductory textbooks and the tendency of their authors to be methodologically or religiously sectarian,[1] teachers of such courses usually resort to a selection of works available in paperback. Among her respondents Vande Kemp found astonishingly little consensus on basic reading in this area. Of 49 such courses, only 17 required James's acknowledged classic *The Varieties of Religious Experience*, 14, Freud's *The Future of an Illusion*, and 10, Allport's *The Individual and His Religion*; only 8 other titles were chosen by 4 or more of the 49 instructors. The great majority of these courses, furthermore, were taught in religion departments, presumably by persons relatively untrained in contemporary psychology's theories and methods. Psychologists, on the other hand, are almost invariably unschooled in the history and theory of religion. Representatives of either group, of course, may exhibit parochialism within their own domain.

The German Literature

The prominence of Freud in Vande Kemp's findings is a reminder of the major, even leading role that European perspectives have come to play in the American psychology of religion. The importance internationally of the depth psychologies of Freud and Jung is underscored in a trend analysis carried out by the late Danish theologian and psychologist of religion Villiam Grønbaek (1970). Using 24 'important' books in the psychology of religion published in America and Europe between 1950 and 1967, Grønbaek found that the following names occurred most frequently and in this order: (1) William James, (2) Sigmund Freud, (3) Gordon Allport, (4) Werner Gruehn, (5) Edwin Starbuck, (6) Carl Jung, (7) Karl Girgensohn, (8) Philipp Lersch, (9) André Godin, and (10) Rudolph Otto. It is striking, first of all, that the top three contenders in Grønbaek's list are the same as those Vande Kemp found. It is telling, moreover, that six of Grønbaek's list of ten are from the German literature; three others are Americans—all of whom had studied in Europe—and one, André Godin, is a Belgian who has published in both French and English. If the psychology of religion was first set into motion in America, it would appear at present to have its intellectual center of gravity in Europe.

Freud's views on religion, expressed in a series of books and papers (e.g., 1913, 1927, 1939) and echoed in the writings of a number of his disciples, are well enough known to require only the briefest summary here. Religious beliefs and practices, he said, are rooted in the fears and wishes of childhood, foremost those that constitute the Oedipus complex. God the father is a re-creation of the omniscient and omnipotent father of infancy, who first inspired the love and fear that characterize the religious devotee's attitude toward the divine. The irrationality of religion's motives and the repression that keeps hidden its all-to-human origins are betrayed, Freud argued, by the air of inviolable sanctity that surrounds religious ideas and by the compulsive qualities of sacred rites reminiscent of neurotic 'ritual.'

The literature inspired by Freud's writings on religion has today grown to enormous proportions, easily exceeding a thousand books and articles in German, English, French, and a number of other languages

(Beit-Hallahmi 1978, Meissner 1961, Nase and Scharfenberg 1977, Spiegel 1972). At first this literature consisted chiefly of elaborations or criticisms of the themes that Freud enunciated. Over time, however, increasing attention was given to pre-Oedipal elements in religion, to religious traditions and phenomena neglected by Freud, and to the potentially constructive character of the psychoanalytic critique. Today, major revisions in psychoanalytic theory have brought in their train new and essentially positive efforts to clarify the psyche's role in religion. Foremost among these are Erik Erikson's (1958, 1969, 1977) studies from the viewpoint of ego psychology; a number of works from the perspective of object-relations theory (e.g., Guntrip 1969, Henderson 1975, Rizzuto 1979); and a growing international literature inspired by the 'new narcissism' of the late Chicago psychoanalyst Heinz Kohut (Heimbrock 1977, Homans 1979, Kakar 1978, Randall 1976, Spiegel, 1978). Also noteworthy is the spate of critical studies advocating dialogue between theology and psychoanalysis (e.g., Homans 1968, Müller-Pozzi 1975, Preuss 1971, Scharfenberg 1968, 1972, Zahrnt 1972). As Meerwin (1971) points out, however, the invitation to dialogue has come, with few exceptions, from theologians, not psychoanalysts.

Although Jungian psychologists may be no more inclined than the Freudians to initiate exchange with theologians, analytical psychology's fundamental interest in religious symbols guarantees a continuing and explicit basis for dialogue. In sharp contrast to Freud, with whom he was associated for a limited period of time, Jung argues that religion is an essential psychological function that one neglects only at considerable risk.

Underlying the personal unconscious, according to Jung, is a deeper-lying region, the collective unconscious, out of whose depths arise the myths and symbols that constitute humanity's religious traditions. Over millennia of time, Jung hypothesizes, recurrent experiences have gradually formed the structural elements of the collective unconscious, the archetypes, which have come to serve as the basis for recognizing and experiencing anew the persons and situations that compose human reality. In the individual psyche the archetypes are at first wholly unknown and undifferentiated. With time, however, as a result of external events as well as natural inner tendencies, the archetypes tend to be projected into an indefinite variety of corresponding images, among the most important of which are the various religious symbols. By means of these images, the individual gradually differentiates and comes to terms with the archetypes, which represent both dangers and opportunities in the human situation. Complementary to differentiation is the tendency toward integration, toward the equilibrium and wholeness that is represented by the archetype of the self and its multifarious images, including the Buddha and Christ.

In the past, says Jung, the process by which one moves toward the actualization of the self, the individuation process, was directed and promoted above all by religious rituals and teachings. An understanding of the content of these traditions is thus essential if one is to grasp, as Jung and his disciples sought to do, the dynamics of this fundamental psychic activity. The rather considerable international literature that is the outcome of this effort, along with the responses of theologians and other scholars, is helpfully reviewed by Heisig (1973) in an exhaustive and highly critical survey of 442 books, chapters, and articles. The bibliography to Hummel's (1972) comparative study of analytical psychology and theological anthropology, though limited to the German literature, is also valuably comprehensive.

Although Jung's psychology has not yet stimulated the multitude of revisions that Freud's has prompted, the work of James Hillman, formerly the Director of Studies at the C.G. Jung Institute in Zurich, deserves mention here as a promising further development. Hillman advocates an 'archetypal psychology' that is chiefly concerned with 'soul-making,' that is, with the nurturing of the deepest possibilities of our natures. By 're-visioning' psychology, Hillman seeks to free the soul from partial identifications—most notably with the heroic ego—and to foster the soul's life through a non-interpretive understanding of the imaginal process. Among the soul's diverse images are the Gods, and thus psychology, if it is to be genuinely one of depth, must be religious and theistic—polytheistic, in fact, given the soul's 'native polycentricity' (Hillman 1975: 167)—though not in any literal sense. Such a psychology, Hillman adds in direct criticism of Jung, must also be wary of any literal understanding of its own concepts and techniques, so that what in reality are archetypal structures in process are mistaken for universal axiomatic laws. Largely ignored just as Jung's work has been by academic psychologists, Hillman's archetypal psychology is gaining increasing attention from scholars of religion (Moore 1980).

An Austrian and a Swiss, respectively, Freud and Jung retain to this day their leading positions of influence within the German psychology of religion. Independent of their work, however, and sometimes in opposition to it, is an equally significant descriptive literature, contributed by both psychologists and scholars of religion. In the seven volumes of the revived *Archiv für Religionspsychologie* published between 1962 and 1978, Freud and Jung are hardly more frequently cited than Karl Girgensohn (1921) and his student Werner Gruehn (1960), both Protestant theologians renowned for applying Oswald Külpe's method of systematic experimental introspection to religious experience. Although Girgensohn and his associates, collectively known as the Dorpat school of religious psychology, maintain that their 'experimental' method sets their program apart from all others, they share with other descriptive investigators a reliance on self-observation, an emphasis on individual uniqueness, and a desire to foster a mature religious life.

Members of the Dorpat school presented to a variety of subjects a series of religious stimuli—most often hymns, poems, or brief, striking sentences. The subjects were asked to report as accurately as possible their experience of these materials. In his own classic study, Girgensohn (1921) concluded that religious experience is not simply a vague or undefinable feeling, but that it consists, rather, of two essential elements: (1) intuitive thoughts of the divine that are recognized or accepted as one's own, and (2) the personal conviction that the object of these thoughts constitutes an unquestionable reality. The religious experience is marked, Girgensohn also observes, by certain transformations of the self. In proportion to the advancement of the experience, the self undergoes enlargement and intensification, to the point, in exceptional cases, of becoming extinguished as it merges with the divine.

Occasionally modified to accommodate a more diverse group of subjects, the Dorpat school's method was assiduously employed for more than a decade by an international group of scholars, including Grønbaek. World War II, however, drastically curtailed the work of the school, and today it is considered by many to be nothing more than a curious historical phenomenon. Its program is nonetheless still actively advocated and widely discussed (Bolley and Clostermann 1963, Gins 1976, Godin 1959, Müller-Pozzi 1975, Vëto 1971).

Most descriptive psychologists of religion have considered a range of methods to be more or less equally valid, so long as religious experience remains well in view. Their common goal is to 'understand' (*verstehen*) religious experience, not by means of reductive causal explanation, but by 'reliving' the experience empathically, in order to discern the meaningful connections that give structure and coherence to the human world as it is lived by each individual. Valuable in itself, such an understanding is thought to provide a vital foundation for all further scholarly study of religion. Some emphasize as well its potential for enriching individual religious lives.

Outside German-speaking circles probably the best known of the German descriptive studies are Rudolph Otto's *Das Heilige* (1917, translated as *The Idea of the Holy*) and Friedrich Heiler's *Das Gebet* (1918, in English, *Prayer*). Numerous other studies belong here too. Most of the investigations of childhood and adolescent piety are primarily descriptive, including Spranger's (1924, 1925) enduring contributions and the more recent works of Thun (1959, 1963, 1969), whose investigations extend to the piety of old age. Self-consciously phenomenological studies are represented by Albrecht (1951) and Walther (1976) in two parallel inquiries into mystical experience, and the *verstehende* approach of Dilthey and Spranger has been employed in a noteworthy and wide-ranging work by Trillhaas (1953). Although religiously somewhat parochial, Pöll's (1965, 1974) systematic analysis of religious experience is representative of much of this literature. Among American humanistic psychologists, Allport (1950), who was a student of Spranger's, shows most clearly the influence of the German descriptive tradition.

The current of influence flows the other way as well. The correlational and factor-analytic procedures that are today a *sine qua non* for the conduct of research among certain American psychologists and sociologists of religion have been adopted by some German investigators, including Boos-Nünning (1972), Fuchs and Oppermann (1975), and Holl and Fischer (1968). Given, however, the continuing dominance in the German literature of theologians and other scholars of religion, it is unlikely that the quantitative approach will soon displace the dynamic and descriptive ones.

Mention should be made, finally, of the relatively modest German literature on religion and psychiatry. As Heimann's (1961) essay demonstrates, the psychiatric interest in religion is linked historically and conceptually with the trends we have just surveyed, as well as with the field of pastoral care. In fact, however, it has developed in relative isolation, reflecting its specialized interest in exceptional states and pathological processes. Weitbrecht's (1948) standard work focuses in particular on conversion, treating it as a subtype of personality change. One of Weitbrecht's students, Günter Schüttler (1971, 1974), traveled to India and Japan to carry out field observations and psychiatric evaluation of a group of Tibetan oracle priests and another of Zen masters. The phenomena considered in these and other works include asceticism, inspiration, possession, mystical ecstasy, stigmata, and speaking in tongues. Attention is also given to peculiarities of religiousness that mark certain well-defined forms of psychopathology.

The French Literature

Historically, the best known work on the psychopathology of religion was carried out by French psychiatrists and psychologists, including Charcot, Ribot, and Janet. It was their sometimes too facile reduction of exceptional religious experience to pathological states, in fact, that inspired James's famous refutation of 'medical materialism.' The same tendency prompted in the French literature a spate of critical Catholic works that urge subtler discriminations among religious states and challenge the presumption that psychology is able to comprehend the whole of mystical experience. Room must be left, they argue, for the activity of God, which only philosophy and theology are said to be competent to discuss.

The Catholic response to the efforts to develop a psychopathology of religion has not, however, been limited to criticism. Long sensitive to the subtleties of the spiritual life, the complications that can distort it, and the difficult task of directing it, Catholic scholars have undertaken a variety of positive investigations that fall well within the psychology of religion. Particularly noteworthy is the series *Études Carmélitaines*, founded in 1911 as a serial and reconstituted in 1936 as a succession of monographs, most of which record the proceedings of a series of conferences on psychology of religion sponsored by the Discalced Carmelites. The latter volumes, containing contributions from philosophers, theologians, historians of religion, psychologists, and medical specialists, are organized around such themes as stigmatization, mysticism, Satan, contemplation, the boundaries of human capacity, the role of sensation in religious experience, and the relation of liberty and structure (e.g., Jésus-Marie 1948, 1954). Interrupted during the war, this series of monographs finally came to an end in 1960 after the retirement of its long-time editor, Father Bruno de Jésus-Marie.

The volumes in the *Études Carmélitaines* evince the trend among Catholic psychiatrists and psychologists to retain supernatural causes among their diagnostic categories. Unlike Charcot, Ribot, and Janet, accordingly, they are inclined to distinguish 'true' and 'false' religious occurrences, including conversion, mystical experience, miraculous cures, and possession (e.g., Lhermitte 1956). Yet at least a few have been reluctant to employ supernatural explanation, as Siwek (1950), a Jesuit who was a student of Janet's, demonstrates in his study of the twentieth-century stigmatist Theresa Neumann of Konnersreuth.

Although the significant French work of the most recent decades remains largely in the hands of Catholic scholars, the themes that now dominate the literature are familiar to us from the American and German traditions: the theories of Freud and Jung, the use of questionnaires and statistical analysis, an interest in religious development and education. As in the other major literatures, we find here systematic studies of the background, principles, and implications of the depth psychologies of religion, including that of Jung (Hostie 1955, van de Winckel 1959) and especially that of Freud (Beirnaert 1964, Bellet 1973, Pohier 1972, Tauxe 1974). Where depth psychology is not found wanting by these authors, they are likely to see it as a means of purifying and promoting the Christian faith. The practical concerns underlying many of these works are even more explicit in a second area of reflection and research, religious development and education. Most notable are the *Lumen Vitae*

Studies in Religious Psychology edited by the Belgian Jesuit psychologist of religion André Godin (e.g., 1959, 1964, 1972), in which appear numerous reports of empirical research as well as articles of theoretical import. On the Protestant side are two works by scholars associated with the University of Geneva: the widely cited book on the child's religious sentiment by former director of the J.J. Rousseau Institute Pierre Bovet (1925), a work augmented in its second edition (1951) by chapters on religious education; and a more recent investigation of adolescent piety by Edmond Rochedieu (1962), the successor to Georges Berguer (1946), a Protestant pastor in France and Geneva who was the first scholar anywhere to occupy a chair in the psychology of religion.

The widespread respect among French-speaking psychologists of religion for the quantitative research techniques developed chiefly in America is evident not only in the *Lumen Vitae* series but also in the works that have won the Lumen Vitae Quinquennial Award in the psychology of religion, administered by the recently reconstituted *Commission internationale de psychologie religieuse scientifique* (Deconchy 1967; Dumoulin and Jaspard 1973; Rulla, Imoda, and Ridick 1978). Statistical methods akin to those employed in these works, including factor analysis, have also found a home at the Center for the Psychology of Religion of the Catholic University of Louvain. The work of this Center, which was founded by Father Antoine Vergote, is represented in a special issue of the bilingual journal *Social Compass* (Vergote et al. 1972) as well as in a series of studies exploring the relation of parental figures to the representation of God (Vergote and Tamayo 1981).

The possibilities of employing in religious research the even more exacting techniques of experimental and quasi-experimental psychology are being explored in a series of investigations of religious orthodoxy by Catholic theologian and psychologist of religion Jean-Pierre Deconchy (1977, 1980), who is Director of Research of the Paris-based National Center for Scientific Research. Experimentation of a rather different sort, employing physiological measures and non-Western practitioners of yoga, has been carried out over many years by Thérèse Brosse (1963), once head of the cardiology clinic of Paris University's faculty of medicine.

A Worldwide Endeavor

It is probably safe to say that there are today works on the psychology of religion in most of the world's major languages. One may confidently add, however, that the great majority of these works are dependent in fundamental ways on the literatures we have just reviewed in brief—though they are, of course, no less valuable in their own right for being so. An Italian textbook by Milanesi and Aletti (1973), for example, features the views of James, Allport, Freud, Jung, and Fromm. In Spain, a modified version of the Allport and Ross intrinsic-extrinsic Religious Orientation scale was employed by Jesús Amón (1969), a Jesuit psychologist at the University of Madrid, to assess the relation of extrinsic religiousness and anti-Protestant prejudice. The intrinsic-extrinsic distinction likewise plays a role, along with measures of authoritarianism, dogmatism, and rigidity, in Lange's (1971) correlational studies in Amsterdam of the religious practices and social attitudes of a sample of Jews, Catholics, and Protestants. In Sweden, the related perspectives of James, Allport, and Clark (1958), along with the role theory of Swedish theologian and psychologist of religion Hjalmar Sundén (1959), are brought to bear on the religious development of Nathan Söderblom by Hans Åkerberg (1975). In Japan and India, finally, the physiological and quantitative techniques of Western psychologists have been used to study representatives of Eastern religious traditions (Akishige 1977, Hirai 1974, Rajamanickam 1976). Although such publications as these may employ familiar theories and methods, there is nevertheless much to be learned from their application to different phenomena and in other cultures. Some of these works, moreover, such as Sierksma's (1956) incisive analysis of religious projection from the viewpoint of the psychology of perception, offer fresh perspectives of fundamental importance.

The spread internationally of most of the leading theories and methods in the psychology of religion and the occasional appearance of collaborative works (e.g., Godin's volumes, and Brusselmans et al. 1980) have not yet changed the reality of the three major traditions, nor have they diminished the value of acquaintance with all three. Indeed, the problem of the language barrier seems only to grow, given the recent work, for example, in the Scandinavian countries and the Netherlands. There is the further difficulty simply of gaining physical access to the myriad journal articles and books in which the literature has appeared over the decades, for few libraries are likely to have more than a small fraction of these widely scattered sources.

Some Fundamental Issues in the Psychology of Religion

The barriers of language and geography are not, unfortunately, the only problems that trouble contemporary psychologists of religion. There is, of course, the fundamental contrast already observed between understanding and explanation, between empathic comprehension from within and causal analysis from without. Implicated in this issue are other, more specific ones, upon which well-informed and thoughtful scholars continue to disagree.

The Definition of Religion

The task of defining religion, some scholars have maintained, is in the end a hopeless one. Yet not to undertake it is to risk proceeding on the basis of a seriously inadequate understanding of the object of one's study. Most psychologists of religion agree that religiousness involves a combination of cognition, emotion, and action, though one or another of these three traditional elements is commonly emphasized. The conviction is widespread, for example, that religious experience is primary and that its articulation in words and outward actions is a secondary expression that, if taken alone, would allow little discrimination between the 'truly religious' and those whose piety is, however well-intended, largely imitative or derived. One identifies religious persons primarily, then, in terms of the experiences they report, not through what they believe or the religious rituals in which they report participation. Although some argue that religion necessarily entails experience of the divine, others have identified it with any intensified and deeply serious attitude toward the world of experience, out of which emerges, however inchoately, a sense of life's meaning.

Beyond the task of formulating a general definition of religion lies another one, no less problematical: devising some means by which one may observe it in the lives of particular persons. How does one assess the piety of an individual, especially in a way that allows comparison with that of another? Modern positivistic psychology's distrust of introspective and empathic modes of research has led to the development of a complex science of psychological assessment, an essential element of which is the attitude scale (Shaw and Wright, 1967). Scales of this type usually consist of a series of statements with which respondents are asked simply to agree or disagree. Their answers allow the calculation of quantitative scores as well as the carrying out of a variety of statistical manipulations. Beyond providing an operational definition of religion for correlational studies, these scales have served, when subjected to the complex statistical technique of factor analysis, as a means for testing assumptions about religion's dimensionality. Although a few investigators continue to hold that religiousness is a single dimension, however it may be measured, most have concluded that multidimensional scales approximate reality more closely. At the same time, there is growing appreciation for the element of arbitrariness in the whole undertaking (Dittes 1969, King and Hunt 1972).

The measurement of piety's dimensions has become the keystone for most of the research carried out in England and America. Questions about the adequacy of the various means of quantification, therefore, are critical for an evaluation of this literature. Although it is a truism that all psychological measurement devices are at best *relatively* reliable and valid, depending in part on the context in which they are employed, those assessing religious attitudes seem peculiarly vulnerable to criticism. There are of course those who doubt that quantification of piety is a legitimate or useful enterprise in the first place. To quantify, they argue, is invariably to distort and mislead. The reduction of religious faith to numbers on a scale, they aver, is the final triumph of the banality of modern technology.

A more moderate view might assert the usefulness of quantitative research at the same time that it recognizes the dangers it involves, especially if misinterpreted. The strength of the quantitative approach lies in the explicitness with which it carries out its operations, and thus the ease with which they can be reproduced by other researchers and their results compared. Yet this approach is at the same time far less sensitive to the object of its investigation, for it radically restricts the individual's opportunity to respond and thus reduces the investigator's basis for interpretation. Scales measuring religious belief in particular have been unnecessarily limited, for most of them give the respondent only two alternatives: literal belief and literal disbelief. Even the addition of one or two more subtle alternatives, however, beyond increasing the risk of suggesting the 'right' answer to those eager to impress the investigator, is unlikely to provide sufficient latitude for the diverse populations that will be evaluated by these questionnaires. Furthermore, even if it were possible to represent every theological position, one would need in addition some indication of how important the selected belief is to the respondent's total outlook.

The same problems hold true for scales measuring other dimensions of religiousness. The more specific the inquiry about one's religious practices or the extent of one's knowledge, say, of the Scriptures, the narrower the concept of religiousness the scale is able to operationalize. Too general a set of items, on the other hand, so reduces the variability of scores in some populations that the scale will be useless in the search for piety's correlates. The task facing the operationalists, in sum, is an enormously difficult one. They must compose scales of a specificity precisely appropriate to the populations they wish to study, with alternatives acceptable to every respondent (if not also to the historian of religion). This collection of scales, moreover, must be sufficiently diverse to allow each respondent to indicate the ways in which he or she gives expression to the personal faith—the inner experience of transcendence—that lies at the heart of the religious life (Smith 1963). At the same time psychometric evidence must be forthcoming that demonstrates a level of reliability and validity sufficient for the purposes intended. The fact is, of course, that research proceeds apace even though these standards have nowhere been approximated. Its value is accordingly a matter for considerable discussion, as at least some of those who carry it out realize.

The quantitative psychologists are not the only ones with definitional problems. Freud is another who set limits on his analysis by adopting too narrow a definition of religion. For him, religion is two things only: a set of dogmatic and unchallengeable beliefs, above all belief in a father-God who is loved and feared, and the unreflective carrying out of rigidly prescribed ritual. When his friend Romain Rolland suggested to Freud that he had overlooked the true origin of religious sentiments, the 'oceanic' feeling of unboundedness, Freud (1930: 72) could only speculate that such feelings, wholly unknown to him, might represent the ego's defensive 'restoration of limitless narcissism' in the face of a threatening world. More than that he was unwilling to say. It has been the task of the psychoanalysts following him to expand the range of religious phenomena to which the theory has been applied, though their efforts have not always been convincing.

The Selection of Subjects

The religious persons Freud had in mind when he wrote *The Future of an Illusion* are clearly not the same ones that James assembled in the pages of the *Varieties*. Nor are the typical respondents to the quantitative psychologist's questionnaire. How one defines religion, it is apparent, determines in large measure where one will look for its representation. One has the choice, first of all, between religious persons and religious contents. Whereas Starbuck and James elected to focus on persons, albeit rather different classes of them, Stratton (1911) based his analysis primarily on the sacred writings of the world's religious traditions. Jung likewise opted for a psychology of religious contents—what he calls 'the psychology of religion proper' (Jung 1952, in 1969: 464)—while recognizing the legitimacy of a predominant interest in individuals.

If one is convinced, on the other hand, that religion is known best of all through its manifestation in personal lives, there is yet the question of which persons will tell us the most about its nature. Much like the French alienists, James (1902: 6, 39) argues for studying the 'unmistakable and extreme' cases, the '"geniuses" in the religious line,' who indeed commonly show signs of pathological disturbance. It is in their experience, he maintains, that piety first springs into life, and through them above all that one can hope to clarify the nature of religion's fruits, positive and negative.

Although interest in exceptional religious experience remains alive today, many contemporary psychologists of religion are convinced that a general psychology of religion must be founded on the study of ordinary piety, however habitual or second-hand it may be. Samples are drawn wherever they can be found—in college and seminary classrooms, local churches, homes for the delinquent or the aged, and so on. Data may also be compiled from national surveys or public records. In every case, statistical or content analysis is directed to the end of characterizing trends in piety and its correlates that may be generalized to larger populations, though precisely who constitutes these populations is often unclear.

If there is today a preference for the assessment of unexceptional piety, there is nevertheless hardly a category of person whose religiousness has not been explored, at least in the Western world. The field as a whole has been surprisingly catholic, though one may regret the lack of balance and integration. Unfortunately, however, many persons have been chosen for study simply because they were close at hand. It is noteworthy, therefore, when researchers such as King and Hunt (1972) make exceptional efforts to assemble carefully selected and well-specified samples. In such cases one knows at least to whom the results may be legitimately generalized. Their efforts should also remind one that the question of whom (or what) one studies is fundamental to the investigation of religion.

The Faith of the Investigator

No less fundamental is the researcher's own faith. We have already noted the marked tendency for psychologists of religion themselves to be religious, embracing in some cases a conservative Christian theology that plays an explicit role in their professional work. Even those of a more liberal bent have made plain that their research is shaped and directed by their personal religious concerns. Conservative or liberal, the critics will say, the religious psychologist cannot be trusted to be a disinterested investigator of religion. The ideal standpoint, it has been suggested, is that of the skeptic or agnostic: both the religiously committed and the atheist are thought likely to impose the character of their own perspectives on their research.

It is surely no coincidence that negative evaluations of religion have come from psychologists who have personally and vehemently rejected traditional religious forms and expressions (e.g., Leuba, Watson, and Skinner), whereas analyses essentially favorable to religion have been carried out by scholars known for the depth of their piety (e.g., Otto, Heiler, and Pratt). Must both groups therefore disqualify themselves? Otto and Heiler have each argued that the fruitful study of religion is impossible for individuals who have never known religious feelings. Such persons, agrees Pfennigsdorf (1927: 15), will risk getting lost in the complexities of the material, mistaking insignificant elements for major ones, for example; they are also likely to make uncritical use of measures that are inappropriate to religious experience. The meaning of religious phenomena is in large measure subjective, he argues, so that one must approach them first of all on the basis of one's own experience.

The objective psychologist, who in principle eschews all subjective modes of comprehension, is not likely to agree. Psychologists have studied a host of subjects, including animals, human infants, and the mentally ill, whose subjective experience remains largely or wholly unknown to normal adult human beings. Careful observation, experimental manipulation, and cautious interpretation have nevertheless made it possible to gain some understanding of the lives of these subjects. Might not these techniques serve equally well in the study of religious persons?

If the investigation of religion is possible by certain means without one's having "been there" oneself, surely first-hand acquaintance is the best safeguard against presumption and insensitivity. It may be that certain forms of religious experience or practice can in fact be comprehended by the psychologist who claims to be irreligious, but just as surely other forms lie beyond such a researcher's unknowing grasp. Yet the same may be true of the religious psychologist, if such an individual is similarly characterized by a narrowly bounded faith. At bottom, it would seem, it is a matter of where one's limits lie, for no one is capable of fully understanding another person, a fact that Otto and Heiler would be among the first to acknowledge.

The Choice of Basic Categories

The defining of religion and the choosing of subjects for study are undoubtedly influenced by how intimately the psychologist of religion knows the religious life. So too, perhaps, is the task of selecting the categories one shall use for analysis. Dittes (1969) suggests that in this regard there are two fundamental strategies. On the one hand, the investigator may employ the descriptive language of the person of faith; one accepts for scholarly use, at least at the outset, the traditional categories of religious experience and conduct. On the other hand, one may deem it more useful to begin with the categories of psychology as they have been developed in the study of other phenomena. This starting point, says Dittes, is likely to be chosen by persons who, seeing no essential difference between religious and nonreligious phenomena, seek to demonstrate that general theories of behavior are adequate for the religious varieties as well. To one impressed above all by the unparalleled richness of the religious life, however, such an approach will likely appear crassly reductionistic and procrustean.

Elsewhere Dittes has himself opted for giving priority to psychology's categories. 'Until we can use these more scientific constructs,' he says, 'our understanding of what religion is will be impoverished' (Havens 1968: 7). The same point of view is advanced by Pruyser (1968), who maintains that the reliance on religion's own categories has led the psychology of religion into an intellectual cul-de-sac. Goodenough (1965), by contrast, argues for a fundamental rethinking of psychology in the light of a sympathetic understanding of the diverse manifestations of religion. 'The business of the "psychology of religion,"' he says, 'is not to fit religious experiences into the pigeonholes of Freud or Jung or into the categories of *Gestalt* or stimulus-response or any other, but rather to see what the data of religious experiences themselves suggest' (1965: xi).

The issue is largely the one with which we began this chapter: description versus explanation. It is also a question of where one locates the psychology of religion within the scholarly arena. Is it primarily a subfield within psychology, so that one is justified in giving priority to the methods and theories of contemporary psychology, or is it more properly considered a helping discipline within *Religionswissenschaft*, where the emphasis will likely be placed on faithfulness to religious phenomena? In the American and French literatures, the accent has been on the field's psychological roots; among German writers, by contrast, the psychology of religion has been viewed primarily as an aid to scholars of religion, who are generally suspicious of any theoretical or methodological imperialism. Although a balance between respect for religious manifestations and astute employment of psychological categories would seem to be possible, it has proved so far to be an exceptional achievement.

The Question of Truth

Profoundly implicated in every issue we have reviewed here—if indeed it is not the fountainhead of them all—is a final and most difficult question: what may the psychologist of religion say on the matter of religious truth? Freud won the disapprobation of theologians for presuming to judge religion an illusion, albeit one that by chance may happen to be true. Jung has likewise been sharply criticized for foreclosing the question of religion's objective validity.

The problem here, according to Scheler (1921), is not one of a particular theorist's point of view, but of the whole enterprise of an explanatory psychology of religion. By its very nature, Scheler maintains, such a psychology inevitably calls into question the reality of religion's object. Beyond this 'spurious' and 'atheistic' approach is another, however, the descriptive one. Yet even the 'merely descriptive' psychology of religion, he claims, is possible only within individual religious communities. 'There are therefore as many psychologies of religion as there are *separate confessions*' (1921: 159).

Scheler's counsel of despair, however, seems not to have discouraged others from seeking to develop a generally valid psychology of religion, be it descriptive or explanatory. Yet his concern with psychology's attitude toward the religious object is widespread, especially on the continent. In a well-known and highly praised paper that is still discussed today, University of Geneva psychologist Theodor Flournoy (1903) set forth as one of the psychology of religion's fundamental principles the 'exclusion of the transcendent.' The psychologist of religion, according to this principle, must leave aside all judgments about the existence of religion's transcendent objects, neither affirming nor denying their reality. Wobbermin's (1928) added warning that one nevertheless must somehow take into account the decisive significance of the transcendent in the fundamental structure of religious consciousness seems, on the other hand, to have gone largely unheard. As Müller-Pozzi (1975: 37) observes, Flournoy's principle has given the psychology of religion a purely negative disposition: it specifies only what lies outside the field's competence, not what its positive contributions may be.

Agreeing that the question of truth is not the psychologist's to answer, Heimann (1961) notes that contemporary researchers are nonetheless concerned with distinguishing genuine religiosity from spurious or pseudoreligious forms. The question is in part a practical one, for its answer, however tentative, will shape the decisions and conduct of psychotherapists and pastoral counselors. Genuine piety, according to Heimann, is marked by a correspondence between the spiritual aspirations of the person and the likelihood of their realization, given the individual's capacities and determination. To make such a judgment, clearly, one must possess in large measure both perspicacity and wisdom.

Separable from the question of genuineness is the even more perplexing matter of pathology. Worldwide, a large portion of the literature in the psychology of religion concerns itself with pathological phenomena; in most cases the fact of psychic disorder is unmistakable. Occasionally, however, the subject of these studies is a person whose 'madness' has inspired a significant religious movement. The followers of such a person may themselves come in for scrutiny. 'One must be capable of distinguishing the pathological and the useless from what is valuable and worth preserving,' writes Jung (1943: 45), 'and that is one of the most difficult things.' Toward the end of making such a discrimination, Trillhaas (1953: 177–179) offers seven criteria. Pathological religiousness, he says, is characterized by (1) unusually long and intense episodes; (2) unclear and illogical thought patterns combined with remarkably self-confident faith; (3) behavior that violates general legal and ethical ideals; (4) marked egocentricity, with the conviction that the revelation, which may include special instructions, is one's private possession; (5 striking variation in the content of religious experience from one phase to the next in the underlying disorder, without continuity between phases; (6) incommunicability of the highly personal experience to the empathic understanding of others; and (7) partialness in the degree to which the experience fills the person's life, with corresponding inconsistency in behavior.

Even while seeking to distinquish genuine piety from spurious forms or healthy varieties from pathological ones, the psychologist of religion must bracket the reality of faith's object. To make reference to that object, however, without at the same time taking some evaluative stance toward it seems nearly impossible. Our very language, including the word religion itself (Smith 1963), misleads us. Simply to point out that someone 'believes' something is subtly to imply that the belief in question is subject to doubt. To speak of God without qualification or comment is to give the impression that one is taking for granted a particular theological viewpoint.

The difficult issues that we have reviewed here spring in large part, according to Ulrich Mann (1973: 39), out of the troublesome nature of religion itself. If Heimbrock (1978) is right that in scarcely any other field of study have the questions of object, method, and goal received more diverse answers or been the source of more controversy than in the psychology of religion, it nevertheless shares these difficulties to a large degree with other subfields in the study of religion. The 'situation of crisis' in which the psychology of religion has found itself since its earliest days, concludes Mann, is inherent in the field. There is simply no way to escape it.

Methods in the Psychology of Religion

The unavoidability of these difficulties is most evident in the practical matter of choosing one's methods. For psychology in general, the question of method has been bound up from the beginning with a fundamental dilemma. Unlike the chemist or physicist, who may be able to point with ease to the phenomenon under investigation, the psychologist's object, the human psyche, appears frustratingly private and intangible. Furthermore, the human capacities that make possible the planning and carrying out of research are in psychology the very focus of investigation. The instrument of research is itself the object. On the one hand, then, what one is investigating, impalpable though it be, has already a familiarity that may beguile the unsuspecting; on the other hand, every deliberate effort to rise above the familiar and start anew, scientifically, seems doomed to fall back into hopeless subjectivity. Psychology, some have argued accordingly, can never be a science, at least not one on the model of physics or chemistry.

The century-long search for methods universally acceptable for psychological research remains to this day unfulfilled. The situation as Stern described it many years ago is little changed:

> There is hardly a psychological method the correctness or usefulness of which might not be contested in principle or practice, while on the other hand there is a strong tendency to elevate some one method to the status of the sole means of salvation. Both acts, the proscribing of methods and the dictation of methods, are alike harmful to the progress of the science (1935: 47).

Wisdom lies, according to Stern, in remaining task- and problem-centered, drawing undogmatically on whatever methods promise to deepen one's comprehension. Although methodological imperialism is not unknown in the psychology of religion, the field as a whole has been strikingly pluralistic in its quest for understanding.

Whereas in principle the psychology of religion is distinguished from other forms of psychological research only by its object, not its methods, it has proceeded in fact with relative independence from methodological trends in general psychology. Like the psychology of personality, to which in some respects it is closely related, it has been less influenced by positivistic notions of science than has laboratory psychology in America. As in the case of personality psychology, its concerns are thought by many to be too complex and holistic to brook the stringent demands of the experimentalist's methods and theories, though especially in America there has been of late considerable accommodation. As might be expected, it is particularly among scholars whose training is primarily in the study of religion, not psychology, that the field has been promoted with relative indifference to fashions in general psychological research. Some researchers, on the other hand, seem to follow these fashions unquestioningly, with little apparent regard for the difficulties that may be created by doing so.

Observing Individual Piety

From the beginning, the psychology of religion has been said to have two fundamental methods: the observation of religious individuals and the study of traditional content from the history of religion. The first of these has received by far the greater emphasis, though of course the two are intimately related. Both are still employed today.

Self-Observation. The way of observation, many have thought, must begin with one's own experience. Self-observation or introspection was for psychologists at the turn of the century the chief means of psychological research. With the rise of both behaviorism and psychoanalysis, however, the usefulness and reliability of introspective reports were sharply called into question. New, more objective methods of observation were developed by the behaviorists, who were determined to eliminate introspection altogether from their science. The psychoanalysts, by contrast, set about to augment introspection through free association, which emancipates self-observation from the conscious control of the observer. The always-reluctant surrendering of control and the analyst's carefully timed interpretations of the hidden meanings transform traditional introspective evidence, so the psychoanalysts claim, into a vital source of insight. Although the psychoanalysts thus preserve a place for self-observation, they, like the behaviorists, consider it virtually useless in itself.

To those unconvinced by the behavioristic and psychoanalytic viewpoints, however, disciplined self-examination of naive experience remains a major avenue of knowledge. The advantages of self-observation are easy to see, says Pöll:

> It demands no elaborate preparations or safeguards, as is often the case in the psychological experiment. Introspective concentration on the matter at hand is enough, an achievement requiring, to be sure, practice, care, and self-criticism but not apparatus, tests, or statistical calculations. What is decisive, however, is the fact that only self-observation leads one directly to the psychic life. Only in self-observation do we encounter experience as it is in itself and not as it is expressed in words, gestures, and other forms of behavior. By this means we come upon religious awe, joy, and repentance themselves. Moreover, self-observation alone can clearly reveal at least the fundamental forms of experience and therewith likewise the psychic life of others. The same is true in the religious sphere (1965: 45).

A proper understanding of the basic forms of religious experience requires, therefore, that one know them at first hand. Such intimate knowledge of certain forms may serve, furthermore, as a basis for empathically re-living, or at least sensing the character of, those experiences in which one has not oneself directly participated.

Detractors of self-observation, on the other hand, have repeatedly pointed out the difficulties and dangers of such a method. They argue, first of all, that it is impossible to observe psychic events as they are occurring. Intrusion into ongoing experience with the intention of observing it seems inevitably to disturb or transform it. A man earnestly praying to God, for example, who suddenly attempts to observe himself in prayer will at that instant cease praying. If he waits to make his introspective effort until after his prayer has come to a natural conclusion, what will follow, according to Traxel's (1968) argument, will consist only of reflection and interpretation, not observation.

There are other, no less serious problems. There is always the possibility of self-deception, especially when feelings of self-regard are implicated in the experience under observation. A theologically sophisticated person whose introspective gaze is turned, say, to the idea of God may unwittingly overlook the vital substratum of naive images and associations that linger from early childhood. Yet even if the role of such elements is recognized, one may be reluctant to share that awareness with others, fearing that they will judge one's faith immature. Where self-deception, then, has not robbed the literature of a full and balanced account of religious experience, circumspection may bring about the same result.

The vagueness of experience, discussed with unsurpassable eloquence by James (1890) in his famous chapter on the stream of consciousness, presents the would-be self-observer with still another difficulty. The problem lies not only in bringing these fleeting and ill-defined portions of consciousness before the mind's eye, but also in finding words that adequately describe them. We overlook these vague yet important aspects of our experience, says James, because they are unnamed. Our language, in the end, is inadequate to articulate these subtleties. Even when a label is found for some aspect of experience, that label is bound to misrepresent it. 'As soon as we name anything and thus assign it to some definite psychological category, it *is* no longer the same thing that it was before,' writes Stern (1935: 11); it acquires a peculiar rigidity and fixity that cannot be ascribed to mind itself.'

Proponents of self-observation have proved to be no less aware of the risks and shortcomings of this technique. Yet one abandons a method, they argue, not because its application is fraught with difficulties but because a better, more certain one has come along. The fact is, they maintain, self-observation is not simply one method among others, one that we may set aside at will. It is, rather, 'a prerequisite for every [other] method in the psychology of religion' (Stählin 1912: 395). If self-observation has not been employed by the researcher in the quest for hypotheses and the design of the study, it surely enters into the subjects' responses. As Boring (1953: 169) indicates, 'introspection is still with us, doing its business under various aliases, of which *verbal report* is one.' Where its use is unrecognized or unacknowledged, however, it is likely to be employed only casually or to be hamstrung by too-severe limitations. It is time, Bakan (1954) argues, to move toward a 'careful and avowed use' of self-observation, especially if we are to have a psychology appropriate to the tasks at hand—in this context, the study of religion.

Advocates of introspection have long recognized the difficulty, if not the impossibility, of observing experience as it is occurring. In most cases, certainly, observation will have to be indirectly carried out, either immediately after the experience—in a form that Stern calls primary self-remembrance—or sometime later, when of course recollection is likely to be far less reliable. The vicissitudes of memory, however, are variable enough to disallow any simple generalizations about what is possible. Pöll (1965) observes that experiences involving no obvious stimulus—dreams, fantasies, as well as many religious states—possess, like sensory experiences, short-lived 'after-images,' to which one may for a brief time give one's attention. Longer enduring after-effects, more fragmentary in character, may permit a fuller study of certain elements. Such residues, furthermore, along with certain occurrences consequent to the experience, may serve sometime later to awaken anew the original experience, in part or in whole. Marcel Proust's famous recovery of his childhood days in Combray, from the taste of cake soaked in tea, vividly illustrates this possibility. Proust's voluminous remembrances demonstrate as well, it would seem, that language can go a long way in communicating the private transport of so lively a recollection.

Yet how does one verify such a report? Only those phenomena that can be made public and hence observable by two or more investigators are capable of verification, say many contemporary researchers, thereby ruling out all self-observation. Bakan (1954) argues to the contrary, maintaining that verification can be achieved without meeting the 'naive criterion of publicity,' through the introspective reports of other investigators. One may even seek to create, as Girgensohn and his associates did, a uniform set of conditions, so that one observer's report is easily comparable to a series of others. Should one discover that each of these replications produces essentially the same result, and that such verification, furthermore, cannot be attributed to suggestion, one may be confident that the findings have a degree of generality. How large a degree is another troublesome question, yet it is not unique to self-observation, as Bakan points out.

In effect, verification and the assessment of generality occur, however informally, whenever findings from self-observation are examined. One automatically checks another's introspective report against one's own experience. If the two are consistent, the report will immediately appear self-evident. Having the quality of self-evidence does not mean, of course, that the report cannot also be penetratingly original or existentially helpful. Smith (1971) has suggested, in fact, that the social sciences and the humanities substitute for the natural sciences' principle of verification one that might be called the principle of existential appropriability; that is, no statement would be considered true if it cannot be meaningfully appropriated into the lives of those about whom it is made. Such a principle is employed less easily in the case of introspection, where it may not be clear to whom, beyond the self-observer, the statements pertain. Bakan provides, however, a possible corollary: the value of an introspective report may be assessed by the degree to which its suggestion of possibilities enhances the sensitivity of its reader. Knowledge of such possibilities may lead further—to the deepening of the reader's own experience, the goal of much spontaneous self-observation in the history of religion.

Indeed, Pöll maintains that psychologists will find religion a particularly fruitful area for self-observation, especially given the long history of merciless self-examination on the part of religious aspirants. Such unrelenting concern for the quality of one's spiritual life entails, of course, certain presuppositions, goals, and value judgments that must be set aside by the disinterested psychological observer. Yet the object of study—the inner psychic life—is in both cases the same. Each for its own purposes, moreover, is peculiarly aware of the tendencies toward self-deception and self-justification. Together with the unusual familiarity and the complex personal associations that accrue with ritual practice, this long-standing concern with accurate introspection, Pöll concludes, allows the application of self-observation in the psychology of religion with exceptional proficiency and reliability.

Yet even in this field there are no proponents of the exclusive use of introspection. Findings obtained in such a way, it is agreed, must be checked and supplemented by other methods, though most of them bring the investigator or the subjects back, at some point, to the task of self-observation. Even when one employs physiological indices, such as EEG recordings, or certain unobtrusive measures requiring no verbal response from one's subjects, one is likely to be forced to rely on introspective evidence, if only when it comes time to interpret the meaning of one's results. Limited though they are, therefore, by human subjectivity, most of these techniques nevertheless sufficiently increase the degree of control and accuracy to make their use highly desirable. They are more objective, many would say, for they separate the observer from the object of study. Yet it must be remembered that the more distance that is placed between a phenomenon and the individual who observes and records it, the more opportunity there will be for error. None of these further methods is as direct as unalloyed self-observation.

Self-Report. The first and for a time most widely used method of studying the religious life of others, the self-report, obviously relies heavily on the subjects' own introspective capacities as well as their willingness to employ them. Although self-report is a term ordinarily used to refer to any data or information provided by the subject, it will be used here in a more restricted sense. For our purposes, a self-report is a precise record of any freely expressed verbal communication, whether written or spoken, that is intended by the subject to represent a defined range of personal experience or reflection. So delimited, this rubric excludes standardized tests, which typically allow only agreement or disagreement with a series of standard questions, as well as projective techniques, which by design seek to circumvent the subject's intentions.

Among those sources of data that constitute self-reports as defined here, the most important distinction is between the spontaneous and the elicited. Spontaneous reports have the great virtue of having come into being independent of the investigator's inquiry. Unshaped by leading questions and less commonly burdened by perfunctory prose, these writings are a rich source of exceptional self-observation. Yet such reports are available from only a limited range of persons and, far from being truly spontaneous, they are often written for specific purposes, ones not always evident to the reader. Moreover, they often leave out much that a researcher would want to know. It is common, therefore, for psychologists of religion to elicit self-reports from a broader, more typical range of subjects and, on some occasions, to follow up the subjects' responses with a series of individualized and more probing questions.

Virtually all 'spontaneous' self-reports constitute what are called human or *personal documents*, including letters, journals, and topical or comprehensive autobiographies, as well as certain artistic productions (Allport 1942). It is possible, of course, to elicit such documents as well, by assigning the keeping of a diary, say, or by distributing open-ended questionnaires. Yet unless the subjects are involved in the task as an end in itself, the results may well be disappointingly pedestrian. At their best, however, personal documents are unrivaled as a source of intimate, accessible, and fascinating data. For James (1902: 501–502), they alone promise entrée into the private recesses of personal feeling, 'the darker, blinder strata of character, ... the only places in the world in which we catch real fact in the making, and directly perceive how events happen, and how work is actually done.'

If the personal document is the means *par excellence* by which one may become acquainted with the concrete reality of individual lives, it is at the same time a source of data with potentially serious shortcomings. At the time it is recorded, the personal document is already shaped and edited by the perspective, motives, and verbal abilities of its writer. Every document is necessarily selective, and whether or not it is so intended, such selectivity will likely help to cast a particular light on the author. It is not uncommon, for example, for diarists to exercise their art primarily at times of frustration or unhappiness. What is included, moreover, may be designed, unconsciously or deliberately, to deceive the reader. Simple lapses of memory may serve the same end. Even in cases of penetrating self-awareness and radical honesty, however, one must still contend with the conceptual framework employed by every writer, which serves not only as a basis for selecting and emphasizing certain elements but also for formulating their relations to one another, filling in gaps, and interpreting, finally, the significance of the whole. Such interpretation may in fact be largely arbitrary. If one is nevertheless determined to meet these difficulties, especially by drawing on supporting evidence from other sources, there is still the problem of scarcity. In spite of the diverse motives that prompt the formulation of personal documents, obtaining useful ones is ordinarily difficult and expensive at best (Allport 1942).

In reviewing the case against the personal document, Allport emphasizes that its insufficiencies must not be evaluated apart from either the measures that can be taken to compensate for them or the limitations of other methods. From Allport's point of view, the personal document's relative advantages greatly outweigh its shortcomings. Above all, it provides the psychological investigator with 'the needed touchstone of reality' (1942: 143), especially in the domain of subjective meaning, a region of particular importance for the psychology of religion. 'It is safe to say,' writes Allport, 'that [the religious life] has never been studied with even partial adequacy by any means other than the personal document' (1942: 38). In it, one has preserved the organismic wholeness that is commonly lost with other research techniques in psychology. Where the document has been written over time, moreover, as in the case of the diary and some autobiographies, one has an unparalleled opportunity for longitudinal study. Personal documents, Allport argues, provide the particulars upon which all general psychological understanding depends. Indeed, he hypothesizes that the goals of science—commonly thought to be understanding, prediction, and control—can be achieved more effectively by means of the 'idiographic' study of single cases than by traditional 'nomothetic' methods, those designed to establish general laws.

Allport does not, however, advocate the abandonment of nomothetic techniques. Rather, he emphasizes the value of employing both approaches to psychological events. The manner in which idiographic study of personal documents and nomothetic analysis of highly structured questionnaire responses can complement each other is illustrated by two investigations published nearly a half century apart, both bearing on the personal rejection of a traditionally religious outlook. On the one hand is Vetter and Green's (1932) questionnaire investigation of 320 male members of the American Association for the Advancement of Atheism; on the other is Åkerberg's (1978) study of Swedish political scientist and newspaper editor Herbert Tingsten, who, when he died in 1973, left behind a corpus of autobiographical writings that describes a life of profound nihilism, chronic anxiety, ill-defined guilt, and deep fear of personal annihilation in death. The outstanding trends in the lives of Vetter and Green's atheists are astonishingly confirmed in nearly every respect in Tingsten's own life: the position of the first-born; a parent of more than ordinary piety (his mother); a troubled childhood (debilitating illness in Tingsten's case); the death of a parent within the first two decades (his mother, when he was 14), an adolescent 'conversion' to atheism (by about age 16), a high degree of education, and politically liberal views.

Without knowing that a disproportionately high percentage of members of an atheist organization share these life trends, one might not think to consider their role in forming Tingsten's own atheist views. Indeed, Vetter and Green's avowed atheists themselves seemed not to recognize the influence of early personal and social factors in their antireligious attitudes, but credited instead their later reading and reflection. Tingsten, it should be said, noted both the role of his scientific education and his mother's death in his own growing conviction that life is without meaning.

Yet Åkerberg's study of Tingsten is not simply one more instance to add to Vetter and Green's statistics. On the contrary, only in this study, and especially in the deeply moving autobiographical passages that are used to illustrate the themes in Tingsten's life, do we encounter a living personal reality. From Vetter and Green's study we have no idea what place atheistic sentiments have in the total economy of each subject's life, nor do we learn, for example, how those subjects who lost a parent in childhood or adolescence reacted to that event. There is no mistaking these matters in Tingsten's case. From Åkerberg's study, too, we learn something of the course of Tingsten's nihilistic dread throughout his life and the measures he took in his efforts to escape it. One has, then, an opportunity to gain insight into the dynamics of the atheistic outlook in one person's life, an opportunity that Vetter and Green's anonymous and static data do not provide.

One can well imagine that Vetter and Green would have designed a somewhat different questionnaire had Tingsten's writings been available to them. They would surely have wanted to know if other atheists share his inexplicable sense of sin and dread of annihilation. Are they haunted, too, by 'an impetuous seeking without a goal'? Under what circumstances is equanimity found or 'grace' experienced? Is their 'atheism' merely hostility toward particular traditional religious ideas or is it, as in Tingsten's case, a thoroughgoing loss of a sense of life's meaning? A more open-ended questionnaire would undoubtedly be required, and from it would most certainly issue a new collection of personal documents underscoring crucial if sometimes subtle variations in life circumstances and personal outlook. One would come to understand more of the life experiences of 'atheists' at the same time that one would grow more cautious in generalizing about them.

Early in the century the *open-ended questionnaire* was the chief means by which psychologists of religion gathered their data. Sharing most of the advantages of the spontaneous self-report, the replies to such a questionnaire have several additional virtues: they are parallel to each other in content and structure, which are determined beforehand by the investigator; they are potentially available in large numbers and from persons of nearly every walk of life; and they may be obtained under a great variety of circumstances, as the need arises. On the other hand, the questionnaire reply is no less dependent than the spontaneously produced document on its writer's introspective capacities, memory, self-knowledge, verbal ability, and candor. Although one has more opportunity to ask what one wants to know, there is no guarantee that the answer, if it is forthcoming, will be full and reliable. Moreover, with certain populations the questionnaire will tend to elicit largely conventional expressions or orthodox declamations. Yet even if the response is formulated in relatively original terms, it is likely to exhibit a clarity and order that misrepresents the respondent's experience. The very posing of questions will likely suggest a particular form and content for the answers and may at the same time yield a document misleading in its emphases.

To these problems must be added one more: the fact of selective returns. Even with a relatively undemanding questionnaire and a group of subjects actively interested in promoting their own viewpoints, Vetter and Green received replies from fewer than 60 percent of the persons in their random sample—a percentage, as they note, that is exceptionally *high* for a mailed questionnaire. By contrast, of the 550 questionnaires that Pratt (1907) distributed, only 15 percent were returned. Today, a 50 percent return rate is considered good, though it is clearly low enough to require special efforts to determine how representative that proportion of respondents may be.

If one has the time and opportunity, *interviewing* one's subjects may serve as a way around some of the difficulties of the questionnaire. In face-to-face conversation, one's subjects will likely give answers that are fuller, more spontaneous, and less subject to editing for syntax, consistency, and coherence. Moreover, even if one carefully employs a standard series of questions, one may also gently encourage the reticent subject to expand on certain points, just as one may probe for the personal meaning of conventional or obscure expressions. One also has the opportunity to observe the subject's expressive behavior as the answers are given; facial expressions, gestures, and posture, along with the subject's manner of speaking, can give to the astute observer important clues to the attitudes that lie behind the words, thereby providing leads to further questioning. The interview is thus potentially more sensitive to individual differences at the same time that it casts light on the adequacy of the prepared questions themselves.

The interview yields a self-report as defined in this chapter only when the subject's own words are faithfully recorded, today most commonly by electronic means. Apart from this requirement, the interview as a means of gathering self-reports may be conducted in a variety of ways. Piaget's semi-clinical interview, which combines a standard set of questions with the clinician's technique of free inquiry, has been employed by Elkind (1964) to explore the spontaneous meanings that children between the ages of 5 and 14 ascribe to their own religious denominations. A similar technique was used by Goldman (1964), whose questions were directed to reveal his six- to seventeen-year-old subjects' thinking about three pictures with religious content and three Bible stories. In Germany, Thun (1959, 1969) has employed less structured forms of interviewing as a means of eliciting reports of religious experience and reflection. With children he conducted the interviews as class discussions on particular topics; his interviews with elderly subjects, by contrast, were carried out individually and in most cases in two lengthy sessions, the second of which was directed to such themes as past experience, interests, ideals, conscience, death, prayer, church, and the nature of God. Even less structure and more intense personal association was the rule in Coles's (1971) remarkable interview study of the poor in the northern cities of the United States. Eschewing representative samples and statistical analysis on the one hand and insensitive reductive interpretation on the other, Coles relies heavily on the words of three informants—two women and the minister of one of them—to make evident how intimately the poor and suffering have come to know God and Jesus Christ, and how changes in life's circumstances can affect that intimacy.

Whether one limits one's interviews to the posing of a few selected questions to anonymous respondents or extends it to the point of becoming a participant-observer in the subjects' lives, this manner of gathering self-reports is obviously time-consuming to an exceptional degree. The problem of establishing rapport, moreover, which comes into play whenever a subject's cooperation is required, becomes especially critical in the context of an interview. The advantage of the extended interview lies not only in the longer protocols that result but also in the opportunity it provides for the growth of familiarity and trust, vital ingredients for the development of rapport. Yet one must also be certain that interested encouragement, whether in the form of further questions or simple gestures of acknowledgment, does not become a major factor in shaping the content of the interview. The task of the interviewer becomes increasingly difficult as the subject matter comes to deal less with factual matters and more with questions of attitudes and values.

The often large quantity of material gathered by means of self-report can be handled in any of several ways, depending on the character of the data as well as one's purposes. Where the number of subjects is small, it is possible to allow each of them to emerge as a separate personality, represented by lengthy quotations and supplementary life-history material (e.g., Coles 1971, McDowell 1978, Thun 1969). More commonly, the self-reports of a relatively large number of subjects are used in an essentially inductive manner to identify fundamental stages or types, or to illuminate the structural elements of an experience, around which, then, the research report is organized. Brief excerpts from the documents of several different writers, who are likely to be identified by little more than age, sex, and perhaps school year or occupation, serve to illustrate each type or element (e.g., Goldman 1964, Guittard 1953, Schmid 1960). It is possible, of course, to combine these approaches, as Schüttler (1974) demonstrates in his interview study of enlightenment in Zen Buddhist practice.

An idiographic approach requires by definition an emphasis on particular personalities, though the individual case study can also serve the nomothetic goal of explanation in terms of one or another theory. In a few cases, personal documents have been allowed to stand virtually alone, with little commentary or interpretation. As Girgensohn (1921) discovered, however, self-reports that seem to the investigator to be unequivocally clear in their significance may be far from transparent to other readers. Whether one's purposes are idiographic or nomothetic, then, some structure and interpretation would seem to be highly desirable. When one is elaborating the personal documents into a formal life history, organization and conceptualization are essential (Watson 1976).

A full and accurate understanding of one's documents—if such is ever possible—requires far more than a casual reading of them. Many investigators have relied upon some form of systematic intuiting, whether it be genuinely phenomenological in character or guided by some set of presuppositions. An intuitive approach relies heavily, of course, on an intimate knowledge of one's materials as well as on highly developed capacities for empathy and discernment. Other researchers have sought more objective means of dealing with the extended document's idiosyncratic subjectivity, employing techniques of content analysis, rating scales, and a variety of statistical procedures (e.g., Pahnke 1966).

Standardized Questionnaire. The difficulties both of obtaining detailed and usable self-reports and then of analyzing their content have led to the widespread substitution of the standardized questionnaire and related measurement devices. Not only do these techniques require far less time and effort from the respondent, thus making cooperation more likely, but they also eliminate altogether the subjective evaluation process. Indeed, it is possible to have one's respondents enter their agreement or disagreement with the questionnaire statements on a machine-scorable answer sheet, so that each respondent's answers pass directly from that page to the computer. Sophisticated statistical analysis is then possible, including structural analysis of the questionnaire itself as well as calculations of the degree of relatedness between the questionnaire's scales and other social and personality variables, once they too have been operationally defined.

Questionnaires assembled to measure individual differences in religiousness range from very brief scales such as Yinger's (1977) scale of non-doctrinal religious attitudes to far more complex instruments, including King and Hunt's (1972) factor-analytically derived scales of diverse religious attitudes and behavior and Mallory's (1977) questionnaire on spirituality, a large part of which consists of quotations from the writings of St. John of the Cross. For convenience's sake, if not also out of conviction, many investigators have assumed that religiosity is a single dimension along which people are widely scattered. According to this point of view, a variety of indices—such as church attendance, frequency of prayer, attitudes toward 'religion' or 'the church,' religious beliefs, occurrence of religious experience, knowledge of the Scriptures, and adherence to religious norms—are effectively measuring the same thing, though perhaps not equally well. It is of no great consequence, then, which measure one uses.

The relatively low correlation typically found among these measures, however, and their failure to show the same pattern of relation to other variables, raises serious doubts that the unidimensional assumption is correct. The application of factor analysis—a complex statistical procedure that, since the development of the high-speed computer, has been commonly used to evaluate the interrelation of items on a questionnaire—has in many cases confirmed the hypothesis that religiousness is multidimensional. Yet an occasional factor-analytic study reasserts the existence of a single religiosity factor or at least a general one. As Dittes (1969) points out, the dimensionality of a questionnaire depends in large measure on the kinds of items that compose it and the nature of the subjects who respond to it. A questionnaire that is made up of items expressing conventional religious attitudes, that contains as well a number of non-religious items, and that is completed by a religiously heterogeneous group of respondents will likely yield a single 'religious factor.' If, however, the questionnaire is wholly composed of sophisticated religious items and is administered to a homogenous group of religiously knowledgeable and committed persons, one may expect the questionnaire to yield a more complex factorial structure. King and Hunt (1972), for example, found 10 meaningful factors and Mallory (1977) discovered 13.

Once religiousness has been operationally defined by means of a standardized questionnaire—one, we may hope, that has proved itself acceptable in terms of reliability and validity (see Standards 1974)—the main task of this approach in the psychology of religion can be undertaken: the identification of piety's correlates. The easiest way of uncovering such relationships is the technique of contrasting groups. Two or more classes of people are identified that differ on some fundamental dimension: sex, age, educational attainment, socioeconomic status, profession, denominational affiliation, psychiatric history, criminal record, country of citizenship, and so on. Where such differences are not obvious or a matter of record, one may ask acquaintances of one's subjects to assign them to one group or another. After obtaining scores on one's questionnaire from a representative sample of persons in each of these groups, one may look for mean differences that are 'statistically significant,' that is, that are great enough in comparison to the variability of scores within the groups to allow one to conclude with a high level of confidence that the samples one has drawn are not, in terms of piety, from the same population. Such group differences may provide important clues to the nature and dynamics of religious faith, clues sufficiently ambiguous, however, to allow a range of interpretations.

Useful though group membership has proved to be, it is at best a crude measure of individual differences. More subtle discriminations are made possible by the use of standardized personality and attitude questionnaires, many of which have been formally published and widely researched. By such means one may explore the relation of piety to intelligence, prejudicial attitudes, dogmatism, neurotic tendencies, introversion-extraversion, locus of control, fear of death, achievement orientation, political attitudes, as well as a host of other, less commonly employed variables.

Although consistent findings have issued out of this research, their generality is an important but neglected question. The tendency toward fundamentalist literalism in the writing of items for religiosity questionnaires has prejudiced the results from the outset, practically guaranteeing, for example, a negative correlation with intellectual capacity or a positive one with dogmatism. Hunt (1972a) has argued for adding a 'mythological' dimension to these scales, and Greeley (1972) urges yet another, a 'hermeneutic' one, which would more clearly refer to the transcendent. In fact, every questionnaire option raises the question of hermeneutics, as Hunt (1972b) points out. It is a matter, in the end, of how many interpretive options are required to accommodate a diverse group of respondents. Given the extraordinary range of individual differences in human piety, one can well imagine that no existing questionnaire is wholly satisfactory.

Many of the personality and attitude questionnaires used in these correlation studies are similarly problematical. For example, Shostrom's (1966) Personal Orientation Inventory, a putative measure of self-actualization that is today one of the most widely—and uncritically—used personality tests in the correlational psychology of religion, is in fact a test of dubious value. The extreme, categorical statements that compose this questionnaire represent an undefended ethical and metaphysical position, many elements of which would win a sociopath's happy approval. The negative correlations often found between measures of piety and the POI's scales, coefficients that are commonly interpreted to religion's disadvantage, may in fact be accounted for by the test's emphasis, not on genuine self-actualization, but on loosely principled self-interest and power. In a correlational study with the Allport-Vernon-Lindzey Study of Values, for example, an investigation that Shostrom himself cites, the POI scales proved to be most positively related, on the average, to the Political or power scale, and most negatively correlated with the Social scale, which is intended as a measure of altruistic love. No attitude or personality questionnaire should be used in any context without first carrying out a well-informed and thorough evaluation of the evidence for what it measures. One should be particularly wary of the test manual's claims in this regard as well as of the labels attached to the test's various scales. Regrettably, much of the correlational literature in the psychology of religion suffers from too casual a use of measuring instruments, including those designed to assess the diverse expressions of religious faith.

The use of one or another form of self-report or standardized questionnaire to evaluate an individual's religiosity presupposes that most people are capable of providing a reliable account of their inmost feelings and attitudes. Yet it is precisely this assumption that Freud and the clinical psychologists who have followed him have most vigorously called into question. Comparative religionist W.C. Smith (1959: 39) likewise challenges any simple reliance on self-report: personal faith, he avers, 'cannot adequately be expressed in words, not even by a man who holds it devoutly.' To comprehend the faith of others, he says, 'we must look not at their religion but at the universe, so far as possible through their eyes. It is what the Hindu is able to see, by being a Hindu, that is significant' (Smith 1963: 138).

Projective Methods. Coming to know how another perceives the world, albeit in a rather more limited sense, is precisely the goal of projective techniques. In order to encourage individuals to disclose the chief elements, organization, and meanings of the personal world in which each of them lives, an ambiguous or relatively unstructured set of complex stimuli is presented to each of them for organization and interpretation. Because no particular responses are compelled by these materials, it is assumed that the order imposed by the subject inevitably reveals something of the character of that individual's private world of experience, a world that may otherwise remain wholly inarticulate. Furthermore, because the purpose of the projective test is more or less disguised, it is thought by its users to be less vulnerable than other assessment techniques to efforts to create a deliberate impression. By those of psychoanalytic persuasion, it is also thought to tap unconscious layers of the psyche and thus to provide material unavailable to introspection. Whereas the standardized questionnaire presents a sharply limited range of predetermined and conventional meanings from among which the respondent must choose, the projective test allows for an indefinite number of meanings, including the most highly idiosyncratic and richly elaborated. The task of interpreting an individual's responses is correspondingly more complex and the subject of considerable controversy.

On the relatively rare occasions when projective methods have been introduced into the psychology of religion, they have most often been used in one of two ways: to assess the psychological status of persons of a particular religious outlook or to explore the religious views of individuals of a particular general class (e.g., children). The first of these approaches employs standard projective techniques, chiefly the Rorschach inkblot test and the Thematic Apperception Test (TAT). The Rorschach has served, for example, to evaluate Protestant seminarians (Helfaer 1972), Pentecostal adherents (Wood 1965), and psychotic patients with religious delusions (Lowe 1953). It has also been used to explore group differences, such as those between religious conservatives and liberals (Dreger 1952) and those among groups varying in level of meditation experience (Brown and Engler 1980). The more highly structured pictures of the TAT are commonly used in conjunction with the Rorschach, as in Lowe's and Dreger's studies, but they have also been employed separately, as in Schüttler's (1971) investigation of Tibetan monks. A variety of other standard projective methods have been drawn into the psychology of religion as well, including the Rosenzweig Picture-Frustration Study, the Szondi Test, Koch's Tree Test, the animal test, the Draw-a-Person Test, and sentence completion.

The reasonable expectation that ordinary projective methods might occasionally yield explicit religious imagery or themes, especially from unusually pious individuals, has in most cases not been fulfilled (Attkisson, Handler, and Shrader 1969; Pruyser 1968). Accordingly, when projective methods are utilized to assess religiousness *per se*, rather than some other personality trends, they are usually modified to ensure that religious themes will be forthcoming. Thus TAT-type pictures with obvious religious elements have been used by several investigators (Goldman 1964, Godin and Coupez 1957), word association has been carried out with religious concepts (Deconchy 1967), 'letters to God' have been elicited from parochial elementary school children (Ludwig, Weber, and Iben 1974), and drawings of God or other religious themes have been sought from children, adolescents, and psychiatric patients (Bindl 1965, Rizzuto 1979). The texts and pictures so obtained provide a basis for judgments about religious concerns and development, both for individual subjects and for particular groups as a whole.

Correlations between religiosity scores derived from projective methods and those of existing standardized questionnaires are low enough—Ludwig and Blank (1969), for example, report ones ranging from 0.22 to 0.37—to suggest that the two methods are assessing different aspects or dimensions of piety. Whether or not the projective approach presently comes closer to assessing how an individual sees the universe is surely a moot question. In principle, however, it would seem to have the advantage. One must nevertheless remember that the partial abandonment of structure, while reducing the likelihood of dissimulation and response set and providing more latitude for individual response, also reintroduces the complicated problems of scoring and interpreting idiosyncratic personal content. It is these difficulties that standardized questionnaires are designed to minimize.

Naturalistic Observation. Except for spontaneous personal documents, all the methods we have so far considered depend upon a measure of cooperation from the individual observed. Yet informing potential subjects of one's plans to study them, especially when self-reports are required, is most likely to introduce a degree of self-consciousness, if not also defensiveness, that may seriously distort one's findings. One is usually dependent, moreover, on the limited capacities of one's subjects for systematic and accurate self-observation. The events observed, finally, commonly lie in the past, so that one must also contend with the vicissitudes of memory and recall.

To catch phenomena when and where they spontaneously occur, while minimizing as much as possible the disturbing presence of the observer, is the goal of naturalistic observation. Although this rubric is associated more commonly with sociological investigation, it has been employed on occasion by psychologists as well. Indeed, one may view some forms of psychotherapy as a variant of it, as Rapaport (1959) does when he identifies the basic method of psychoanalysis as participant observation. That is, the phenomenon of transference brings vital relationships from the past into the consultation room and casts the therapist into the dual role of 'significant other' and trained observer. By means of participant observation and the use of such techniques as free association and dream analysis, the therapist seeks to make these transferred relational patterns conscious and thereby to give the patient insight into them. For the psychology of religion, the outcome has been a series of case studies that serve at least to illustrate, if they do not also test, the principles of the psychoanalytic viewpoint (see, for example, Edelheit 1974; also Lubin 1959).

The method of participant observation in its more usual sense can be found in a study by Festinger, Riecken, and Schachter (1956), who observed at close range a small millennial group convinced that a great flood was shortly to inundate a large portion of the Western hemisphere and that the group's members, as faithful believers, would be carried out of harm's way by superior beings from another planet. The observers that Festinger and his associates managed to insinuate into the group feigned conviction at the same time that they tried to avoid acts of participation that would shape the group's conduct and destiny. Exhausting though their impossible task proved to be, the observers managed to learn much about the group members and to document in considerable detail the long wait for orders, the final preparations, and the reactions to disconfirmation. In a similar if somewhat less dramatic study in which intentional deception was not employed, Lofland (1966), who was himself the participant observer, was for a time cast in the role of 'studying the precepts.' Once it became evident, however, that he was not likely to convert to the viewpoint of the Korea-based doomsday cult, which was later to achieve considerable notoriety, its members forced his withdrawal. For yet another naturalistic investigation, in which participation would have been virtually impossible, Schüttler (1971) gained permission to observe and photograph a Tibetan oracle ceremony, as well as to interview several high-ranking priests. The Dalai Lama apparently assented to this research because of his disdain for such folk practices.

The problem of observing phenomena in their natural setting without changing or shaping them has impelled some social scientists to search out 'non-reactive' measures, for use in combination with other techniques. Work of this sort is rare in the psychology of religion, but a study of TeVault, Forbes, and Gromoll (1971) illustrates what can be done. Five of the most liberal and five of the most conservative Protestant congregations in a midwestern city in America were carefully chosen to assure that they constituted an otherwise homogeneous sample of middle-class churches in predominantly or exclusively white residential neighborhoods. Sunday morning during the main service, the investigators determined the proportion of cars in each church parking lot that had a locked driver's door. They found that the percentage of locked cars was significantly higher in the lots of the conservative churches than in those of the liberal churches (41 percent as compared to 33). If one is not inclined to accept this finding as evidence that 'conservative church members, repressing their own unacceptable urges, project them onto others,' one cannot deny that it is suggestive of how the religious conservative views and relates to the world.

Unfortunately, naturalistic observation is rarely so unobtrusive or so clearly defined and quantified as in this study. The complexity, unpredictability, and transiency of the phenomena studied by Festinger and his associates are far more typical. It is these very qualities that deter many psychologists from undertaking this form of observation. Too many unmeasured and thus statistically uncontrollable variables play simultaneous roles in the proceedings, and one seldom has the opportunity—or, when it presents itself, feels justified in taking it—to modify any of these variables. Rokeach's (1964) experimental manipulation of the interactions and delusions of three mental patients each of whom believed he was Christ is a rare instance of intrusion into naturally occurring (if also abnormal) processes.

Experimentation. According to some psychologists, the degree of control and accuracy of measurement that is required for truly scientific research, including the testing of hypotheses about cause and effect, can never be achieved in a natural setting. Even the correlational approach, though it adheres more faithfully to contemporary standards of psychometric practice, falls short of the ideal, for it too disallows firm conclusions about the causal ordering of events. Only experimentation as it is understood in the physical sciences—not, for example, as the Dorpat school uses it—is capable of establishing beyond a doubt the cause-effect relations that lie at the heart of psychological explanation. Proponents of this point of view, which constitutes one of the 'two disciplines of scientific psychology' (Cronbach 1957), by and large disdain the concern for individual differences that characterizes the other, correlational discipline. They seek, rather, to observe the effects of systematically controlled changes in laboratory conditions on selected dependent variables. Subjects are chosen in a manner that minimizes the role of individual differences; committed as the experimentalists are to the most rigorous standards of observation and measurement, they are inclined to emphasize the effects of highly accessible, environmental factors and to discount or ignore the more vaguely defined and roughly measured variables that concern the personality psychologist.

Many persons simply take it for granted that experimental methods are not applicable in the psychology of religion. Even if it is possible to introduce aspects of religiousness as experimental variables—and a relatively large literature stands as testimony that it is—there is strong sentiment in many quarters that experimentation with religion for scientific purposes is unethical if not also sacrilegious. Even the benign 'experimentation' of the Dorpat school was undertaken with some trepidation: to preserve the sanctity of the proceedings, some members of this tradition began and ended the 'experiments' with prayer (Vetö 1971).

The size of the experimental literature in this field depends upon how one defines both experimentation and religion. If one is willing to include only those studies in which the independent variables are genuinely under the experimenter's control and the dependent variable is an unmistakable dimension of piety, one will be hard pressed to find more than one or two examples. Undoubtedly the best known of these is Pahnke's (1966) study of the potential role of drugs in mystical experience. In this experiment, careful efforts were made to control for personality factors, religious background, past religious experience, as well as the subjects' expectations and the setting of the experiment itself. The experimental group was presumed to be distinguished from the control group only by the fact that its members were given 30 milligrams of psilocybin, whereas the control group subjects received an identical-appearing capsule of nicotinic acid, the side effects of which were intended to give the control subjects the impression that it was they who had received the psychedelic drug. The dependent variable, elaborately measured by a lengthy questionnaire and content analysis of essay and interview data, was the subjects' experience during a Good Friday service. The self-reports of the experimental group proved indeed to show significantly more of the hallmarks of mystical experience than did those of the control group.

If, on the other hand, one casts a net large enough to include experimental studies of meditation (which most American psychologists of religion, curiously, seem not to associate with their domain of research) as well as studies where religion is among the *independent* variables or where the independent variables are to a large degree *not* under the experimenter's control—so-called quasi-experimental studies—one will discover a literature of considerable proportions (e.g., see Bock and Warren 1972, Darley and Batson 1973, Deconchy 1980, Funderburk 1977).

Yet however one sets the boundaries, complications and doubts remain. The ethical and epistemological issues are only now gaining an adequate hearing (Batson 1977, Batson and Deconchy 1978). There are practical difficulties, too: a woman who agrees to speak in tongues for a scientific observer discovers that, under these circumstances, she experiences no inner exhilaration; a Zen monk finds that the electrodes attached to his scalp are a distraction that prevents his usual course of meditation; a widely respected yogi, reputed to have attained the rare state of *samadhi*, rejects experimental investigation as presumptuous and trivial; the subjects in an elaborately double-blind study—Pahnke's—suddenly realize which group they are in. According to Koepp's (1920) argument, searching for other subjects or redesigning one's system of controls, helpful though they might be for such particular difficulties as these, will not solve the fundamental dilemma of all experimental research in the psychology of religion: any religious phenomenon brought into the laboratory—that is, any such phenomenon that is called forth, not for its own sake, but for scientific purposes—will inevitably be changed, to the point, says Koepp, that it will lose its essentially religious character. At the very best, he concludes, the experiment may indirectly touch upon matters that are of secondary importance in the religious life. Yet research design today is far more sophisticated than Koepp most likely anticipated. It has proved possible, for example, to conduct quasi-experimental research in naturalistic settings (e.g., Hood 1977). Recent trends, both in research and in discussions of method, suggest that the last word has yet to be spoken on these issues.

Studying Content and Tradition

The research interests of many psychologists of religion are by and large limited to the varied expressions of personal faith. Committed to the contemporary understanding of empirical investigation, which is defined in terms of established observational techniques, these researchers assume that historical materials lie outside the arena of psychological investigation (e.g., see Girgensohn, 1921: 5–12). Others, however, see in the cumulative materials of the world's religious traditions a rich mine of data for psychological analysis. Koepp (1920), for one, has argued that the comparative history of religion is an essential source of phenomena for psychological investigation, given especially the impossibility, in his view, of any direct observation of living religious experience. From Jung's (1969) perspective, it is not simply a matter of finding data where one can; rather, he distinguishes two kinds of psychology of religion, one concerned with the religious person, the other, with religious contents. Still others emphasize the reciprocal dependence of the history and the psychology of religion, the former providing the materials, the latter, the modes and categories of analysis (see Hellpach 1951, van der Leeuw 1926).

Comparative and historical materials have been used by psychologists of religion in a variety of ways. Early in the century, the work of some scholars in this field showed a convergence of psychological and anthropological perspectives. Wundt's (1905–1909) massive study entitled *Mythus und Religion*, which centers on a psychology of mythic apperception, is entirely dependent for its data on historical and anthropological research. Psychological interest in religion's origins and the testimony of comparative data likewise arose in England and America as well as in France, where the psychology of religion was to claim Durkheim's classic work *The Elementary Forms of the Religious Life*, published in 1912, as a major resource of its own.

The authors of such works were fascinated above all by reports on the practices of 'primitive' tribes. Stratton (1911), by contrast, was drawn chiefly to the sacred literatures of the world's religious traditions. Rejecting in a brief aside his contemporaries' reliance on the questionnaire, especially given the narrow range of persons reached by it,

Stratton turned instead to 'the prayer, the hymn, the myth, the sacred prophecy,' which, he believed, 'still furnish to the psychologist the best means of examining the full nature of religion in its diverse forms' (1911: v–vi). Stratton concludes in this strikingly original work that at religion's heart is the struggle with the conflict of psychic opposites, a conflict laid to rest in some but still a present reality in others.

Yet another variety of historical investigation draws thematically on the records of particular religious events as its primary source of data, records that occasionally include personal documents and eye-witness accounts, as in the famous seventeenth-century case of possession at Loudun. Not surprisingly, as this example illustrates, these studies focus chiefly on exceptional phenomena, including—in addition to demon possession and exorcism—speaking in tongues, religious revivals, and a variety of ecstatic practices. One may also find investigations of one or another religious movement, including case studies of their leaders and perhaps psychological evaluations of their adherents.

Whereas one might expect the psychoanalytic literature on religion to consist largely of individual case studies, in fact the bulk of it focuses on religious contents, not on individual persons. One may find psychoanalytic interpretations of religious rituals, shamanism, biblical stories and figures, religious movements, concepts of divinity, religious symbols, holidays, and sacred art. The overrepresentation of Jews among psychoanalysts is reflected in a preponderance of elements from the Jewish tradition, although there are also occasional works on themes from the Christian, Hindu, and a scattering of other traditions. Analytical psychology, beginning with Jung, likewise strongly emphasizes religious content, but in this case the accent is on Christian rather than Jewish elements. Jung and his followers were especially interested in Gnostic and alchemical symbols, particularly in their connections with the Christian tradition.

Widespread though the use of historical materials and traditional content therefore is in the psychology of religion, no generally accepted methods for their evaluation or interpretation have been established. Not uncommonly, depth psychologists introduce individual case material in conjunction with historical content, the psychoanalysts to emphasize the putative infantile dynamics of the traditional elements, the Jungians to demonstrate the timeless, archetypal, even religious qualities of individual dreams and fantasies. However fascinating such comparisons may be, experimental psychologists consider them far from adequate tests of the respective theories. At best, it is argued, they serve an illustrative function. By those who have found the depth-psychological approaches illuminating, however, the clinical and comparative studies, whatever their technical shortcomings, have produced far more suggestive accounts of the psychodynamics of religion than have the efforts of the correlational and experimental psychologists. The clinical viewpoint, argue Hiltner and Rogers (1963), is an essential source of hypotheses, derived both systematically and heuristically; the experimentalists, as they take on these more complex problems, can provide the needed checks and controls.

The possibility of a more systematic approach to traditional content is illustrated by Young's (1926) analysis of Protestant hymns. Young classified 2922 hymns from seven conservative-Protestant hymnbooks in terms of their dominant appeal or motive. The most common theme proved to be 'infantile return,' a turning back to God the all-powerful father who protects and consoles; second most common was 'future reward,' the joyful anticipation of heaven, often expressed in quite literal terms. Together these themes account for nearly 58 percent of the hymns, and many others bear a close relation to one or the other of these motifs. Here is evidence, says Young, for the validity of the psychoanalytic claim that religion reflects the conflict between infantile wishes and the demands of reality. This investigation also illustrates how historical materials may be used to test hypotheses derived from the study of individual piety.

Techniques or Hermeneutics: Some Reflections on Method

There is little doubt that concern with method can have a salutary effect on the conduct of research. It encourages investigators to think more critically about the means by which they make their observations and, in that light, the significance and limits of their findings. More self-conscious about the potentially distorting roles of their own points of view and personal needs, they are better able to appreciate the discipline of using precisely specified techniques shared by a scientific community. These common procedures, moreover, allow the comparison of one study with another and thus the accumulation of evidence bearing on a single area of investigation.

Yet absorption in the technicalities of method can too easily lead to a methodological imperialism that blindly denies legitimacy to other approaches. It can likewise result in a rigidity of technique that unknowingly violates, through insensitive intrusion or misrepresentation, the phenomenon it seeks to comprehend. Grønbaek (1970) warns particularly against unthinking appropriation of modern scientific techniques by the psychology of religion; there is a danger, he says, of becoming *less* scientific, so that one fails to do justice to the uniqueness of the religious life. A truly scientific attitude, thoughtful scholars have emphasized again and again, does not simply adopt methods that have proved successful in one domain and use them in another; rather, it seeks to identify the means of investigation that are most appropriate to its object.

It may also be the case that such means will have none of the appearance of conventional methods. Coe (1916) makes this point in discussing the third, psychological part of Höffding's *The Philosophy of Religion* (1901). Höffding, he says,

> makes little use of anthropology, or of sacred literatures, or of religious biographies, or of question-list returns; yet his analysis of the religious experience is among the most noteworthy. The reason is that, though he adduces few new data, he sees far into common facts. Now, this far-sight of his is not an accident; it is rather the ripe fruit of long experience with psychological facts and problems (1916: 55–56).

Höffding's 'method,' then, is an extraordinary mind both richly furnished and discerning, one capable of seeing the commonplace in a new light, of making connections between facts previously thought unrelated. A world-famous psychologist and the outstanding Danish philosopher of his day, Höffding counted himself a methodological pluralist. His broad sympathies are likewise reflected in his sensitivity to a wide range of individual and historical differences in piety as well as to a great diversity of nuances that he says lie beyond the abstractions of psychological analysis.

Höffding's example underscores for the psychology of religion the critical importance of human understanding, of an interpreting mind. Although portions of the field are today still burdened by the literal-mindedness of positivistic psychology as well as its conviction that operational procedures are an adequate solution for the problem of meaning, there is growing recognition of the centrality of hermeneutics to any genuine psychology of religion. In Germany, where hermeneutics has its deepest roots, psychologists of religion, especially those of the *verstehende* tradition, have long recognized the importance of interpretive understanding (see Pöll 1965). More recently, the essentially hermeneutical character of the depth psychologies has become the subject of close analysis, above all by Ricoeur (1965) in his widely discussed study of Freud, but by others as well, including Heimbrock (1977, 1978), Homans (1970), and Müller-Pozzi (1975), who are concerned chiefly with the psychoanalytic interpretation of religion, and Heisig (1979), Homans (1969), Hummel (1972), and Wehr (1974), who explore the Jungian perspective. Worthy of note, too, is a somewhat earlier work by Sierksma (1950), who discusses the *verstehende* approach in relation to Freudian psychoanalysis and Jung's analytical psychology.

Although they may be loathe to admit it, correlational and experimental psychologists are no less involved in the process of interpretation. Elaborate instrumentation and statistical procedures, far from solving the hermeneutical question, only compound it, by removing human (and animal) responses from their natural context of meaning and transforming them into highly abstract graphs and numbers. When researchers report that their results are statistically 'significant,' or, in a flight of interpretive fancy, that their animal subjects are exhibiting 'superstitious' or 'ritual' behavior, they are using language in a way that serves to obscure rather than clarify meaning. Regardless of theoretical or methodological commitment, in sum, the psychologist is at some point engaged in the task of interpreting evidence, and thus in hermeneutics. To ignore the important issues of interpretation in psychology, argues Hudson (1975: 12), 'is to do our best to ensure the triviality of whatever research we undertake.' In the psychology of religion, regrettably, concern with hermeneutics has come almost exclusively from the side of theology and religious studies, not from psychology.

A LOOK TO THE FUTURE

So unreciprocal a concern with hermeneutics—that is, with the theory of interpretation, not merely the exegetical task of applying a particular interpretive standpoint—calls to mind other important differences among the practitioners of the psychology of religion. Some insist foremost on precision and clarity; others, on speculative depth and mystery. The former are likely to emphasize the creedal and behavioral sides of religion; the latter, the experiental and mythic. For some, 'religion' calls up all the features of a particular Christian denomination, whereas for others it signifies nothing less than the sum total of the elements composing the world's religious traditions, or perhaps some essence underlying these. In some quarters, the search comes to an end when piety, thought finally to be unmasked, is proved to follow the same laws as other psychic events; in others, satisfaction lies only in the sudden opening outward of a new vista, when one finally sees how the world can appear from another, perhaps radically different perspective. The ultimate test and fulfillment of the psychology of religion, some would say, lies in its capacity to promote the spiritual life, by aiding religious education and pastoral care. Such practical and too-often sectarian concerns, others would reply, are a serious hindrance to any truly comprehensive psychology of religion.

Such differences as these are inevitable, given the multiplicity of perspectives in psychology itself, the enormous complexity of religion, and the diversity in educational background and professional identity of scholars in the field. The personal equation surely plays an important role as well. One's own religious outlook, even if it is a relatively inchoate one, cannot but influence the questions one asks, the theories and methods one adopts, the conclusions one draws. At another level, religious outlook implies a host of personal characteristics, such as temperament, quality of intellect, dominant motives, and degree of empathy and social concern, that combine to shape one's vision and hence one's conduct of research.

According to Jung, the personal factor in psychology is a reality as significant as it is unavoidable. One's psychology constitutes a 'subjective confession,' Jung says; it is testimony to what one has seen and heard within the vast range of human experience. To emphasize the subjective factor in psychology, however, is not to deny the possibility of meaningful communication or even agreement on essential matters. Yet dialogue among researchers of differing persuasions, if it is to yield genuine progress, requires that its participants recognize the relativity and limitations of their own points of view. One might expect psychologists of religion before all others to appreciate the multitude of factors that condition any fundamental commitment, whether it be religious or scientific. Among such specialists, however, explicit recognition of the personal element in their own work, including discussion of both its potential contributions and its dangers, is still far too uncommon. It is even rarer among the amateurs—coming usually from the side of psychology—who, for reasons of their own, are momentarily given to holding forth on the nature of religion or to applying a favorite theory or technique to one more area of human experience.

There is nevertheless evidence of progress. The cause of dialogue among psychologists of religion promises to be well served, for example, by the recent transformation of two formerly Catholic associations into officially non-sectarian ones. One of these, known today as Psychologists Interested in Religious Issues, was accepted in 1975 as a division of the American Psychological Association. The other, the *Association internationale d'études médico-psychologiques et religieuses*, draws the majority of its members from French-, Spanish-, and Italian-speaking countries. Along with the *Internationale Gesellschaft für Religionspsychologie*, a small organization of scholars from Germany and a dozen or so other countries, these groups provide a forum for researchers of diverse backgrounds and persuasions.

Yet to whatever degree these organizations succeed in transcending their parochial origins and promote the informed scholarly dialogue upon which true advancement of the psychology of religion will depend, they cannot hope to compensate for a lack of support within educational institutions. Formal graduate study in the psychology of religion is today hardly possible anywhere outside schools of theology, the traditional setting in which almost all appointments in this field have been made. Departments of psychology or of religious studies, where the psychology of religion would far less likely be associated with pastoral care and other applied or sectarian concerns, have by and large failed to provide alternative contexts. Given the typical psychologist's attitude of suspicion or even hostility toward religion, it is not surprising that departments of psychology are loathe to hire psychologists interested in religion, let alone ones who might inaugurate special programs in the area. Would-be students of the psychology of religion often return the compliment: most of the courses in the standard curriculum in psychology, they judge, are useless for any genuine comprehension of the deepest and most interesting aspects of humankind. Departments of religious studies, if they do not tacitly share this sentiment, are in any case rarely prepared to offer intensive work in the psychology of religion. Limited budgets and long-standing departmental priorities, often shaped by a sectarian past, do not permit the hiring of a specialist broadly trained both in the history of religion and in psychology, if indeed such a person can be found. At best, a single introductory-level course, sometimes in the department of psychology but more often in religious studies, is offered by persons without training beyond that level themselves.

One should not wonder, then, that at least in America hardly anyone has assayed more than a small, accessible portion of the field's voluminous and wide-ranging literature; that standards of scholarship in the psychology of religion are generally lower than in psychology or religious studies; that there is a corresponding disregard for the field and its practitioners; that in turn there are few professorships or chairs in the area; that financial support for advanced work and research likewise is hardly to be found; and that those promising young scholars who might reverse these trends too often elect another, less problematical area of study. The situation in England and on the continent is apparently little different (see Deconchy 1970, Grønbaek 1970, Scobie 1977).

On balance, it must be observed that some of the world's most eminent psychologists have actively contributed to the psychology of religion. Moreover, several of the leading graduate psychology programs in America have in recent years awarded the Ph.D. for dissertations in the area. It is clear that a good measure of the prejudice against the field is of the uninformed and reflexive type, with which the study of religion in general has long had to contend. There are signs, too, that scholars of religion are increasingly turning to psychology for leads to a fuller comprehension of piety's diverse manifestations. The leads are in fact there: the challenge lies in finding and developing them.

To meet this challenge, students of the psychology of religion will need to become well acquainted with a large portion of the field's own literature; to master the theories and methods of psychology, past and present, with a critical eye to their strengths and weaknesses; to inform themselves to the fullest degree possible in the history of religions; to witness at first hand, and sympathetically, a broad range of contemporary piety; and to prepare themselves for critical reflection upon every aspect of their undertaking, from the statement of goals to the final interpretation. Beyond instilling in the individual researcher a healthy sense of humility, the awesome demands of such an agenda should serve to underscore the dependence of the psychologist of religion upon other specialists, in psychology and in the study of religion, as well as the importance of cooperative effort among scholars who share a commitment to broad, flexible, and disinterested investigation. By means of such collaboration, the psychology of religion may yet fulfill its promise, both as a field of scholarly inquiry and as a source of practical insight.

[1] The author has sought to provide a more adequate balance of viewpoints and phenomena in his own forthcoming book, tentatively entitled 'Psychology of Religion: An Historical Introduction.' Many of the themes and issues mentioned here are discussed in greater depth in this longer, more comprehensive work.

Bibliography

Åkerberg, H. *Omvändelse och kamp: En empirisk religionspsykologisk undersökning av den unge Nathan Söderbloms religiösa utveckling 1866–1894*. Lund: Studentlitteratur, 1975.

Åkerberg, H. 'Attempts to Escape: A Psychological Study on the Autobiographical Notes of Herbert Tingsten 1971–1972.' In T. Källstad (ed.), *Psychological Studies on Religious Man*. Stockholm: Almqvist and Wiksell, 1978, 71–92.

Akishige, Y. (ed.). *Psychological Studies on Zen* (2 vols.). Tokyo: Komazawa University, 1977. [Volume 1 first published in 1968.]

Albrecht, C. *Psychologie des mystischen Bewusstseins*. Bremen: Schünemann, 1951.

Allport, G.W. *The Use of Personal Documents in Psychological Science*. New York: Social Science Research Council, 1942.

Allport, G.W. *The Individual and His Religion: A Psychological Interpretation*. New York: Macmillan, 1950.

Amón, J. *Prejuicio antiprotestante y religiosidad utilitaria*. Madrid: Editorial Aguilar, 1969.

Argyle, M., and Beit-Hallahmi, B. *The Social Psychology of Religion*. London: Routledge and Kegan Paul, 1975.

Attkisson, C.C., Handler, L., and Shrader, R.R. 'The Use of Figure Drawings to Assess Religious Values.' *Journal of Psychology*, 1969, *71*, 27–31.

Bakan, D. 'A Reconsideration of the Problem of Introspection.' *Psychological Bulletin*, 1954, *51*, 105–118.

Batson, C.D. 'Experimentation in Psychology of Religion: An Impossible Dream.' *Journal for the Scientific Study of Religion*, 1977, *16*, 413–418.

Batson, C.D., and Deconchy, J.-P. 'Psychologie de la religion et expérimentation.' *Archives de Science Sociales des Religions*, 1978, *46*, 169–192.

Beirnaert, L. *Expérience chrétienne et psychologie* (2nd ed.). Paris: Éditions de l'ÉPI, 1966. (First edition, 1964.)

Beit-Hallahmi, B. *Psychoanalysis and Religion: A Bibliography*. Norwood, Pa.: Norwood Editions, 1978.

Bellet, M. *Foi et psychanalyse*. Paris: Desclée de Brouwer, 1973.

Berguer, C. *Traité de psychologie de la religion*. Laysanne: Payot, 1946.

Bindl, M.F. *Das religiöse Erleben im Spiegel der Bildgestaltung; Eine entwicklungs-psychologische Untersuchung*. Freiburg: Herder, 1965.

Bock, D.C., and Warren, N.C. 'Religious Belief as a Factor in Obedience to Destructive Commands.' *Review of Religious Research*, 1972, *13*, 185–191.

Bolley, A., and Clostermann, G. *Abhandlungen zur Religions- und Arbeitspsychologie; Werner Gruehn zum Gedächtnis*. Münster: Aschendorff, 1963.

Boos-Nünning, U. *Dimensionen der Religiosität: Zur Operationalisierung und Messung religiöser Einstellungen*. München: Chr. Kaiser; Mainz: Matthias-Grünewald, 1972.

Boring, E.G. 'A History of Introspection.' *Psychological Bulletin*, 1953, *50*, 169–189.

Boucouvalas, M. 'Transpersonal Psychology: A Working Outline of the Field.' *Journal of Transpersonal Psychology*, 1980, *12*, 37–46.

Bovet, P. *The Child's Religion*. Trans. G.H. Green. New York: Dutton, 1928. (Original French edition, 1925.)

Bovet, P. *Le sentiment religieux et la psychologie de l'enfant* (2nd ed.). Neuchâtel: Delachaux et Niestlé, 1951.

Brosse, T. *Études instrumentales des techniques du yoga: expérimentation psychosomatique*. Paris: École francaise d'Extrême-Orient (Dépositaire: Adrien-Maisonneuve), 1963.

Brown, D.P., and Engler, J. 'The Stages of Mindfulness Meditation: A Validation Study.' *Journal of Transpersonal Psychology*, 1980, *12*, 143–192.

Brusselmans, C. (ed.). *Toward Moral and Religious Maturity*. Morristown, N.J.: Silver Burdett, 1980.

Campbell, J. *The Masks of God* (4 vols.). New York: Viking Press, 1959–1968.

Capps, D., Rambo, L., and Ransohoff, P. *Psychology of Religion: A Guide to Information Sources*. Detroit: Gale Research, 1976.

Capps, D., Ransohoff, P., and Rambo, L. 'Publication Trends in the Psychology of Religion to 1974.' *Journal for the Scientific Study of Religion*, 1976, *15*, 15–28.

Carstairs, C.M. *The Twice-Born; A Study of a Community of High-Caste Hindus*. London: Hogarth Press, 1957.

Clark, W.H. *The Psychology of Religion: An Introduction to Religious Experience and Behavior*. New York: Macmillan, 1958.

Coe, G.A. *The Psychology of Religion*. Chicago: University of Chicago Press, 1916.

Coles, R. *The South Goes North*. Boston: Little, Brown, 1971.

Cronbach, L.J. 'The Two Disciplines of Scientific Psychology.' *American Psychologist*, 1957, *12*, 671–684.

Darley, J.M., and Batson, C.D. '"From Jerusalem to Jericho": A Study of Situational and Dispositional Variables in Helping Behavior.' *Jounal of Personality and Social Psychology*, 1973, *27*, 100–108.

Deconchy, J.-P. *Structure génétique de l'idée de Dieu chez des catholiques français*. Bruxelles: Lumen Vitae, 1967.

Deconchy, J.-P. 'La Psychologie des faits religieux.' In H. Desroche and J. Seguy (eds.), *Introduction aux sciences humaines des religions*. Paris: Cujas, 1970, 145–174.

Deconchy, J.-P. La Psychologie sociale expérimentale et les comportements religieux. *Annual Review of the Social Sciences of Religion*, 1977, *1*, 103–132.

Deconchy, P.-J. *Orthodoxie religieuse et sciences humaines*. Suivi de (Religious) Orthodoxy, Rationality, and Scientific Knowledge. The Hague: Mouton, 1980.

Dittes, J.E. 'Psychology of Religion.' In G. Lindzey and E. Aronson (eds.), *The Handbook of Social Psychology* (2nd ed., vol. 5). Reading, Mass.: Addison-Wesley, 1969, 602–659.

Dreger, R.M. 'Some Personality Correlates of Religious Attitudes as Determined by Projective Techniques.' *Psychological Monographs*, 1952, *66*, No. 3 (Whole No. 335).

Dumoulin, A., and Jaspard, J.-M. *Les médiations religieuses dans l'univers de l'enfant: Prêtre et*

Eucharistie dans la perception du divin et l'attitude religieuse de 6 à 12 ans. Bruxelles: Lumen Vitae, 1972.

Edelheit, H. 'Crucifixion Fantasies and Their Relation to the Primal Scene.' *International Journal of Psycho-Analysis*, 1974, *55*, 193–199.

Elkind, D. 'Piaget's Semi-Clinical Interview and and the Study of Spontaneous Religion.' *Journal for the Scientific Study of Religion*, 1964, *4*, 40–47.

Erikson, E.H. *Young Man Luther: A Study in Psychoanalysis and History*. New York: W.W. Norton, 1958.

Erikson, E.H. *Gandhi's Truth: On the Origins of Militant Nonviolence*. New York: W.W. Norton, 1969.

Erikson, E.H. *Toys and Reasons: Stages in the Ritualization of Experience*. New York: W.W. Norton, 1977.

Festinger, L., Riecken, H.W., Jr., and Schachter, S. *When Prophecy Fails*. Minneapolis: University of Minnesota Press, 1956.

Flournoy, T. 'Les principes de la psychologie religieuse.' *Archives de Psychologie*, 1903, *2*, 33–57.

Fowler, J.W. *Stages of Faith: The Psychology of Human Development and the Quest for Meaning*. San Francisco: Harper and Row, 1981.

Freud, S. 'Totem and Taboo: Some Points of Agreement Between the Mental Lives of Savages and Neurotics.' In *The Standard Edition of the Complete Psychological Works of Sigmund Freud*, Vol. 13. London: Hogarth Press, 1953, 1–161. (First German Edition in one volume, 1913.)

Freud, S. 'The Future of an Illusion.' *Standard Edition*, Vol. 21, 1961, 1–56. (First German edition, 1927.)

Freud, S. 'Civilization and Its Discontents.' *Standard Edition*, Vol. 21, 1961, 64–145. (Original German edition, 1930.)

Freud, S. 'Moses and Monotheism: Three Essays.' *Standard Edition*, Vol. 23, 1964, 7–137. (Original German edition, 1939.)

Fromm, E. *Psychoanalysis and Religion*. New Haven: Yale University Press, 1950.

Fuchs, A., and Oppermann, R. 'Dimensionen der Religiosität und Bedeutungsstruktur religiöser Konzepte.' *Archiv für Religionspsychologie*, 1975, *11*, 260–266.

Funderburk, J. *Science Studies Yoga; A Review of Physiological Data*. Glenview, Ill.: Himalayan International Institute, 1977.

Gins, K. 'Inhalt oder Anzahl religiöser Erlebnis-Phänomene? Zur Frage nach dem Untersuchungsgegenstand empirischer Religionspsychologie.' *Archiv für Religionspsychologie*, 1976, *12*, 150–175.

Girgensohn, K. *Der seeliche Aufbau des religiösen Erlebens; Eine religionspsychologische Untersuchung auf experimenteller Grundlage* (2nd ed.). Corrected and supplemented by W. Gruehn. Gütersloh: C. Bertelsmann, 1930. (First edition, 1921.)

Godin, A. (ed.). *Research in Religious Psychology: Speculative and Positive*. Brussels: Lumen Vitae, 1959.

Godin, A. (ed.). *From Religious Experience to a Religious Attitude*. Chicago: Loyola University Press, 1965. (First Published, 1964.)

Godin, A. (ed.). *Death and Presence: The Psychology of Death and the After-Life*. Brussels: Lumen Vitae, 1972.

Godin, A., and Coupez, A. 'Religious Projective Pictures: A Technique of Assessment of Religious Psychism.' *Lumen Vitae*, 1957, *12*, 260–274. [Reprinted in Godin, 1959.]

Goldman, R. *Religious Thinking from Childhood to Adolescence*. London: Routledge and Kegan Paul, 1964.

Goodenough, E.R. *The Psychology of Religious Experience*. New York: Basic Books, 1965.

Greeley, A.M. 'Comment on Hunt's "Mythological-Symbolic Religious Commitment: The LAM Scales."' *Journal for the Scientific Study of Religion*, 1972, *11*, 287–289.

Grønbaek, V. 'Die heutige Lage der Religionspsychologie.' *Theologische Literaturzeitung*, 1970, *95*, 321–327.

Gruehn, W. *Die Frömmigkeit der Gegenwart; Grundtatsachen der empirischen Psychologie* (2nd ed.). Konstanz: Friedrich Bahn, 1960. [First edition, 1955.]

Guittard, L. *L'évolution religieuse des adolescents*. Paris: Editions Spes, 1954.

Guntrip, H. 'Religion in Relation to Personal Integration.' *British Journal of Medical Psychology*, 1969, *42*, 323–333.

Havens, J. (ed.). *Psychology and Religion: A Contemporary Dialogue*. Princeton: Van Nostrand, 1968.

Heiler, F. *Prayer; A Study in the History and Psychology of Religion*. Trans. S. McComb. New York: Oxford University Press, 1932. (Original German edition, 1918.)

Heimann, H. 'Religion und Psychiatrie.' In H.W. Gruhle, et al. (eds.), *Psychiatrie der Gegenwart: Forschung und Praxis*, Vol. 3: *Soziale und angewandte Psychiatrie*. Berlin: Springer, 1961, 471–493.

Heimbrock, H.-G. *Phantasie und christlicher Glaube: Zum Dialog zwischen Theeologie und Psychoanalyse*. Kaiser: Grünewald, 1977.

Heimbrock, H.-G. 'Wahrheit in der Wirklichkeit? Ein Literaturbericht zur Religionspsychologie.' *Theologia Practica*, 1978, *13*, 148–158.

Heisig, J.W. 'Jung and Theology: A Bibliographic Essay.' *Spring: An Annual of Archetypal Psychology and Jungian Thought*, 1973, 204–255.

Heisig, J.W. *Imago Dei: A Study of C.G. Jung's Psychology of Religion*. Lewisburg, Pa.: Bucknell University Press, 1979.

Helfaer, P.M. *The Psychology of Religious Doubt*. Boston: Beacon Press, 1972.

Hellpach, W. *Grundriss der Religionspsychologie* (*Glaubensseelenkunde*). Stuttgart: Ferdinand Enke, 1951.

Henderson, J. 'Object Relations and the Doctrine of "Original Sin."' *International Review of Psycho-Analysis*, 1975, *2*, 107–120.

Hillman, J. *Re-Visioning Psychology*. New York: Harper and Row, 1975.

Hiltner, S., and Rogers, W.R. 'Research on Religion and Personality Dynamics'. *Religious Education*, 1962, *57* (4, Research Supplement), 128–140.

Hirai, T. *Psychophysiology of Zen*. Tokyo: Igaku Shoin, 1974.

Höffding, H. *The Philosophy of Religion*. Trans. from the German edition by B.E. Meyer. London: Macmillan, 1906. (First Danish edition, 1901.)

Holl, A., and Fischer, G.H. *Kirche auf Distanz; Eine religionspsychologische Untersuchung über die Einstellung Österreichischer Soldaten zu Kirche und Religion*. Wien: Wilhelm Braumüller, 1968.

Homans, P, (ed.). *The Dialogue Between Theology and Psychology*. Chicago: University of Chicago Press, 1968.

Homans, P. 'Psychology and Hermeneutics: Jung's Contribution,' *Zygon/Journal of Religion and Science*, 1969, *4*, 333–355.

Homans, P. *Theology after Freud: An Interpretive Inquiry*. Indianapolis, Ind.: Bobbs-Merrill, 1970.

Homans, P. *Jung in Context: Modernity and the Making of a Psychology*. Chicago: University of Chicago Press, 1979.

Hood, R.W., Jr. 'Eliciting Mystical States of Consciousness with Semistructured Nature Experiences.' *Journal for the Scientific Study of Religion*, 1977, *16*, 155–163.

Hostie, R. *Religion and the Psychology of Jung*. Trans. G.R. Lamb. London: Sheed and Ward, 1957. (Original French edition, 1955.)

Hudson, L. *Human Beings: The Psychology of Human Experience*. Garden City, N.Y.: Anchor/Doubleday, 1975.

Hummel, G. *Theologische Anthropologie und die Wirklichkeit der Psyche*. Darmstadt: Wissenschaftliche Buchgesellschaft, 1972.

Hunt, R.A. 'Mythological-Symbolic Religious Commitment: The LAM Scales.' *Journal for the Scientific Study of Religion*, 1972, *11*, 42–52. (a)

Hunt, R.A. 'Reply to Greeley.' *Journal for the Scientific Study of Religion*, 1972, *11*, 290–292. (b)

James, W. *The Principles of Psychology* (2 vols.). New York: Henry Holt, 1890.

James, W. *The Varieties of Religious Experience; A Study in Human Nature*. New York: Longmans, Green, 1902.

Jésus-Marie, Fr. Bruno de (ed.). *Satan*. Paris: Desclée de Brouwer, 1948. [Modified English edition, 1951.]

Jésus-Marie, Fr. Bruno de (ed.). *Nos sens et Dieu*. Paris: Desclée de Brouwer, 1954.

Jung, C.G. 'On the Psychology of the Unconscious.' In *Collected Works*, vol. 7 (2nd ed.). Princeton: Princeton University Press, 1966, 1–119. (Fifth German edition, 1943.)

Jung, C.G. *Psychology and Religion: West and East* (2nd ed.). Vol. 11 of the *Collected Works*. Princeton: Princeton University Press, 1969.

Kakar, S. *The Inner World; A Psycho-analytic Study of Childhood and Society in India*. Delhi: Oxford University Press, 1978.

King, M.B., and Hunt, R.A. *Measuring Religious Dimensions: Studies of Congregational Involvement*. Dallas: Southern Methodist University, 1972.

Koepp, W. *Einführung in das Studium der Religionspsychologie*. Tübingen: Mohr (Paul Siebeck), 1920.

Lange, A. *De autoritaire persoonlijkheid en zijn godsdienstige wereld*. Assen: Van Gorcum, 1971.

Lhermitte, J. *True and False Possession*. Trans. P.J. Hepburne-Scott. New York: Hawthorne, 1963. (Original French edition, 1956.)

Lofland, J. *Doomsday Cult: A Study of Conversion, Proselytization and Maintenance of Faith* (enlarged ed.). New York: Irvington, 1977. (Original edition, 1966.)

Lowe, W.L. 'Psychodynamics of Religious Delusions and Hallucinations.' *American Journal of Psychotherapy*, 1953, *7*, 454–462.

Lubin, A.J. 'A Boy's View of Jesus.' *Psychoanalytic Study of the Child*, 1959, *14*, 155–168.

Ludwig, D.J., and Blank, T. 'Measurement of Religion as Perceptual Set.' *Journal for the Scientific Study of Religion*, 1969, *8*, 319–321.

Ludwig, D.J., Weber, T., and Iben, D. 'Letters to God: A Study of Children's Religious Concepts.' *Journal of Psychology and Theology*, 1974, *2*, 31–35.

Mallory, M.M. *Christian Mysticism: Transcending Techniques; A Theological Reflection on the Empirical Testing of the Teaching of St. John of the Cross*. Assen: Van Gorcum, 1977.

Mann, U. *Einführung in die Religionspsychologie*. Darmstadt: Wissenschaftliche Buchgesellschaft, 1973.

Maslow, A.H. *Religions, Values, and Peak-Experiences*. Columbus: Ohio State University Press, 1964.

McDowell, V.H. *Re-creating: The Experience of Life-Change and Religion*. Boston: Beacon Press, 1978.

Meerwein, F. 'Neuere Überlegungen zur psychoanalytischen Religionspsychologie.' *Zeitschrift für psychosomatische Medizin und Psychoanalyse*, 1971, *17*, 363–380.

Meissner, W.W. *Annotated Bibliography in Religion and Psychology*. New York: Academy of Religion and Mental Health, 1961.

Milanesi, G., and Aletti, M. *Psicologia della religione*. Torino: Elle Di Ci, 1973.

Moore, T.W. 'James Hillman: Psychology With Soul.' *Religious Studies Review*, 1980, *6*, 278–285.

Müller-Pozzi, H. *Psychologie des Glaubens. Versuch einer Verhältnisbestimmung von Theologie und Psychologie*. München: Kaiser-Grünewald, 1975.

Nase, E., and Scharfenberg, J. (eds.). *Psychoanalyse und Religion*. Darmstadt: Wissenschaftliche Buchgesellschaft, 1977.

O'Flaherty, W.D. *Women, Androgynes, and Other Mythical Beasts*. Chicago: University of Chicago Press, 1980.

Otto, R. *The Idea of the Holy; An Inquiry into the Non-Rational Factor in the Idea of the Divine and Its Relation to the Rational*. Trans. J.W. Harvey. London: Oxford University Press, 1923; 2nd ed., 1950. (First German edition, 1917.)

Pahnke, W.N. 'Drugs and Mysticism.' *International Journal of Parapsychology*, 1966, *8*, 295–314.

Pfennigsdorf, D.E. *Der religiöse Wille. Ein Beitrag zum psychologischen Verständnis des Christentums und seiner praktischen Aufgaben* (2nd ed.). Leipzig: Deichert, 1927.

Philp, H.L. *Freud and Religious Belief*. London: Rockliff, 1956.

Philp, H.L. *Jung and the Problem of Evil*. London: Rockliff, 1958.

Pöll, W. *Religionspsychologie; Formen der religiösen Kenntnisnahme*. München: Kösel, 1965.

Pöll, W. *Das religiöse Erlebnis und seine Strukturen*. München: Kösel, 1974.

Pohier, J.-M. *Au nom du Père...; Recherches théologiques et psychanalytiques*. Paris: Les Éditions du Cerf, 1972.

Pratt, J.B. *The Psychology of Religious Belief*. New York: Macmillan, 1907.

Preuss, H.G. *Illusion und Wirklichkeit; An den Grenzen von Religion und Psychoanalyse*. Stuttgart: Ernst Klett, 1971.

Pruyser, P.W. *A Dynamic Psychology of Religion*. New York: Harper and Row, 1968.

Rajamanickam, M. *A Psychological Study of Religious and Related Attitudes of the Student and Professional Groups in South India*. Annamalainagar, Tamilnadu: Annamalai University, 1976.

Randall, R.L. 'Religious Ideation of a Narcissistically Disturbed Individual.' *Journal of Pastoral Care*, 1976, *30*, 35–45.

Rapaport, D. 'The Structure of Psychoanalytic Theory: A Systematizing Attempt.' In S. Koch (ed.), *Psychology: A Study of a Science*, vol. 3. *Formulations of the Person and the Social Context*. New York: McGraw-Hill, 1959, 55–183.

Ricoeur, P. *Freud and Philosophy; An Essay on Interpretation*. Trans. D. Savage. New Haven: Yale University Press, 1970. (Original French edition, 1965.)

Rizzuto, A.-M. *The Birth of the Living God: A Psychoanalytic Study*. Chicago: University of Chicago Press, 1979.

Rochedieu, E. *Personnalité et vie religieuse chez l'adolescent; Étude de psychologie religieuse*. Neuchâtel: Delachaux et Niestlé, 1962.

Rokeach, M. *The Three Christs of Ypsilanti; A Psychological Study*. New York: Alfred A. Knopf, 1964.

Rulla, L.M., Imoda, F., and Ridick, Sr., J. *Structure psychologique et vocation*. Rome: Presses de l'Université Grégorienne, 1978.

Scharfenberg, J. *Sigmund Freud und seine Religionskritik als Herausforderung für den christlichen Glauben*. Göttingen: Vandenhoeck und Ruprecht, 1968.

Scharfenberg, J. *Religion zwischen Wahn und Wirklichkeit; gesammelte Beiträge zur Korrelation von Theologie und Psychoanalyse*. Hamburg: Furche, 1972.

Schaub, E.L. The Psychology of Religion in America During the Past Quarter-Century. *Journal of Religion*, 1926, *6*, 113–134.

Scheler, M. *On the Eternal in Man*. Trans. B. Noble. New York: Harper and Row, 1960. (First German edition, 1921.)

Schmid, L. *Religiöse Erleben unserer Jugend. Eine religionspsychologische Untersuchung*. Zollikon: Evangelischer Verlag, 1960.

Schüttler, G. *Die letzten Tibetischen Orakelpriester: Psychiatrisch-neurologische Aspekte*. Wiesbaden: Franz Steiner, 1971.

Schüttler, G. *Die Erleuchtung im Zen-Buddhismus. Gespräche mit Zen-Meistern und psychopathologische Analyse*. Freiburg: Karl Alber, 1974.

Scobie, G.E.W. 'The Psychology of Religion: A Religious Revival?' *Bulletin of the British Psychological Society*, 1977, *30*, 142–144.

Shaw, M.E., and Wright, J.M. *Scales for the Measurement of Attitudes*. New York: McGraw-Hill, 1967.

Shostrom, E.L. *Personal Orientation Inventory: An Inventory for the Measurement of Self-Actualization*. San Diego: Educational and Industrial Testing Service, 1966.

Sierksma, F. *Phaenomenologie der religie en complexe psychologie*. Assen: Van Gorcum, 1950. [Also published as *Freud, Jung en de religie*, 1951.]

Sierksma, F. *De religieuze projectie; Ene antropologische en psychologische studie over de projectie-verschijnselen in de godsdiensten*. Delft: Gaade, 1956.

Siwek, P. *The Riddle of Konnersreuth; A Psychological and Religious Study*. Trans. I. McCormick. Milwaukee: Bruce, 1953. (French edition, 1950.)

Smith, W.C. 'Comparative Religion: Whither—and Why?' In M. Eliade and J.M. Kitagawa (eds.), *The History of Religions; Essays in Methodology*. Chicago: University of Chicago Press, 1959, 31–58.

Smith, W.C. *The Meaning and End of Religion; A New Approach to the Religious Traditions of Mankind*. New York: Macmillan, 1963.

Smith, W.C. 'A Human View of Truth.' *Studies in Religion*, 1971, *1*, 6–24.

Spiegel, Y. (ed.). *Psychoanalytische Interpretationen biblischer Texte*. München: Chr. Kaiser, 1972.

Spiegel, Y. (ed.). *Doppeldeutlich, Tiefendimensionen biblischer Texte*. München: Chr. Kaiser, 1978.

Spranger, E. *Psychologie des Jugendalters*. Leipzig: Quelle und Meyer, 1924.

Spranger, E. *Types of Men; The Psychology and Ethics of Personality*. Trans. P.J.W. Pigors. Halle: Max Niemeyer, 1928. (Trans. of the 5th German edition of *Lebensformen*, 1925.)

Stählin, W. 'Die Verwendung von Fragebogen in der Religionspsychologie.' *Zeitschrift für Religionspsychologie*, 1912, *5*, 394–408.

Standards for Educational and Psychological Tests. Washington, D.C.: American Psychological Association, 1974.

Stern, W. *General Psychology from the Personalistic Standpoint*. Trans. H.D. Spoerl. New York: Macmillan, 1938. (Original German edition, 1935.)

Stratton, G.M. *Psychology of the Religious Life*. London: George Allen and Unwin, 1911.

Strommen, M.P. (ed.). *Research on Religious Development: A Comprehensive Handbook*. New York: Hawthorn, 1971.

Sundén, H. *Die Religion und die Rollen. Eine psychologische Untersuchung der Frömmigkeit*. Berlin: Alfred Töpelmann, 1966. (Original Swedish edition, 1959.)

Tart, C.T. (ed.). *Altered States of Consciousness: A Book of Readings*. New York: John Wiley and Sons, 1969.

Tauxe, H.C. *Freud et le besoin religieux*. Lausanne: L'Age d'homme, 1974.

TeVault, R.K., Forbes, G.B., and Gromoll, H.F. 'Trustfulness and Suspiciousness as a Function of Liberal or Conservative Church Membership: A Field Experiment.' *Journal of Psychology*, 1971, *79*, 163–164.

Thun, T. *Die Religion des Kindes* (2nd ed.). Stuttgart: Ernst Klett, 1964. (First edition, 1959.)

Thun, T. *Die religiöse Entscheidung der Jugend*. Stuttgart: Ernst Klett, 1963.

Thun, T. *Das religiöse Schicksal des alten Menschen*. Stuttgart: Ernst Klett, 1969.

Traxel, W. *Über Gegenstand und Methode der Psychologie*. Bern: Hans Huber, 1968.

Trillhaas, W. *Die innere Welt; Religionspsychologie*. München: Chr. Kaiser, 1953.

Vande Kemp, H. 'Teaching Psychology/Religion in the Seventies: Monoply or Cooperation? *Teaching of Psychology*, 1976, *3*, 15–18.

van der Leeuw, G. 'Ueber einige neuere Ergebnisse der psychologischen Forschung und ihre Anwendung auf die Geschichte, insonderheit der Religionsgeschichte.' *Studi e materiali di storia della religioni*, 1926, *2*, 1–43.

van de Winckel, E. *De l'inconscient a Dieu; ascèse chrétienne et psychologie de C.G. Jung*. Paris: Editions Montaigne, 1959.

Vergote, A., et al. 'Psychologie de la Religion/Psychology of Religion.' *Social Compass*, 1972, *19*, No. 3.

Vergote, A., and Tamayo, A. (eds.). *The Parental Figures and the Representation of God; A Psychological and Cross-Cultural Study*. The Hague: Mouton, 1981.

Vetö, L. 'Bedeutung und Grenzen der experimentellen Methode in der Religionspsychologie.' *Archiv für Religionspsychologie*, 1971, *10*, 275–285.

Vetter, G.B. *Magic and Religion; Their Psychological Nature, Origin, and Function*. New York: Philosophical Library, 1958.

Vetter, G.B., and Green, M. 'Personality and Group Factors in the Making of Atheists.' *Journal of Abnormal and Social Psychology*, 1932, *27*, 179–194.

Walther, G. *Phänomenologie der Mystik* (3rd ed.). Olten: Walter, 1976. [First edition, 1923.]

Watson, L.C. 'Understanding a Life History as a Subjective Document: Hermeneutical and Phenomenological Perspectives.' *Ethos*, 1976, *4*, 95–131.

Wehr, G. *Wege zu religiöser Erfahrung; Analytische Psychologie im Dienste der Bibelauslegung; Eine Anregung*. Darmstadt: Wissenschaftliche Buchgesellschaft, 1974.

Weitbrecht, H.J. *Beiträge zur Religionspsychopathologie, insbesondere zur Psychopathologie der Bekehrung*. Heidelberg: Scherer, 1948.

Wobbermin, G. 'Die Methoden der religionspsychologischen Arbeit.' In E. Abderhalden (ed.), *Handbuch der biologischen Arbeitsmethoden*, Abt. 6, Teil C/1. Berlin: Urban und Schwarzenberg, 1928, 1–44.

Wood, W.W. *Culture and Personality Aspects of the Pentecostal Holiness Religion*. The Hague: Mouton, 1965.

Wundt, W. *Mythus und Religion* (3 vols., 2nd ed.). Constitutes vols. 4–6 of *Völkerpsychologie: Eine Untersuchung der Entwicklungsgesetze von Sprache, Mythus und Sitte*. Leipzig: Alfred Kröner, 1910–1915. (First edition, 1905–1909.)

Yinger, J.M. 'A Comparative Study of the Substructures of Religion.' *Journal for the Scientific Study of Religion*, 1977, *16*, 67–86.

Young, K. 'The Psychology of Hymns.' *Journal of Abnormal and Social Psychology*, 1926, *20*, 391–406.

Zährnt, H. (ed.). *Jesus und Freud; ein Symposion von Psychoanalytikern und Theologen*. München: Piper, 1972.

3

Sociological Approaches (1)

MICHAEL HILL

Wellington

In attempting to map out the broad features of the sociology of religion over the past three decades, the question of selectivity immediately arises. Despite its imperialistic claims on other disciplines and its international—or at least, western—growth, sociology has shown a marked tendency to internal schism.

Sociologists tend to approach their work from the vantage point of some particular school or tradition and through the filter of their own cultural context. It has been argued from a study of major sociological journals, for instance, that what might appear to be the 'internationalization' of sociology could be more accurately perceived as its 'Americanization' (Oromaner 1970: 331). Of course, given the intense concern within the discipline to establish the validity of the sociological approach when its scientific status appears to be undermined by its social location, the need for some vantage point is better understood. It is also true that debates generated by different schools of thought have been a fruitful source of research: an excellent example of this is the elaboration of a sophisticated typology of organizations within Christianity as a result of the dialectic between insights drawn from a European context and those made in North America (M. Hill 1973a: 47). The plain fact remains, however, that to some extent all sociological accounts are 'parochial.'

I make these introductory comments because, while attempting to provide as balanced and as representative a statement as possible of recent developments in the sociology of religion, some selectivity will be unavoidable. A brief summary of my own 'parish' might indicate the likely biases in this paper. First, my approach to the study of religion has been shaped by a sociological training in Britain. As a result, for reasons which I will clarify in the next section, my work has not been oriented towards the extensive use of statistical data, either in large-scale survey research of the type found in North America, or of a demographic nature, as is often employed in other parts of Europe. Rather, the importance of historical source material has always been central to the sociological tradition on which my research has been based (M. Hill 1973b). Second, and linked with this, the major theoretical influence I have encountered is that of Max Weber, with the result that the area of 'religion' as demarcated sociologically has been more closely attached to a specific social and historical context than the more universal definition of religion adopted by Durkheim and by later functionalists. Third, the major focus of the sociological studies which will be considered here is on Christianity: a not surprising concentration, given the fact that the development of sociology occurred in societies in which Christianity had traditionally been the dominant religion.

These, then, are the perspectives that have shaped my perception of, and selection from, recent developments in the sociology of religion. In the discussion that follows, it is not intended that these perspectives should restrict the choice of themes and examples in the sociology of religion but rather that they should provide a general sense of direction. Let us now explore a central element in any sociological undertaking, namely the methods adopted by sociologists in the study of the particular area of society with which they are concerned.

Methods

A major distinction between sociologists is the extent to which they use statistical data in their research. In the study of religion this distinction has emerged with great clarity in the different ways in which North American, British, and other European sociologists have approached their task. As a general rule it can be said that North American sociologists have frequently attempted to quantify their data as well as relying on large-scale survey techniques to a much greater extent than their British counterparts. The latter, in contrast to the macro approach of their North American colleagues, have been more inclined to use historical material, community studies and the micro 'anthropological' approach of close and detailed analysis of religious groups, especially small, local, sectarian groups. On the European continent, especially in France, researchers have frequently resorted to longitudinal studies, which involved the use of large-scale demographic statistics, which were often subjected to rigorous analysis over a period of years.

There are a number of important exceptions to these three broad approaches, but as broad characterizations of particular strains within the sociology of religion they are reasonably accurate. One of the explanations for this divergence of research methods is the prosaic question of availability of research funding. In North America there has been a substantially larger pool of institutional research funding than in Britain, and the very expensive deployment of large-scale survey research has been a viable option. By contrast, in Britain sociologists have either used history as a research laboratory or have refined the focus of their research in order to study communities and small-scale religious groups. Elsewhere in Europe, the establishment of socio-religious research institutes by religious organizations, especially the Roman Catholic hierarchy, has made possible the collection and analysis of extensive demographic data.

It is worth examining important studies in each of these three environments. I will first look at surveys in the United States, then at demographic studies in France, and finally at the micro approach of British sociologists of religion. One of the most notable and influential pieces of research in the United States was Gerhard Lenski's *The Religious Factor* (Lenski 1961). In analysing the 'religious factor,' Lenski was taking up one of the classical hypotheses of sociology—Weber's suggestion of a link between economic activity and religious profession (Weber 1976)—and testing its validity using a random sample of Detroit residents drawn from a variety of ethnic and religious backgrounds. Although in his initial formulation of the relationship between economic activity and religious adherence, Weber thought that 'victorious capitalism ... needs [religion's] support no longer' (Weber 1976: 181–182). Lenski nevertheless found there was a contemporary link between worldly success and Protestant affiliation, though only for white Protestants. Using similar research techniques, Greeley (1963) countered this conclusion: his findings were that American Catholics were just as likely as American Protestants to be educated and to aspire to business success. In a subsequent study (Greeley 1966a) he compared the influence of Catholic and secular education on students' aspirations and achievements, once again finding—as Weber's initial formulation would suggest—that the 'Protestant ethic' thesis does not hold in contemporary society.

Using similar methods of large-scale survey research, Glock and Stark of the University of California have examined the present-day religious situation of the United States (1965). In particular, they have examined the dimensions of religious experience and practice in an attempt to discover how widely each is distributed and how they are related. Their work can be viewed against the background of an interpretation of religion which has become increasingly important in recent years, namely that while religious institutions may atrophy, religiosity—variously defined by different sociologists—may show a great deal of resilience. Using a battery of attitudinal measures on religious beliefs and social perceptions, the researchers found significant divergence between what their respondents knew about their religion, how far they believed what they knew, how actively they practised a public or private form of religion, and whether or not they had had any transcendental experience. Glock and Stark's survey method has also been applied to the analysis of Christian beliefs and anti-semitism (Glock Stark 1966). Again, by distinguishing between different types of Christian commitment—and especially by constructing a Religious Dogmatism Index—the researchers were able to isolate the attitudinal factors associated with negative religious images of the contemporary Jew. A subsequent study drew attention to the eclectic and unstructured nature of much religious belief (Stark Glock 1968).

Quantitative methodology has also played a significant role in the study of religion in continental Europe. Especially in France and in the case of Roman Catholicism, the use of large-scale statistical data has long been established. There are two main sources for the development of a *sociologie religieuse* (a term which is discussed on page 99) since the second world war. On the one hand the historian and canonist Le Bras, as a result of his interest in the social and historical context within which canon law was required to operate, embarked on a massive research project to analyse the religious behaviour of the French population. The records of dioceses and national archives provided an extensive statistical picture of changes in religious practice (Le Bras 1955; 1956). The other source for the statistical approach was the strong emphasis on missionary activity within the French church. As well as having an active concern in foreign missions, the Roman Catholic Church in France has always seen its home base as a 'mission country,' and the disruption of the second world war raised the problem in an acute form. In particular, attention was focussed on the different patterns of religious practice in rural and urban areas. Prominent among those studying religion in a rural environment was Boulard (1960), whose most notable contribution was a map of religious practice in rural France. The geography—or, perhaps more accurately, the sociography—of religion remains a relatively undeveloped area in which Boulard's work is still the most extensive exploration. Like Glock and Stark, though on a geographical basis, he attempted to categorize levels of religious practice. Thus he distinguished between category A, B, and C areas. Category A areas were those of majority practice, where more than 50 percent of the population attended Easter Communion and Sunday Mass; category B areas were those of minority practice but seasonal conformity—the familiar 'hatch, match, and dispatch' of residual religiosity; while category C areas were mission areas in which a minimum of 20 percent of children were not baptized or did not attend religious instruction.

On the urban industrial front, researchers such as Godin and Daniel, Pin and Houtart have produced comparable studies (see Jackson 1974). Their findings suggest that in France the major cause of declining religious practice has been industrialization rather than urbanization, though an adaptive response by the church seems capable of blocking or slowing down the more general trend of 'dechristianization' (a frequently used equivalent of 'secularization'). Another finding which gives statistical confirmation to some studies in Britain which have attempted to assess levels of religious participation is that small towns show rather higher rates of activity than large ones, though the nature of the town is an important variable (D.A. Martin 1967: 46–7). The major characteristic of these French studies is the use of large-scale statistical data of a demographic, historical and 'official' form: without wishing to trivialize it, we might label it ecclesiastical market research. By contrast, the approach in the United States has typically involved survey research of the contemporary population in order to tap attitudinal variables which are not confined within the boundaries of a single religious institution.

The statistical approach has occupied a much smaller part of the sociological study of religion in Britain. Data derived from survey research has frequently been small-scale and associated with community studies, though this has sometimes enabled sociologists to assemble data in a comparative framework in order to establish broad national trends (D.A. Martin 1967: chap. 2). In Scotland, however, the study of religion has been notably advanced by the use of a similar historical-demographic approach to that of the French researchers in the work of Highet (1950). The main source of large-scale statistical data on religion can, however, be found in the mass observation and market or audience research type of study. For instance, an early piece of research which identified some of the confusion and fluidity in people's religious beliefs—which have been explored in more recent studies—was the product of an opinion research organization which had originally provided attitudinal data for government agencies (Mass Observation 1948).

Another source of data has been the responses made to questions about religious belief and social attitudes by opinion research organizations such as Gallup Poll. While these kinds of statistics provide relatively unsophisticated insights into the complex area of religious belief, they can provide general indicators of attitudes and behaviour, and some secondary discussion of them is available (B. Martin 1968). Rather more detailed analysis is given in two extensive audience research surveys which took the opportunity to examine the wider context of respondents' religious beliefs, adherence and practice and to link these with social characteristics and attitudes (ABC Television 1964, ITA 1970).

Partly as a result of the way in which academic disciplines have developed in Britain, sociologists have always found fruitful areas of common interest with anthropologists and historians, and this is amply demonstrated by the methods adopted in the study of religion. If one had to single out a British 'tradition' in the sociology of religion it would be in the study of sectarian movements using a similar approach to that of the anthropological monograph. The origin of the tradition is closely associated with Wilson, whose pioneering study remains a model (1961) for this type of research, and many subsequent studies owe some debt, either directly to him or to his work. A recent addition to the British literature on sectarian movements gives an assessment of this method:

> It is a curious fact about the historical development of sociological studies of religion in Britain that greater aggregate effort has been expended on the study of small, so-called sectarian movements than on studies of larger religious groups. Perhaps because the sect approximates to the anthropologist's tribe, many graduate students in sociology have come to regard the opportunity to study one as a form of doing field-work. Indeed, the sect presents many advantages to the would-be field-worker in sociology: it is restricted in size, sometimes limited in geographical dispersion, often lacking a long history, usually publishing ample literature, occasionally lacking the kind of professional leaders who might deter the less-than-intrepid researcher and being sufficiently restricted in the scope of its activities to facilitate overall judgements of its performance. (Beckford 1975: ix)

Significantly, the major weakness which the author does identify in such studies is one which has also been attributed to British anthropology, namely the relatively weak emphasis on a comparative perspective. However, Wilson's more recent work adopts just such a perspective (Wilson 1973).

A recognition of the importance of history for sociology has always been a well-established feature of British sociology, and has produced impressive results in the area of religion. In particular, both sociologists and historians have examined the role of religious beliefs and organization in shaping, and being shaped by, political and economic factors.

Historians of the labour movement in Britain had long pointed to the implications of certain religious movements, especially evangelicalism, for the development of working-class consciousness (though they might disagree about the extent or precise nature of this relationship). Interest in the period of industrialization, with all that it implied for the testing of sociological hypotheses about 'the religious factor,' was decisively rekindled in the early 1960s with the publication of Thompson's provocative study of artisan and working-class society between 1780 and 1832. As a result, the mutual interchange of ideas between historians and sociologists grew markedly, aided on the positive side by the richness of the historical data and the weighty precedent of such figures as Weber and Halévy, and on the negative side by the absence of funds for any other kind of research on religion. As one commentator pointed out at the time, '... sociology—and funds for social research—has a bias towards the immediate and publicly accredited areas of social problems. Religion has not been seen as a field for applied sociological virtue' (MacRae in Martin, 1967: 8).

Whatever the explanation, in this particular aspect of the study of religion the overlap between sociological and historical interest was substantial, and left a vaguely demarcated boundary. On a practical level, the division of labour perhaps tended to leave the historian with the task of examining detailed membership records while the sociologist used the results to establish broader explanations, but sociologists often adopted the strategies of the historian. A good example of the latter is Moore's study, *Pit-Men, Preachers and Politics*, of the effects of Methodism in a Durham mining community (Moore 1974).

Though history and sociology have a close affinity, especially in the latter's early development, they have also shown a degree of rivalry and, at times, suspicion and hostility. This is partly due to sociology's imperialistic tendency to lay claim to the territory occupied by other academic disciplines, and partly to sociologists' often-expressed belief that conventional history leaves something to be desired: as one prominent sociologist used to remark with genuine delight, 'Sociology is history with the facts left out; history is sociology with the brains left out.'

In the study of religion, however, there has been considerable co-operation between the two disciplines and various facets of the historical method have proved of immense value to sociologists. It is of interest to note, however, that the cross-fertilization has been easiest between sociologists and historians with a radical perspective. An example of a historian whose approach to seventeenth century religious and political movements adopts this perspective is C. Hill (1968). His work provides many seminal insights for sociologists, and it is useful to compare it with the brief pilot study of the same period written by a sociologist of religion (D.A. Martin 1965). When utilizing historical methodology, then, sociologists have been more at ease with those approaches to history which entertain broad categories and comparative interpretations: in this respect, the study of religion as a universal social and historical phenomenon has particularly benefited from such collaboration.

Sociology's Stance

The debate over sociology's 'value freedom,' or lack of it, is perennial, passionate and often based on mistaken premisses. It becomes especially acute in the study of religion, and the reason for this lies at the heart of sociology as an academic discipline. In its nineteenth-century origins, sociology was a conscious attempt to replace traditional religious and mythical perceptions of the world—'primitive' worldviews—with modern, scientific accounts. Sociologists of the positivist persuasion tended to see themselves as mature, rational analysts of the social world and they tended also to project this self-image on to the subject of their enquiry, *homo sociologus*, who thus became a calculating social animal capable of, though not always exhibiting, a rational perception of his natural and social environment. The task of sociology was to promote this perception, which implied that fictitious and immature worldviews—principally those associated with magical and religious beliefs—must be exposed and disposed of. This stance was of course ethnocentric, because it claimed that the sole source of valid knowledge lay in the experimental procedures of Western science; it was also sometimes élitist, for it suggested that while the scientific vanguard (including the sociologists) might be able to cope with a rational comprehension of the world, the masses (at home and abroad) might need to cling to their superstitions if a stable social order was to prevail. Indeed, 'order' neatly gives a key to the confrontation between early sociology and traditional religion, for had not the latter explained and underpinned the social order for centuries, and would not sociology make this redundant by stressing the existence of the scientific laws regulating society?

The positivistic stance of sociology was greatly modified at the end of the nineteenth century but was not totally obliterated. Certainly, there developed a much more relativistic conception of sociological 'truths' *versus* alternative definitions of reality. With the discovery of the unconscious and an awareness that social action could not be evaluated exclusively against the yardstick of rational, scientific calculation, the possibility of treating religion as an authentic and socially significant source of motivation was opened up (see M. Hill 1973a: 35–43). Some of the most impressive sociological studies of religion were in fact made in the period 1890–1920. But the rational profile of *homo sociologus* still retained its central position in the development of sociological thought.

Durkheim, for example, who saw religion as the essence of the social bond, is quite unambiguous about the 'real' origin of our ideas of the sacred: they come from, and are symbols of, society itself. Weber gave religion a major role in his theory of society and his comparative studies of Christianity and Eastern religions show a high degree of sensitivity to the nature and social impact of these belief systems; but he described himself as being religiously 'tone-deaf' and his most consistent concern was with the demystification (*Entzauberung*) of the world. In the work of these and later sociological theorists, a rationalistic emphasis survived, with the result that religion either tended to be consigned to some residual category of 'non-rational' action or at least to be regarded as socially off-centre in comparison with other institutional areas such as the economic and the political. As late as the mid-1960s one prominent sociologist of religion in Britain was able to write: '... to care about religious phenomena argues an abnormality, an intellectual perversion. In other words, the sociologist of religion is an academic deviant living by a non-existent subject' (D.A. Martin 1969: 62).

Elsewhere, I have examined the question of neutrality and commitment as it affects the sociology of religion in terms of three possible attitudes which the observer of religious phenomena might adopt (M. Hill 1973a: chap. 1). I shall summarize this discussion before concluding my review of sociology's stance by suggesting one important feature of it which might well be seen as inimical to religion—or at least to certain forms of religion. First, I should emphasize that I think there is an important distinction between the adjective before and the noun after the word 'sociology:' religious sociology and the sociology of religion are two different disciplines. While their use of empirical material may overlap and their research concerns may be mutually supportive, there is a basic difference in the stance they adopt. For religious sociology, the process of defining research problems is closely identified with ecclesiastical or theological concerns, an excellent example of this being the work of Le Bras discussed above.

When these concerns have been generated by the offical church hierarchy, the research problem has usually focussed on the factors influencing the effective deployment of resources and manpower, ecclesiastical productivity, or pastoral concern. When the concerns have been generated by unofficial interest groups, and especially by radical theologians in the Roman Catholic Church, the official response has sometimes been surprisingly sharp, an instance being the attacks by Pope Paul on 'sociology.' However, the fact that the target of the attacks is a very particular form of 'sociology' is borne out by Hebblethwaite's comment: 'On the whole, [these attacks] do not worry professional sociologists, who fail to recognize their own work in what is being so vigorously denounced.' (Hebblethwaite 1975: 97). In contrast with market-research and pastoral concerns, sociologists who study religion—though they might well import value-judgements into their work—must ultimately submit their research to the scrutiny of other sociologists and argue its significance against a body of wider sociological theory rather than arguing its utility against a background of ecclesiastical policy. In religious sociology, the term 'sociology' refers to a battery of pastoral and ecclesiastical techniques; in the sociology of religion it refers to an autonomous academic discipline.

Turning to our three hypothetical observers, at one extreme is a stance that offers little prospect of a viable sociological enterprise. This is the stance which regards religious phenomena as out of reach of human scrutiny, and above all as uncontaminated by the influence of the wider social environment. Since the social environment is an arena of prime concern for sociologists, such a stance would effectively seem to rule out any possible contribution on their part to the study of religion. I suppose one could label this a fundamentalist or theologically conservative position, and although it might in principle be applied to the study of all religious groups and beliefs, it is more common to find it in a version that applies to one community. Generally, the adherent of this stance employs it in a protective way to the area of his own religious commitment while declaring a sociological open season on other forms of commitment. An example of this can be found in the work of the Roman Catholic sociologist, Werner Stark, who defends his own group against sociological scrutiny in the following way:

> [The Universal Church] refuses to be turned by the influences which impinge on it from the secular environment: it keeps its eyes on the beyond, in relation to which the here-and-now appears relatively so valueless, so uninteresting, as hardly to merit any attention, let alone to justify intensive preoccupation (Stark 1967b: 5).

Contrast this with his characterization of sectarian religion:

> Marxists are, by and large, within their rights when they claim that sect movements are phenomena of an ongoing class struggle in societies within which the class conflict as such has not yet become conscious (Stark 1967a: 5).

Likewise, the sectarian claim to direct inspiration is the result of a 'philosophy of sour grapes' of the educationally and culturally deprived (Stark 1967a: 130). The extent to which truth claims have been incorporated into this extreme stance can best be gauged by Wilson's remark that this analysis of sectarianism represents 'an extraordinary, extra-sociological judgement' (1967: 220).

Significantly, the Marxian approach which Stark recommends in the study of sects lies at the opposite extreme from the protective commitment of the first (conservative) stance and is an example of the second perspective a hypothetical observer might adopt in the study of religion. If the first extreme is inimical to sociology, the second approach is inimical to religion; but like the first it tends to import extra-sociological judgments. Our second observer maintains that religious beliefs and symbols, so far from being out of range of human scrutiny and explanation, are on the contrary so much a product of their social environment that they can be 'explained away' entirely in socioeconomic terms. In other words, we can give a comprehensive account of religion in empirical, sociological language: religion is not 'real' in any other sense. Given such an epiphenomenalist stance, religion is reduced to a product of a more substantial reality located in the social environment.

The most prominent example of this stance is, of course, the Marxist-Leninist theory of religion (Acton 1958). Religion is seen as an oppressive and unnatural social system—and simultaneously an important ideological instrument for preserving that system by drugging its victims with fantasy wish-fulfilments of future salvation when they might otherwise be engaging in practical struggle to realize their goals. A vivid analogy of the place religion has in this schema would be a cinema screen: religion is an image projected on a grand scale, which mystifies its audience. Even though it is unreal and insubstantial it cannot be obliterated by standing in front of the screen: instead, the theory argues, you must locate its *real* source—the projection-room of social and economic life—if you wish to destroy the image. As in the first stance, this extreme involves the use of extra-sociological judgments, for instance in distinguishing 'true' from 'false' consciousness or in attributing objectively-available material 'interests' to different social groups. It has nevertheless been an important source of sociological interpretations of religion, if not in a thoroughgoing form then sometimes in the guise of 'creeping epiphenomenalism' (Martin 1969: 63).

The third hypothetical observer adopts a *via media* which has been influential in shaping the role of sociology in the study of religion. While denying *both* that religion is incapable of being studied by sociological techniques *and* that it is capable of being explained completely in terms of the social location and interests of its participants, this third stance argues rather for a division of labour. The observer *qua* sociologist adopts a perspective that is different from, though not necessarily incompatible with, the perspective of the committed adherent or the theologian—or, for that matter, the historian or psychologist who may study religious phenomena. To this extent, the sociologist accepts that his competence is limited by the language, techniques and theoretical apparatus of his own discipline. Furthermore he should be aware of the areas in which the judgments he makes overstep these boundaries; indeed, partisanship and partiality are issues of lively debate in sociology at large, as a brief glance at the Review section of any of the major journals will reveal. Thus, while the sociologist may be concerned with 'outward and visible' social signs which to the committed adherent may appear trivial and irrelevant, this is not because they are seen as being *all* that religion comprises, but that they are aspects of religion which fall particularly within the scope of sociological competence. This also implies, incidentally, that sociologists should be prepared to acknowledge their limitations when confronted by enthusiastic ecclesiastical entrepreneurs, who have occasionally tended to view the subject as some new revelation.

Despite my contention that sociology should be accepted as one among a number of perspectives on religion, and allowing for the likelihood of demarcation disputes over points of interpretation (a criticism which theologians have made of Weber, for example, is that he did not fully grasp the nuances of Calvinist doctrine) there is a sense in which the sociological approach to religion is disruptive. The following is an assessment by Berger—one of the most perceptive contemporary writers on religion—and his co-authors of the moral basis of sociology:

> Sociology is essentially a debunking discipline. It dissects, uncovers, only rarely inspires. Its genius is very deeply negative, like that of Goethe's Mephistopheles who describes himself as a 'spirit that ever says no'. To try to change this character is to destroy whatever usefulness sociology may have—especially its moral and political usefulness, which comes from being held in balance, simultaneously and within the mind of the same person, with the affirmations of moral passion and humane engagement (Berger *et al.*, 1974: 207).

To portray sociology as a critical discipline is to suggest the possibility of conflict in its encounter with religion. Conflict is further opened up by a seeming paradox in the sociological approach, and this relates to my remarks on sociology's stance at the beginning of this section. There, I pointed to the undermining of sociology's original ethnocentric, rationalistic definition of reality—an undermining which made possible the treatment of religion as a significant area of social activity. However, for this to be possible sociology had to adopt a relativistic stance towards the study of values and beliefs, and thus as a methodological principle to exclude the notion of any ultimate source of truth. The acceptance of plural value systems, it has been argued, is one way of weakening the plausibility of any overarching religious system (MacIntyre 1967). Expressed slightly differently, the sociologist who constantly suspends judgment on respondents' expressed beliefs in order to give an authentic account of them is perhaps signifying by means of a professional role his own eclectic moral perspective.

It follows, then, that in the study of religion the sociological approach is likely to be subversive in its initial impact, even if in the long term its concerns may be found to parallel, if not indeed to support, those of the adherents of the religion or religious group in question. On the positive side, sociologists have sometimes been fully prepared to defend minority religious groups in the face of legal, political and media campaigns (see Wilson 1964). But on balance, the following is probably the most characteristic initial encounter which those 'in the truth' are likely to have with the sociologist:

> There is a sense in which sociology is inevitably a subversive enterprise. The very act of reflecting on the behaviour of people and organizations entails that these activities do not bear their meaning and explanation on their face. The sociologist's pursuit of further or different knowledge after he has already been informed of the 'truth' of the matter by the individuals or organizations concerned, displays the fact that he does not accept the 'self-evident', and perhaps even that motivated by malice, he is prepared to tell some entirely different story. (Wallis 1976: v.)

Sociological definitions of religion

Behind any definition in sociology there lies a theoretical premiss or perspective, however tentative or implicit. Every definition contains an element of evaluation because it specifies the boundaries of the phenomenon being studied, the kind of data that are relevant to its study and to some extent an initial prediction of the findings about the phenomenon:

definitions restrict the range of interpretation. One of the most obvious examples of this in the study of religion can be found in different interpretations of the process of secularization, which are heavily dependent on the preliminary definition of religion. This is a topic that will be dealt with in greater detail later in this paper but some preliminary remarks are appropriate here. Secularization can be broadly defined as a decline in, movement away from, or change in religion. Our definition of religion is therefore crucial to our interpretation of the secularization process, as can readily be seen if we take two contrasting definitions and consider their implications.

Thus if religion is defined for sociological purposes as the social activity that goes on within institutions labelled churches, then the data we need to detect a process of secularization would consist of statistics of membership, attendance and adherence, and on this basis we might well view secularization as a major feature, at least of western societies. If, on the other hand, religion is defined as some quantum of 'religiosity' within every individual, then secularization in the sense of a disappearance of religion becomes by definition impossible and could only be used to depict some change in expression or content of this universal feature of human psychology. It is therefore not surprising to find that Wilson, who adopts a predominantly institutional definition of religion in his study of secularization, dismisses the quantum definition as an instance of theological trespassing:

> [Some] posit a fund of 'religiosity' in men and in society, which, like a 'wages fund' or a 'pool of ability' in the context of other arguments, is supposed to remain more or less a constant—but a hypothetical constant the means of measuring which have not yet been discovered. Such a concept obviously draws more strongly on theological than on sociological assumptions about mankind (Wilson 1966: xv).

Since very many of the contemporary approaches to religion in sociology rest on the theories espoused by the classical tradition, it is valuable to look at the definitions of religion—and their implications—given by the founding fathers and especially by sociology's 'holy trinity': Marx, Weber, and Durkheim. For a thinker who proposed that the criticism of religion was the beginning of all criticism, Marx's definition (or, I suppose more accurately, description) of religion is remarkably sentient: 'Religion is the sigh of the hard-pressed creature, the heart of a heartless world, the soul of soulless circumstances. It is the opium of the people.' (in Acton, 1958: 139.) Curiously, the origins of this passage, which is perhaps the best known of Marx's statements on religion, seem to have been theological, echoing on the one hand the words of the Renaissance humanist Sebastian Franck—'God is an inexpressible sigh deep down in the souls [of men]'—and on the other the opium *motif* first used by the Anglican divine, Charles Kingsley. The implications of Marx's definition are, as has been shown, that religion is a mechanism of compensation and the product of a capitalistic social order which—because of the misery and frustration it imposes on its members—creates an image of the world that is 'mysterious.' An example of the work of a contemporary Marxist which shows how a mythical worldview is generated among Melanesian native groups as a result of colonial exploitation can be found in Worsley's study of Cargo Cults (Worsley 1968).

Weber, who followed up many of the initial statements of Marx and who, largely in reaction to the universal scope and theoretical closure of his predecessor, produced a sociology that was relativistic and open-ended, devoted much detailed historical research to religion. His open-endedness (which many find his most infuriating feature) extended to his treatment of religion, however, for as Berger indicates, he never quite reached the point of defining the subject of his research:

> Max Weber ... took the position that a definition of religion, if possible at all, can come only at the end, not at the beginning, of the kind of task he had set for himself. Not surprisingly, he never came to such an end, so that the reader of Weber's opus waits in vain for the promised definitional payoff. I am not all convinced by Weber's position on the proper sequence of definition and substantive research, since the latter can only proceed within a frame of reference that *defines* what is relevant and what is irrelevant in terms of the research. (Berger 1969: p. 176.)

It was possible for Weber to postpone giving a formal definition of religion because his research was always concerned with specific social and historical configurations rather than with religion's universal dimensions. We *know* to a large extent what seventeenth-century Puritanism or eighteenth-century Methodism was; and to a lesser extent we have some conception of the nature of other world religions such as Hinduism and Islam: 'religion' as a separate category is consequently avoidable.

However, it is clear from his work that Weber was most concerned to highlight the dialectical relationship between religious ideas and their social environment. While he was prepared to accept in large part the Marxian definition of religion as a social product—especially in his later writing—he postulated that the impact of a new religious movement as it became incorporated into the motivations of its adherents could have social and economic consequences, albeit unintended, for society at large. The crucial point about the effect of the Protestant ethic was not that it provided a permissive rationalization of ongoing economic activity but that it initially propelled adherents, in pursuit of religious 'interests,' into novel forms of entrepreneurial capitalism. Religion in Weber's works is primarily viewed as a system of *ideas*, especially ideas about salvation and the problem of evil, and hence can be seen in the framework of Weber's general sociology of ideas. Ideas (rather than 'great men') are to a significant extent the autonomous and creative forces which operate the points on the track of history; but unless the ideas ultimately come to coincide with the material interests of their 'public' they are discarded. Some of the most interesting contemporary studies based on, or at least suggestive of, a Weberian definition of religion are those concerned with new religious movements in pre-industrial societies. An example would be Long's research (1968) on the impact of Jehovah's Witnesses on social change in Zambia.

A somewhat higher level of generality is contained in Durkheim's definition of religion:

> A religion is a unified system of beliefs and practices relative to sacred things, that is to say, things set apart and forbidden—beliefs and practices which unite into one single moral community called a church, all those who adhere to them. (Durkheim 1976: 47.)

While Marx was concerned with religion as a social smoke-screen and Weber with religion as a social starter-motor, Durkheim is primarily concerned with religion as a form of social cement. For him, religion—as expressed in its most characteristic institution, the Church—is a means of binding together the members of a society or social group into a moral community. In order to demonstrate that this was a function which had universal significance Durkheim, who saw the development of societies in much the same way as a biologist might see the increasing differentiation of cells in an organism, looked at what was then considered the simplest society of all, that of the Australian aborigine. What he called an 'elementary form' we might term the 'genetic blueprint.' As I suggested earlier (page 98), when he comes to explain the attitudes of respect and awe which adherents exhibit towards the sacred symbols of their religion, Durkheim is sufficiently positivistic to identify as the single 'real' source of such attitudes, society itself. As has been correctly perceived by Towler, this definition directs our attention back towards the Marxian thesis that religion is an expression of social experience and that the religious worldview takes its shape from the shape of the social structure in which it is located (Towler 1974a: 73).

By adhering to the spirit rather than the letter of Durkheim's definition of religion, sociologists have more recently shown the utility of the approach. Swanson, for instance, has attempted to explain (1960) why certain *types* of gods appear in certain *types* of society and he suggests that societies which provide different social experiences lay the bases of the plausibility structures for different types of religious beliefs. In this way Swanson is able to establish correlations between the authority structures of a number of primitive societies and their conceptions of deities, and to show with greater precision than Durkheim attempted how social experience is significant for religious symbolization. In a similar way, Douglas (1970a) has been concerned to account for the degree to which different societies embody a ritualized worldview. Like Swanson, she rejects the evolutionary component of Durkheim's approach, and especially the equation of religious worldviews with primitive societies and secularity with modern complex society. Elsewhere, she has examined the contral theme of maintaining moral boundaries in Durkheim's definition of religion (1970b).

In drawing together the definitional problems faced by sociologists of religion, a useful distinction is made by Robertson (Robertson 1970: 37). He is interested in the *uses* of different types of definition and dichotomizes them into inclusive and exclusive modes. Inclusive definitions of religion are broad in scope, like the Durkheimian one cited above or like the updated functionalist definition of religion given by Yinger: 'Religion, then, can be defined as a system of beliefs and practices by means of which a group of people struggles with [the] ultimate problems of human life' (Yinger 1957: 9). There are two main sources of such inclusive definitions: firstly they are used by sociologists whose conception of a social system strongly emphasizes the need for individuals to be regulated by some shared commitment to a central set of beliefs and values—very much a functionalist conception of society as a moral community; but secondly—and, as Robertson indicates, negatively—they have been used by sociologists whose micro research interests are so finely focussed and circumscribed that definitional problems are remote and the intellectual incentive to use precise definitions is minimal.

Exclusive definitions with a more restrictive and narrow frame of reference are also associated with sociologists who adopt a particular stance either towards society or towards religion. First, those sociologists who deny that social systems are necessarily bonded by similar commitments to a central, core value system, and who see power and force as paramount, may well find an exclusive definition useful in critically analysing the claim that certain beliefs and practices *are* 'religious.' Second, those who wish to examine the tension between religious and non-religious conceptions of the social order are likely to adopt an exclusive definition of religion. I would add that those sociologists, including myself, who have done research mainly in an historical context—in which, albeit only conventionally, religion has generally had a 'firm profile'—may well find a more restricted definition valuable. For instance, I have, following Weber, tended to view religion in terms of a 'bifurcation' of the world and thus would assess my own definition of religion as an exclusive one:

> [Religion is] the set of beliefs which postulate and seek to regulate the distinction between an empirical reality and a related and significant supra-empirical segment of reality; the language and symbols which are used in relation to this distinction; and the activities and institutions which are concerned with its regulation. (M. Hill 1973a: 42–3.)

Definitions are, of course, only as valuable as the clarity they give in demarcating an area and the contribution they make in furthering research. In defence of Weber's reticence it might well be pointed out that his research output *on* religion was infinitely greater than several other sociologists who have devoted themselves to theoretical speculation *about* religion.

All the same, the implications of a definition are rarely trivial, and it is worth looking at the implications of the inclusive/exclusive distinction. Inclusivists tend to be those who see belief systems such as communism and nationalism as belonging to the same species as religion; exclusivists do not see the same identity. One of the reasons why an exclusive definition may well be preferable is that when dealing with the area of churches, denominations and sects on the basis of an inclusive definition, the area will often have to be sub-defined by some stopgap phrase as 'religion as conventionally perceived,' 'commonly understood religion' and 'traditional religious institution.' However, a functional definition may be highly suggestive in identifying 'surrogate' religions—for example, the vast range of 'isms' which confront the consumer in the contemporary mind market (North 1975).

The definitional problem is not one which lends itself to a simple solution; indeed, an ongoing debate about the boundaries of the phenomenon we choose to call 'religion'—if it stimulates a more sensitive approach to the research process—might be a valuable contribution. It can at least be pointed out that such a debate has not prevented the most fruitful collaboration of contemporary sociology, namely that between Berger and Luckmann. While the former is content to work with what he terms a substantive definition—in terms of the positing of a *sacred cosmos*—the latter is a radical inclusivist, defining religion as the capacity of the human organism to transcend its biological nature through the construction of universes of meaning. Berger clearly disagrees with this definition:

> ... I question the utility of a definition that equates religion with the human *tout court*. It is one thing to point up the anthropological foundations of religion in the human capacity for self-transcendence, quite another to equate the two (Berger 1969: 177).

The scope and nature of data

The above review of some of the major considerations in the sociological approach to religion has already touched on a variety of data. It is worth emphasizing this point because there is a widespread misapprehension that *the* source of sociological data is the sample survey, and this has encouraged many enterprising amateurs to undertake small-scale survey research with, in many cases, little initial definition of what information was wanted and why. Frequently, such surveys have been carried out using mailed, pre-coded questionnaires, which is a method unsuitable for collecting anything but fairly crude attitudinal and simple demographic data. Even when interview techniques are employed, recent research suggests that these may only tap surface data such as official denominational adherence, and that more sensitive instruments are needed to elicit more sophisticated data on informal or 'subterranean' patterns of belief (Towler and Chamberlain 1973).

Sociologists are partly to blame for the popularity of the survey myth, for reasons which relate to their occupational experience. There are specialized areas in sociology which command equal academic status but unequal research funds, and undoubtedly among these the sociology of organizations and of industry tend to fare better than most. In comparison, the sociologist of religion has remained largely out in the cold, with the result that any hint of financial support from religious agencies is likely to provoke an enthusiastic response from the sociologist. This, in turn, is likely to be interpreted by the agencies concerned as signifying that a sociological survey (since it is perhaps one of the most obvious hallmarks of the discipline) may provide an original solution to recession in the religious market. In addition to being consulted on the marketing of the product, sociologists are on occasion asked to discover what the product should be; thus, on one memorable occasion a clergyman with a thousand-pound grant from his parochial church council asked the sociology department of a London college to discover what his role should be. Normally on such occasions the sociologist and a research assistant will descend on a parish and, like some latter-day Batman and Robin, try to knock it into shape.

As I have indicated earlier, valuable first-hand data in the sociology of religion have been collected through the survey method, especially in the United States. Such data are highly appropriate when the research problem concerns widely-distributed attitudinal characteristics or readily-identifiable patterns of activity. Any attempt to measure the significance of 'the religious factor' or to distinguish types of religiosity in a large population is likely to require data of this sort. Where the research demands 'submergence' in a community, a combination of in-depth survey data, official records and participant observation is often employed in a cumulative way to build up a detailed sociography of a particular locality. This has been typical of British community studies in which religious beliefs and activities sometimes figure significantly. In both instances the questionnaire method is used with discrimination, and with clearly delimited aims.

The are indeed good grounds for reticence over the use of survey data in the study of religion: first, because it is difficult to explore the subtle casuistry of beliefs at any great depth; and, second, because if a questionnaire has not been designed with a great deal of sensitivity it is not difficult to alienate respondents with strongly-held and articulate beliefs who find the questions either unsophisticated or off-putting.

Official statistics of two main kinds have been used as sociological data, though again they raise problems which I shall discuss. In the first place, there are sources of data on religion which are part of wider enquiries in which religion forms a small part: census data falls into this category. The only occasion on which the English census authorities have got involved in this area of data collection was in 1851, when Horace Mann conducted a specific religious census on church attendance (Pickering 1967). However, in a number of countries a religious question is included on the census: these include Ireland (Macourt 1974), Germany, Canada, and New Zealand (Mol 1972). In the New Zealand census there is a simple question on 'religion' and the respondent is given the option of replying 'object to state.' Insofar as such sources provide valid data for sociological research, this is only after a great deal of secondary interpretation: simple percentage distributions of adherents claiming allegiance to various denominations provide a bland and not very informative picture of the 'religious situation' or distribution of religious denominations in a country. Some general long-range trends can be observed, along with any broad ethnic patterns of adherence, but more detailed observations require a critical quantitative *and* qualitative appraisal of the crude data. Age and sex distributions and specific localities of groups of adherents can provide suggestive hypotheses—such as information about 'peaks' of religiosity. However, the main problem in interpreting Census data is deciding what precisely is *meant* by a particular response: for instance, a high percentage of Anglicans may signify little more than the convention of religious baptism. The corollary of this is that respondents who adopt a sectarian label—'christadelphian,' 'unification church,' for instance—may have in mind a more precisely-defined focus of commitment and may therefore be providing more useful data. Even so, the size of a minority religion often fluctuates rapidly while the wheels of the census department grind extremely slowly, which limits the utility of the data: the 'religious professions' volume of the New Zealand census taken in mid-1976, for instance, did not appear until early in 1980.

A second source of official statistics is the collection made by most religious organizations for their own purposes. Baptisms, confirmations, membership tickets, marriages, and Easter communicants all provide some index of the relative sizes and levels of activity of different religious groups, but once again a critical appraisal is required before such information can be treated as valid sociological data. For instance, if we wish to compare the membership trends over time between a selection of religious bodies, we must first of all establish a 'rate of exchange' or basis of comparison, and this is not easy:

> Both the Roman Catholic and Anglican Churches . . . employ criteria which assume entry by birth-right signalized or realized at Baptism. Religious identity is sometimes treated almost as if it were transmitted physically. By contrast the Baptists acquire members only by adult conviction as signalized in ceremonial immersion. Between these two extremes, Methodist and Congregationalists admit to the religious community in a very limited way by infant baptism but only count those who are definitely adult members. A 'real' Methodist is a 'card-carrying' member. Thus in dealing with Free Church numbers, one must reckon with a fringe of 'friends of the congregation' or adherents (Martin 1967: 35).

Some evidence of the difficulty of maintaining an agreed criterion of membership over time is given by the fact that since Martin made these comments, the Anglican Church has moved more in the direction of adult baptism or confirmation as an indicator of 'real' membership. Even when criteria do remain stable, the sociologist must still investigate the reliability of the data, because some religious bodies are rather more efficient than others at collecting and tabulating statistics.

Historical studies have used official data as a primary source, especially in assessing the relative importance of different denominations in particular periods. One of the pioneers in the use of this kind of data was Wickham, whose research into the influence of the churches—or, more accurately, lack of it—on the emerging urban working class of nineteenth-century Sheffield made effective use of Pew Plans, available places in chapels and Census findings (Wickham 1957). This material is combined with secondary data, such as contemporary newspaper accounts together with local histories and more general commentary, to give a clearly-delineated picture of the process of religious attenuation in the nineteenth century. Subsequent studies have adopted a similar approach, and there are now some extremely interesting pieces of research in progress which involve careful analysis of denominational records: the results of such research bear directly on general hypotheses about the links between religion and social change as discussed by, for instance, Weber and Halévy.

A recent example is the work of Field (1977), whose analysis of the social structure of English Methodism from the eighteenth to the twentieth century, used four main sources: lists of officials; membership books; marriage and baptismal registers; and special surveys. Baxter's research (1974) on the Great Yorkshire Revival of 1792 among the Methodists compared membership lists of Methodist Societies and radical clubs and reached the conclusion—a fascinating one in the light of Thompson's portrayal of Methodism—that members tended to oscillate between radical politics and Methodism, the latter in periods of political repression. While primary data gathered from membership books and registers is a major feature of such studies (especially among researchers whose first discipline is history) secondary data and more general sociological interpretations provide a framework of analysis and a point of integration.

Content analysis has been a relatively common technique for handling data in a number of specialized sociological areas: in the study of infant socialization and child-rearing patterns, for instance, the literature advocating different styles of child care has enabled us to trace the growth and decline of various practices. In the study of religion, data have rarely been subjected to content analysis—though in a very simple way, Weber's use of Calvinist pastoral advice to suggest a gradual modification over time in original Calvinist doctrine might be seen as a form of content analysis. However, a novel source of data has been used by Towler in order to study a particular aspect of contemporary religious symbolism. He was given access to the voluminous correspondence which John Robinson received after the publication of *Honest to God*, and after taking a random sample of letters he used the technique of content analysis to identify the themes to which the letter-writers gave priority (Towler: 1974b). Although the occasion for the correspondents' expression of religious sentiments was specific and the population self-selected, the depth of controversy engendered and the sheer mass of documentary data available open up the attractive possibility of new insights on contemporary religion.

Sociologists who have studied religion have tended to take their data much more extensively from Christianity than they have from other world religions; indeed, Everett Hughes has gone as far as to suggest that if our criterion for selecting data is the extent to which we can test a comprehensive range of sociological hypotheses, we can refine our selection further: 'nearly everything sociologically speaking has happened in and to the Roman Catholic Church' (in Greeley, 1966b: 124). Nevertheless, other world religions have been well served by particular sociologists, either as a result of their interest in particular geographical areas in which other world religions are prominent, or as a result of attempts to test theories and concepts in a comparative context. Islam has provided sociological data which are of general interest, especially since they throw light on theories of political legitimacy. Gellner's work (1969) on the Berbers of the Atlas Mountains deserves mention here, as does Turner's exploration (1974) of the relevance of Islam for Weber's total sociology. There are a number of recent studies of Judaism, often from the viewpoint of the role of religion in the formation and maintenance of an ethnic community: in Britain, Sharot's work (1975) provides contemporary data. Data on Buddhism are available in Spiro's work on Burma (1967, 1970) and in the study by Malalgoda (1976) of Buddhism in Ceylon between 1750 and 1900. In compiling this brief and highly selective review of some of the data which sociologists are drawing from world religions other than Christianity, I have been concerned mainly to show that this is a lively and, indeed, a growing area in the sociology of religion; again, one cannot ignore the paradox that in its early development, sociology was very much concerned with the comparative study of religions and only later became preoccupied with Christianity. It should also be noted that I have avoided a discussion of the anthropological literature because this is appropriate elsewhere, though had this been included a substantial amount of data on world religions would have been evident.

A final comment is needed on an important conjunction of interests between sociologists, anthropologists and social philosophers which has been particularly stimulated by data on primal religions. The interpretation of primal religious data faces, in common with the interpretation of data from world religions, the basic problem of the extent to which—and the sense in which—the belief systems and the actions of the adherents can be labelled 'rational.' This perennial problem, which was of course regarded as being much less controversial in the work of someone like Frazer, has been debated in all these disciplines, and the contributions of some of the major figures in this debate have been collected in the volume *Rationality*, edited by Wilson (1970). The collection draws attention to the fact that the problems faced by anthropologists in interpreting the myth, ritual and symbols of primal religions have a close affinity with those of sociologists faced with the interpretation of religious belief systems (not all of which need necessarily be alien or exotic) in modern societies. While we may make conventional distinctions between the 'primitive' and the 'modern' mind, or between African traditional thought and western science, we must be aware of the continuities and the elements of interpenetration that are also present. Perhaps because they highlight the problems so clearly, the data of primal religions have been very effective in drawing the attention of sociologists to similar problems in their own approach to religion.

Trends in the Sociology of Religion

A review of major recent trends in the sociology of religion—using such criteria as research output and themes in the literature, especially in the rich collection of textbooks on the subject—makes possible a basic distinction between two main perspectives. On the one hand there is the approach to religion which emphasizes the dimensions of power and social change. On the other hand is the view of religion as a source of social and psychological integration. Both have had a significant influence on the way in which sociologists have studied religion, but of the two the first perspective has generated substantially more research and debate than the second. In addition, as I shall go on to demonstrate, while most sociologists of religion who have attempted to provide an overview of their discipline have necessarily had to incorporate insights drawn from both approaches, it is only very recently in the work of Berger (1969) and Luckmann (1967) that a measure of integration has been achieved between these two perspectives.

The power/social change perspective stems initially from the Marxian analysis of religion and more directly from the debate with Marx which was a most significant feature of the work of Weber and his pupil Troeltsch (Troeltsch 1931). The principal focus of such writers was on the dialectical relationship between religion and society and a key insight of their work was that religion was not only a social product, as Marxists had contended, but that the ideas contained in a religious system could themselves exert an independent impact upon society and could thus influence the course of social change in important, if often unintended, ways. Given this stance, sociologists had a very direct concern for the specific historical forms taken by the world religions, and particularly by Christianity. The most influential exponent of the perspective was Troeltsch, who examined the original ideological blueprint of Christianity and showed how the polar elements of Love (radical) and Law (conservative) in the Gospel ethic produced an internal dynamic within the religious system which was subsequently played out on the stage of history. It is important to note that the perspective implied not only a dialectic between religious ideas and the social environment in which they were located—or what Becker in a somewhat inverted analogy termed 'the water of the religious and the oil of the social' (Becker 1932: 617)—but also an internal dialectic within the belief system itself. In this way, the content of the religious message was given an authenticity which it had been denied in the cruder Marxist version.

Two further aspects of the power/social change perspective (both of which are clearly traceable in post-war developments) deserve mention. One is the close affinity between proponents of this approach and liberal Protestantism: once again, Troeltsch sets the archetype for such subsequent researchers as H. Richard Niebuhr and Joachim Wach. Though all three made substantial contributions to the corpus of literature in the sociology of religion, none can be labelled a 'sociologist' in a conventional academic sense. Troeltsch was primarily a theologian and philosopher, Niebuhr a theologian and Wach an impressively eclectic theologian, philosopher, and historian. All, however, shared a liberal Protestant background. The second aspect of this perspective, and one which has been immensely (some would say inordinately) influential in recent trends relates to a basic theological premise. If every revelation is seen to be conditioned by the historical and cultural environment in which it finds expression, it follows that the 'cutting edge' of every religion will be embodied in some concrete organizational form. For this reason, all three writers devoted considerable attention to the different types of organization contained within the various religious traditions. To Troeltsch, who elaborated a distinction first made by Weber, we owe the concepts of church, sect, and mysticism—the latter subsequently being termed the 'cult'—within Christianity; to Niebuhr (1929), the process of denominationalization through which initially sectarian movements adopt a more relaxed, bourgeois style; and to Wach (1947) a more elaborate comparative typology of the 'specifically religious organization of society.'

The second distinct perspective, which has been rather more influential in anthropology than it has in sociology, derives from Durkheim and the functionalist school. As was noted above from its origins sociology was preoccupied with the way in which religion had traditionally given stability and cohesion to human societies, and with the need to replace this 'mythical' basis of social order by means of a rational, scientific account of the laws underlying the social fabric. Though the early positivism of the sociological approach was increasingly eroded, the initial insight was more resilient: religion clearly could function as a maintainer of society and as an integrator and reinforcer of values. Durkheim most notably advanced the view that religion embodied not merely a ritual reaffirmation of social solidarity but was indeed the source of the collective consciousness, of the categories and meanings which men necessarily share as they structure their natural and social environment. Such a theory of religion would evidently be most plausible in the study of stable societies with a high degree of social cohesion rather than in societies characterized by change and fission and for this reason the functionalist approach has been of particular interest to anthropologists, though as I shall later show it has had some impact on the sociological study of religion in modern industrial societies.

An excellent example of the functionalist approach—and one which has been influential in more recent work—can be found in the studies of Radcliffe-Brown (who, incidentally, became acquainted with Durkheim's writings only after completing his fieldwork among the Andaman Islanders). He was concerned to show that any object or event that has a significant impact on the material or spiritual well-being of a society is likely to become an object of ritual attitudes. On this basis he argued that people who are reliant on hunting and gathering for survival have a ritual attitude to the animals and plants which they most need (Radcliffe-Brown 1922). Studies of the role of religion in moden societies which adopt a functionalist approach, while they lack the simple identification of 'needs' that might be possible in a hunting and gathering society, nevertheless focus on areas of social experience which raise similar issues—such as the contention that all societies have certain minimal survival and maintenance needs—and argue that religion functions to fulfil at least *some* of these (Nottingham 1971: 57).

Given these two basic perspectives and the priority which can be attached to them on the basis of recent work in the sociology of religion, the remainder of this paper will be comprised of four main sections: (1)

religious organization; (2) religion and social change; (3) religion and social cohesion; and, (4) an integrated approach and a future prospect. Although not exhaustive in their scope, they do encompass many of the recent trends in the subject.

(1) *Religious Organization*

A review of the research on different types of religious organization, almost exclusively within a Christian context since comparative application raises difficulties (Moberg 1961), is a valuable source of illumination, not only for the approach sociologists have adopted in the study of religion but also for the more general use of concepts in sociological research. What commonly happens is that concepts which are originally designed to achieve a high level of generality are shown by subsequent application to have a more restricted frame of reference, leading in turn to the refinement of more sophisticated and variegated sub-concepts with more limited scope. Thus Troeltsch's dichotomy between the conservative church and the radical sect, with mysticism (the cult) as a more 'modern' offshoot, was developed in a European context in which established, socially inclusive churches typically confronted small, disaffected sectarian groups. Niebuhr found this unsatisfactory in a North American context in which the absence of an established church and the resulting fluidity of religious adherence led, he argued, to the more typical growth of denominations out of former sectarian enclaves. Becker further expanded this into a typology comprising the ecclesia (equivalent to Troeltsch's church), the denomination, the sect and the cult, hypothesizing a similar sect-to-denomination process to that of Niebuhr.

This typology was boldly adapted for comparative analysis by Wach, though his contribution has been very little recognized in more recent work. Far more influential was the adaptation by Yinger (1946), who confined the applicability of his typology to Christianity. Though basically in agreement with previous conceptualizations, he added the subtype of 'established sect' to accommodate those minority religious groups which did not undergo the process of denominationalization, which remained of rather limited membership, and which tended to dominate a large part of the lives of their members: the modal type of the established sect given was the Society of Friends because it conferred a 'visible' identity on its members in their local community. In a later reformulation (Yinger 1957) he retained the original structure of the typology but introduced a further refinement—which in sometimes less codified ways, a number of observers had already indicated—by distinguishing different *types* of sect on the basis of their 'attitude to the world.' The subdivisions he outlined were: (1) acceptance sects, which are generally middle-class in membership and offer a solution to problems which the dominant churches are not tackling, the example given being the Oxford Group Movement; (2) aggressive sects, which anticipate a radical change in the existing social order and consequently tend to run into strong opposition, as did the Anabaptists, leading to the formation of (3) avoidance sects. The latter seek to devalue the importance of this life and to project their aspirations into a supernatural realm, offering compensation to adherents who are usually drawn from underprivileged groups. Not only is this sub-type of sect—an example of which would be the 'holiness' groups in the United States—the most common in contemporary society, it has in common with the first subtype of 'acceptance' sects a tendency to develop into a denomination rather than an established sect.

It was this last hypothesis, suggesting that certain sub-types of sect might retain their distinct sectarian identity while others were more likely to experience the process of denominationalization, which prefaced a substantial volume of research into sectarian processes of change and strategies of maintenance. Much of this research was conducted in a British context using the 'anthropological' approach outlined in the section on Methods, and an early statement of the problem was made by Wilson (Wilson 1959) against the background of previous literature on typologies of religious organization. Wilson's characterization of sectarian groups is based broadly on the tradition stemming from Troeltsch and emphasizes the voluntaristic, virtuoso, and totalitarian features of sectarian commitment. On the basis of different responses to the world, four sub-types of sect can be distinguished (Wilson has subsequently modified this typology to include more sub-types, but for its precision and parsimony the 1959 version remains a valuable point of reference.)

The *Conversionist* sect is primarily concerned with evangelism and is represented by fundamentalist or pentecostal groups in contemporary Christianity, in which some evidence of conversion experience is a prerequisite for full membership: examples are the Salvation Army and Elim Four-Square Gospel. The *Adventist* or *Revolutionist* sect focusses its message on the imminent overthrow of the existing social order and its doctrine combines Biblical exegesis with a diagnosis of 'signs of the times:' Christadelphians and Jehovah's Witnesses would fit within this category. *Introversionist* or *Pietist* sects deflect their members' attention away from the world on to the community of believers, which may be interpreted as an enlightened elect: the Society of Friends and the Amana Society are given as examples. *Gnostic* sects offer some special body of esoteric teaching by means of which their members are shown exotic, often pseudo-scientific means towards attaining culturally prescribed goals rather than being advised to reject or avoid the world: Christian Science could be so classified. It is noteworthy that Wilson, by including this fourth sub-type of sect with its world-accepting stance, has encapsulated a form of religious response which others have viewed as characteristic either of cults (Nelson 1969) or of the 'cultic milieu' (Campbell 1972).

The dialectical component of the power/social change perspective is well demonstrated by the implications drawn by Wilson from the distinction between four sub-types of sect. As he argues, one of the principal sources of tension within sects is the co-existence of an ethic of separation from the world with the injunction which many sects accept to go out and preach the gospel. A concern with evangelism necessitates exposure to the world and the consequent risk that the group's standards of admission and original virtuoso level of practice will be eroded: thus in clear contrast we can observe the interface between Becker's oil of the social and water of the sacred. However, not all sects experience this tension to an equal degree, because Introversionist and Gnostic sects engage in minimal proselytism and admit members either through formalized procedures or on the basis of inter-locking commitments which require no exclusive loyalty to a single group. Adventist sects subject new recruits to a rigorous programme of doctrinal training which acts as a 'filtering' mechanism and tends to prevent any compromise of sectarian doctrine. Therefore it is sectarian groups with a conversionist emphasis which are most likely to resolve the tension between world-avoidance and evangelism in the direction of a denominational structure and belief-system. In particular, the difficulty of filtering new recruits through the mechanism of a subjective conversion experience and the tendency to evolve a specialized ministry in order to mount an effective programme of evangelism combine to erode the sectarian principle of a group of strongly and exclusively committed laity.

Largely as a result of the importance of research in a North American context, the denominational type of organization had usually been regarded as a sect at a later stage of development, its initially high level of commitment having 'cooled' as a result of compromise with the world and adaptation to the needs of the second and subsequent generations of sect members, now the children of originally voluntary members. From the context of English religious history, however, a different process of denominational growth was identified by Martin (1962). If a major feature of sectarian groups is their exclusiveness and especially their monopolistic definition of the community of the saved, then an analysis of the early history of the principal English denominations—Methodists, Congregationalists and Baptists—would suggest that they were devoid of sectarian characteristics. In particular, such groups denied that there could be *any* institutional monopoly on salvation, their basis of organization was fluid and pragmatic and their attitude to the world was reformist rather than the revolutionary/avoidance polarity more typical of sectarian groups: in other words, the 'sociological idea of the denomination is the idea of Her Majesty's Opposition, of disagreement within consensus, except that the opposition is permanently out of office' (Martin 1962: 13).

Martin adopts the concept, introduced by Troeltsch and developed by Wach, of *ecclesiola in ecclesia*—'protest within'—to locate the primary source of denominational organization and ideological stance, and a similar approach has been taken in the study of an historically significant form of 'protest within,' namely the position of religious orders within western Christianity (M. Hill, 1973b). While religious orders share a number of features with sectarian groups—particularly their virtuoso level of commitment, their strong lay element and their world-avoidance—they lack an internal source of authority (since they depend for their legitimation on a larger institutional church of which they form part) and they cannot claim a monopoly on salvation since the boundaries of the moral community must necessarily include members of the institutional church who are not members of religious orders. Nevertheless, when viewed in terms of the religion/society dialectic of the first perspective outlined at the beginning of this section, religious orders exemplify one solution to the tension experienced by a number of sectarian groups. Expressed simply, the conflict between an exclusive ideology and an unsupportive wider social context can be managed in a variety of ways. Perhaps the most common process is for the ideology to be adapted so that it coincides more closely with the norms of the wider society, as occurs in the sect-to-denomination development; or there may be a process of change and mutual interaction between both the surrounding society and the exclusive religious group so that an eventual *modus vivendi* is established—as has been suggested in the example of the Salvation Army.

The means of adaptation found in religious orders has typically been one of social insulation—an example of which is the wearing of special dress—or geographical isolation, which in the case of contemplative orders may be total and lifelong. Such adaptation is characteristic of one sub-type of sect which was included by Wilson in his 1963 typology (see Robertson 1969: 370)—this is the *Utopian* sect. The main feature of Utopian sects is withdrawal from the world in order to remake it to a better specification within the confines of the group. In origin, such communitarian groups have sometimes been trying to avoid social antagonism, although their segregation has also paradoxically served to heighten such antagonism. Though different from religious orders in that utopian sects have an internal source of authority, there are clear affinities between the two types of organization; for instance, the 'heaven on earth' of the sectarian group has parallels with the 'life of angels' practised in the monastic community. A recent treatment of three utopian sects with somewhat different goals—the Shakers, the Oneida Community, and the Bruderhof—shows how utopian movements simultaneously require a high degree of independence from the world but sufficient ties with the world to facilitate evangelism: such movements consequently set up a dialectic which may on occasion result in oscillation between withdrawal and evangelism (Whitworth 1975).

The typology of religious organization has been modified and reformulated in a variety of ways and has stimulated voluminous research on the historical development of, and contemporary processes within, Christianity. Certain implications of this approach can be indicated. Firstly, it is closely bound up with the exclusive definition of religion discussed earlier in this paper because a principal focus is on the clearly delineated historical and institutional forms of Christianity. Secondly, there has been a tendency in the use of typologies to confuse the abstract model with concrete reality and thus to produce a somewhat obsessive morphology in which species and specimens are constantly labelled: a model is an abstraction and is valuable only to the extent that it highlights significant features of an organization or process. Hence one of the most useful and succinct accounts of how research on typologies should be viewed is that of Wilson: 'The sociologist seeks to explain social phenomena in as general and abstract a way as empirical data permit, to which end he evolves concepts, formulates hypotheses, constructs models and organizes theories. He reconstructs social processes in accordance with the factors that appear to operate' (B.R. Wilson 1967: 1). It is worth adding that concepts exist to assist in the explanation of the phenomena being studied rather than to encourage the 'hermetic cloistering' (Beckford 1975: ix) of the researchers.

(2) *Religion and social change*

Research into the impact and dimensions of social change has been so important within sociology generally and the sociology of religion in particular that it would have been possible to have devoted a whole paper to this one theme alone. Furthermore, the focus on social change has provided a most significant source of cooperation between sociologists, social philosophers, anthropologists, and historians. In order to narrow down the area of discussion in this section I will concentrate on one broad topic in the study of religion and social change, namely the links between religious and political beliefs and organization, especially the chronology between millennial movements and radical political movements. This topic has been a major pre-occupation of sociologists of religion in the post-war period, and in simple terms it can be outlined as follows.

If we adopt an interpretation of religious beliefs and organization as *products* of underlying social forces, then the most plausible view of religious movements is that they are off-shoots or appendages of more substantial shifts in the infra-structure of society. The main channel of social change and development is economic and political, so that religious movements may best be seen as distorted expressions or embryonic signs of more substantial social change. In chronological terms, religious movements are more likely to emerge when political movements are already underway or are at least discernible. The contrary interpretation—one which owes much to Weber's study of the links between Calvinism and capitalism—would allow religious movements a more autonomous, if unintended, *impact* on the process of social change. In this case, important religious 'inputs' might be expected before a major social shift occurred. Although somewhat over-simplified in this outline, the question of chronology has been important in studying religion and social change.

Two books, both of which first appeared in 1957, clearly demonstrate this point. Norman Cohn's *The Pursuit of the Millennium* (Cohn 1970) is a study of millennial movements in late medieval Europe. Peter Worsley's *The Trumpet Shall Sound* (1968) is a study of more recent 'cargo cults' in Melanesia. Of particular interest is the very different interpretation of the relationship between millennial movements and radical political movements which each gives.

Cohn's study is concerned with 'the millenarianism that flourished amongst the rootless poor of Western Europe between the eleventh and the sixteenth centuries; and . . . the circumstances that favoured it' (Cohn 1970: 14). He observes that movements of this kind occurred in an environment in which peasant revolts and urban insurrections were very common and, what is more, were often successful. In all the examples cited, Cohn shows how a millennial movement with fantastic, 'unrealistic' goals would typically originate *after* an organized insurrection with limited and 'realistic' objectives had been mobilized. A prophetic leader would exploit the situation by taking over the movement and redefining its goals in apocalyptic terms. Above all, Cohn has been concerned to rebut the idea that millennial movements are appropriately viewed as a pre-political phenomenon: 'It has sometimes been argued that a revolutionary millenarian group fulfils the function of preparing the way for more realistic social movements. This was not the case with the movements which have just been described, for each of these appeared only when an organized insurrection of a decidedly realistic kind was under way' (Cohn 1962: 39)

The interpretation which Cohn explicitly opposes in the last quotation is that of Worsley, whose interest is on the way in which millennial movements act as vehicles for the economic and political aspirations of native groups in a colonial or otherwise deprived situation. He sees the main social location of such movements as being the lowest strata of society, especially uprooted peasants who had become unskilled urban workers or unemployed beggars. The aspirations of the members of these dispossessed groups are potentially revolutionary because they reject the dominant social ideology, and the protest movements which have grown up around them have frequently shown a tendency to engage in violent conflict with the established authorities. As a result, millennial movements have often been proscribed and persecuted by the state as well as by socially acceptable religious groups. At the same time, these movements have served an important political function by integrating previously small, isolated social groups—especially in peasant, tribal and segmented societies—and mobilizing them against the dominant political élite. In colonial societies the European administration provides the focus of opposition by such groups.

The Melanesian 'cargo cults,' based on a fantastic and in Cohn's terms 'unrealistic' belief that the ancestors are about to return with cargo for the natives, thus heralding the overthrow of European dominance, have laid the basis for a broader native unity and consciousness than was possible on a tribal basis. While the cults' overt goals might well be seen as a deflection of more limited and attainable political goals, their unintended consequence—the forging of a broadly-based native unity—has been highly significant for political activity. At this point the notion of chronology is introduced: out of the fantastic utopian goals of such movements there arise 'more advanced movements' with the kind of limited secular political objectives characteristic of national liberation movements. In complete contrast to the Cohn chronology, the latter then 'drain off' the activism of the religious movements, so that in societies in which forms of political organization have developed any residual millennial movements tend to be escapist and quietist.

Another important distinction between Cohn's and Worsley's accounts is the role accorded to the prophet. Both see prophetic leadership as a common feature of millennial movements; indeed, as we saw earlier, Cohn regards the prophet as a key figure who exploits and diverts an already-mobilized political protest by turning it into an apocalyptic struggle under his own leadership. Worsley, on the other hand, regards the prophet more as a 'figure-head' who expresses and symbolizes the aspirations of the members of the religious movement. In this way the leader appeals above the narrower divisions of clan and tribe to a source of legitimacy which, being supernatural, transcends the existing social divisions. 'By this projection on to the supernatural plane [the prophet] thus avoids sectional discord. This is always backed up by specific injunctions to love one another, by calls to forget the narrow loyalties of the past, to abandon those things that divide them and to practise a new moral code of brotherly love' (Worsley 1968: 237)

There is a significant conceptual distinction contained in these conflicting views of prophetic leadership. For Cohn, it is the exceptional presence of the prophet which leads the millennial movement into the pursuit of fantastic and unrealistic aspirations: for Worsley, the prophet serves as a symbolic focus around which the 'realistic' goals of native unity may concentrate and thus he is a figure of much less importance for the direction taken by the religious movement. In particular, Worsley rejects the Weberian concept of charismatic leadership as being an irrational notion which does not adequately explain the social and economic forces underlying radical religious movements (once again, we observe the Marxian view of religion as *product*). It has, however, been pointed out that in testing this approach within a Melanesian context, Worsley had selected a society with little social differentiation and with strong economic preoccupations; in other words, a society in which the impact of charismatic leadership might be expected to be minimal (Wilson 1975). Cohn, by contrast, was concerned with a more differentiated social context—with a society which was more complex than a primitive tribal society though by no means at the level of complexity of a modern industrial society—and it is here that the impact of charismatic leadership might be more readily anticipated.

In discussions of the role of charisma, there is considerable overlap between those whose primary interest is in the linkage between religion and social change and those who are more concerned with the political concomitants of social change. Especially as colonial territories in Africa gained their independence in the 1950s and early 1960s, often with the result that political leaders like Nkrumah in Ghana were thrown into great prominence, it was common for sociologists to identify a transitional period of charismatic leadership as the typical process of development when traditional societies modernized (Apter 1968). Unfortunately for the study of religion and social change, when such figures fell from grace, so did the concept of charisma. While the political significance of charisma in the contemporary world may be made problematic or even highly dubious by the increasingly familiar techniques of propaganda presentation and media manipulation, the concept of charismatic leadership retains much of its utility in the context of religious movements (see M. Hill 1973a: 140–182).

The chronological links between radical religious and political movements have also provided a rich vein of controversy—once again, involving both sociologists and historians—over the political consequences of eighteenth-century Methodism. 'The Weber thesis' has its political corollary in 'the Halévy thesis,' which was first put forward at about the same time as Weber's essay. A premiss of both studies is that religious ideology may exert an autonomous influence in a process of social change, though the difference between them is that until quite recently sociologists had shown little interest in Halévy's work while devoting enormous attention to Weber's.

Halévy was greatly impressed by what he saw as the extraordinary stability of English society during a period in which continental Europe experienced a series of crises and revolutions (Halévy 1924). Though he saw the explanation as a complex one, he identified as a key element the impact of the Methodist and Evangelical revivals. While Methodism permeated down to the disaffected workers, imbuing them with an ethic which would turn them into disciplined and independent artisans and generate upward social mobility, the later Evangelical movement in the Church of England made its impact on the political and commercial élite and laid the basis for the social ethic of Victorian England. Thus Methodism filled a social and ideological vacuum, prevented the polarization of English society *and*—an important component of the Halévy thesis—'creamed off' and politically neutralized precisely that social group which in other societies had been a strong radical force, the rising bourgeoisie. In short, Halévy suggests that Methodism and Evangelicalism together provided a 'transitional creed' which ensured the accommodation of new social groups into the established social order without any major challenge to political stability. Recent research has followed up a number of Halévy's insights, though not always in quite the way that Halévy had put them forward.

A major stimulus to research in this area came in 1963 with the first publication of E.P. Thompson's *The Making of the English Working Class* (1968). If anything, Thompson attributes even greater influence to Methodism than does Halévy, and he also provides an hypothesis (based once again on chronology) which is of sociological interest. Like Worsley, Thompson adopts a Marxian perspective, but he sees as most characteristic the process whereby political activism turns into religious withdrawal. While he finds no difficulty in explaining the appeal of Wesleyan Methodism for the bourgeoisie, since it contained a work-ethic which was particularly well adapted to the aspirations of self-made factory owners and foremen, he thinks it more important to explain how Methodism could simultaneously have exerted the impact it did on wide sections of the proletariat—a problem which is central to Weber's study of the influence of Protestantism. Furthermore, Thompson is quick to point out that Methodism was well able to serve the interests of industrial capitalism since it instilled in its adherents an intermittent display of enthusiasm and emotion which allowed for the methodical, disciplined, and repressed conduct of everyday life: 'Sabbath orgasms of feeling made more possible the single-minded weekday direction of these energies to the consummation of productive labour' (Thompson 1968: 406).

Three explanations are given for the impact of Methodism on the industrial working class in the period 1790–1830. First, there was the impact of direct indoctrination through the Sunday schools with their insistence on discipline and morality. Second, Methodism provided for the new urban migrant a sense of community to replace the traditional community which had been disrupted by social change. Third, and perhaps most interestingly, Thompson sees Methodism as providing ideological compensation whenever revolutionary impulses in the emergent working class were stifled. Since before the 1790s, he contends, there is evidence that the working class held strong radical aspirations, that these would periodically be stifled by counter-revolutionary measures on the part of the established authorities, and that when this occurred religion provided a temporary retreat and compensation. However, 'whenever hope revived, religious revivalism was set aside, only to reappear with renewed fervour upon the ruins of the political messianism which had been overthrown' (Thompson, 1968: 427). Thompson's hypothesis suggests an oscillation or dialectic between political activism and religious pacifism—which he labels 'the chiliasm of despair'—and he gives broad membership statistics to show that waves of revivalism succeeded periods of political activity and coincided with periods of political repression. As was noted above more recent research using the membership lists of Methodist societies and radical clubs tends to support Thompson's argument that religion provided a 'retreat' in times of political repression (Baxter 1974).

Thompson's clearly-drawn polarity between religious revivalism (negative) and radical politics (positive) is questioned by Hobsbawm, whose research interests embrace not only the English labour movement but also the comparative study of millennial movements and peasant revolts in pre-industrial societies (Hobsbawm 1959). Again from a Marxian perspective, he argues that in fact Methodism was never as widespread nor as powerful as Thompson suggests and that a more important reason for the absence of revolution in the period in question was the capacity of the ruling class to make necessary concessions and hence to maintain control. (How far this may in turn have been partly due to the influence of Evangelical groups such as the Clapham Sect is an open question (see Kiernan 1952).) Using the statistical evidence of the 1851 Religious Census, Hobsbawm argues that the different branches of Methodism could only have been expected to exert an influence on popular agitation in the North, Midlands, East Anglia and extreme south-west of England.

The most important objection to interpretations of the sort given by Thompson, however, concerns the use of chronology. Workers in early industrial Britain did not turn towards various religious sects *as an alternative* to revolutionary or radical politics. While religion might sometimes engender passive resignation and a source of consolation in the face of political repression; 'there is another kind of religion which might seize the miserable mass of the people at such times. Preachers, prophets and sectarians might issue what the labourers would regard as calls to action rather than to resignation' (Hobsbawm 1957: 123–4). Religious movements may be quietist *or* activist and the chronological links between religious and political activism may run in parallel. In the nineteenth century, Methodism can be seen as advancing when political radicalism advanced: the periods when Wesleyan Methodism recruited most rapidly were also periods of mounting popular agitation. The effect of Hobsbawm's argument is to suggest that there may be a range of chronological linkages between political and religious radicalism (to the extent that it is possible to make analytical distinctions between the two, a reservation which will be briefly considered at the end of this section).

A final piece of recent research in the general area of political and religious radicalism deserves mention. Moore's study of the effects of Methodism in a Durham mining community comes very close to Halévy's portrayal of the political outcome of Methodist membership. Methodist revivalism was non-revolutionary and its ethics had an individualist emphasis which was congenial to economic and political liberalism. Nonconformity laid the basis for a consensus between bourgeoisie and proletariat and in those areas in which both pitowners and managers and miners belonged to Methodist societies, industrial conflict was muted. Overall, Moore finds that the consensual element produced a social and political context of respectability, restraint and conciliation, thus reducing the possibility of class warfare (Moore 1974).

The distinction between religious and political beliefs and action is a conceptual product of societies in which these institutional areas are differentiated and sometimes formally separated in law. In traditional societies the distinction may be extremely difficult to maintain, and one must constantly strive to clarify the extent to which an observer's categories are being superimposed on those of the actors. Of course, this is a problem which extends beyond the study of religion and social change—an excellent example is the difficulty of reaching any consensus about the boundaries of 'religion' and 'magic'—but it merges in a highly explicit way in the treatment of millennial movements. Despite the frequency with which chronologies of political-religious/activism-pacifism are used in the literature and distinctions such as 'realistic'/'unrealistic' are maintained in relation to the aspirations of such movements, it is as well to be aware that the boundaries they define are tenuous. This discussion will be taken up again in the last section of the paper, but it is appropriate to conclude this section with a statement from a recent study of millennial movements:

> ... I have not pursued the question whether these movements are religious or political. It seems to me obvious that they are both. Too often the "essence" of millenarianism has turned out to be the essence of the discipline from which the observer has come. We deal here not with movements that must be categorized as political, social, economic, or religious. Life does not come so neatly packaged. We deal instead with aspects that, however accentuated, give partial and simplied pictures of richly complex organizations' (Barkun 1974: 4).

(3) *Religion and social cohesion*

The second of the major perspectives on religion—as was suggested earlier—has been more important in anthropology, where the societies studied have generally been more homogeneous and stable than the complex industrial societies studied by sociologists. A review of text-books on the sociology of religion, for example, shows that illustrative material on 'religion as an integrator of society' is often drawn from anthropological research or from studies of traditional societies such as

Greece and Rome. The latter source of material is indeed of more than mere historical significance, for it was the seminal work of Fustel de Coulanges on the role of religion in integrating ancient society that provided a model for the functionalist theory of Durkheim, whose mentor Coulanges was (Fustel de Coulanges 1874). However, simple and traditional societies have not been the only social context in which the Durkheimian theory of religion has been explored, for in both Britain and the United States sociologists have been concerned with the way in which ritual and symbols of a broadly religious nature (in this case adopting a more inclusive definition of religion) have laid the basis for affirmations of social solidarity and a strengthening of social cohesion.

In particular, sociologists have drawn attention to the importance of civic religion and ritual in industrial society. An excellent example of this interest and an application of the functionalist theory of religion is the article by Shils and Young on the meaning of the Coronation (1953). The authors approach the subject from a thoroughgoing functionalist perspective: in all societies, they argue, there is a general moral consensus, though this is rarely formulated and articulated in an abstract way. Furthermore, there is in humans a recurrent need to reaffirm the moral rules by which they live or feel they ought to live, a reaffirmation which involves not only the high-lighting of their sacred character but also a stifling of the ambivalence which people always feel when subject to moral authority; in other words, civilization always has its discontents. Thus the function of the Coronation is to provide a ceremonial occasion for the affirmation of the moral values by which society lives: it is 'an act of national communion.'

Having established this explicit Durkheimian interpretation Shils and Young then provide a more detailed analysis of the Coronation itself. The service is seen as a series of ritual affirmations of the moral values necessary to a well-governed and good society and the key to it is the Queen's promise to abide by society's moral standards, which are seen throughout to have supremacy. A cohesive community is constantly reiterated in the Coronation service and is reinforced by the use of symbols. As evidence that the event *did* generate widespread popular resonance the authors point to—and quote from—the flood of letters protesting to one newspaper about a cartoon which had been churlish enough to suggest that the whole thing had cost a great deal of money. The overall impact of the Coronation is summarized as follows: 'On this occasion one family was knit together with another in one great national family through identification with the monarchy' (Shils and Young 1953: 73).

An observation which is appropriate at this point concerns the distinction between actors' explanations and observers' explanations, because the account which Shils and Young give is in many respects identical with that of the legitimating institutions involved, such as the Church of England. Rituals involving the monarchy are often portrayed by ecclesiastical spokesmen as having widespread social significance and are equally often supported by the traditional legitimation that moral worth and social status are positively correlated. Thus, for instance, a royal wedding is usually portrayed as an event at which all the marriages in a society will be strengthened and reconsecrated. In this sense, a great deal of the mythology surrounding socially élite groups—which Shils and Young accept—comes within the category of 'superstitions and subterranean theologies' described by Martin, who is worth quoting:

> A relatively frequent type [of subterranean theology] concerns ... the impact of *élite* morals on lesser breed behaviour.... Thus a letter in a church newspaper declared that the breaking of Princess Margaret's engagement to a man who had been divorced might 'inaugurate a new era in marital relations'. A somewhat different but equally curious notion of social causation is found in the conviction of one Tory intellectual that the Profumo affair was encouraged by the theology recommended in the works of the Bishop of Woolwich (D.A. Martin 1967: 74).

Simply to point out that the sociological explanation of a situation coincides with that of the actors in the situation is not to say that it is invalid (though there are good theoretical reasons for suspecting that it might be so). Shils and Young have, however, been heavily criticized for their consensual treatment from very much the power/social change perspective. Birnbaum points out that the fundamental proposition of their functionalist approach—that societies *do* have a set of shared moral standards—is nowhere supported with evidence (Birnbaum 1955). Also, their model of society fails to distinguish between simple social systems (of the type Durkheim was concerned with) and complex societies of the modern industrial type. There is also an element of contradiction in the contention, on the one hand, that the shared moral values are rarely articulated and, on the other, that spectators are able to interpret the symbols of the Coronation ritual in a conscious and sophisticated way. A more disturbing difficulty, Birnbaum argues, is that Shils and Young appear to be unclear whether moral standards and beliefs are so important after all: 'Their discussion tends to veer between two propositions. The first holds that the standards themselves are sacred. The second treats their sacredness as a derivative of submission to some other authority held sacred' (Birnbaum 1955: 9). Here the criticism identifies what is perhaps the major flaw in Durkheimian and subsequent functionalist accounts of religion, namely their circularity (see Hill 1973a: 39–40).

A more recent treatment of ritual, which emphasizes its socially cohesive aspect but which also indicates its relevance for social change, is that of Bocock (1974). Using a broad definition of ritual, and exploring it in a mainly British context, Bocock gives an account of civic and religious, political, aesthetic, life-cycle and counter-cultural ritual. His basic approach, an anti-rationalist, 'man shall not live by bread alone' stance, is identical to that of Shils and Young, and although the activities included under the heading of 'ritual' include what conventionally we would term both sacred and secular ceremonies, the main ritual actions of England are seen as being still very much connected with the nationally established Church. The brief attention paid to sport is compensated for by other sociological accounts which see sport not only as a form of ritual activity but more significantly as a type of 'surrogate' religion. Coles provides a direct Durkheimian parallel between British soccer and aborigine ritual (Coles 1975) and Cohen in the United States has examined the way in which American baseball involves an intense affirmation of social solidarity (Cohen 1946).

Turning now to the United States context, it would be no exaggeration to state that the concern of sociologists to identify the mechanisms of social cohesion in a rapidly changing society composed of successive waves of immigrants became an urgent preoccupation. As has been pointed out elsewhere (Robertson 1970: 18) the Durkheimian influence was extensive and reached its peak in the 1950s. At first glance the preoccupation with religion, and especially with what was labelled 'American Civil Religion' (Bellah 1967, 1970, 1975), as a source of social cohesion seems somewhat paradoxical: lacking an established church and incorporating a variety of religious traditions, many with a strong ethnic overlay, the American situation was inherently pluralistic. However, denominational pluralism was seen to have resulted in the coexistence on a relatively tolerant basis of three major religious orientations: Catholic, Protestant and Jewish. Moreover, this coexistence was seen to be highly functional for social cohesion since all three orientations were united by a common commitment to the core values of American society, summed up in the phrase 'the American way of life' or as it has been termed, 'the religion of Americanism.' In such a way, it was argued, religious pluralism could lay the foundation for social cohesion.

As perceived by Bellah, American civil religion is not denominationally-based or confined to particular institutions but is at heart an experiential creed. It can be found in the beliefs and commitments which people exhibit in their everyday lives and is located in various symbols of cohesion such as the Arlington and Gettysburg 'shrines' and the 'sacred' anniversaries of Thanksgiving and the Fourth of July. There is a formal constitutional separation between Church and State, so that any linkage between religion and politics must be indirect—though as Bellah found, politicians constantly draw on religion as a source of legitimation for their actions. In presidential inaugural addresses, for example, God is always invoked, but typically only at the beginning and the end of the speech, and there is no reference to any particular faith or denomination. In this way, the core values and institutions of political life are sacralized and—again the element of circularity—the basic tenets of the major religions are interpreted in the light of political experience: out of this mutual reinforcement emerges civic religion. In addition, the outcome is one which encourages religious freedom: 'Politicians are capable of maintaining that religion ought to be a force in the life of every American while at the same time defending the right of all Americans to choose the particular church in which they worship' (J. Wilson 1978: 178).

Durkheim, of course, had been dealing with societies in which religion was homogeneous and in which there was one, socially-inclusive 'church.' This is clearly not the case in a modern industrial society like the United States, and Wilson succinctly shows how the Durkheimian version has been modified by Bellah in an attempt to make it valid in a contemporary context:

> Bellah has extended and refined the Durkheimian thesis to read as follows: a sacred dimension being considered an inherent part of all social life, the integrative function of religion can be detected even where formal religious unity is absent. This is done simply by locating the source of commonly held feelings of ultimacy and unity. Anything about which people feel a sense of ultimacy is thereby religion. This, of course, makes it very difficult to see any relationship between "religion" and "society", or to see them as separable at all. Bellah, like Durkheim before him, seems to be more interested in the moral foundations of social cohesion than in religion as such; and seems to have dealt with the problem of the relation between religion as defined in this book and other social institutions by explaining it away. Religion cannot 'cause' cohesion because religion *is* cohesion. This would seem to be a less than satisfactory way of coping with the problem of religion in a complex society (J. Wilson 1978: 179).

While it might well be contended by etymological purists that of course religion *is* cohesion, the tautologous solution of Durkheim's analysis will inevitably present problems. Nevertheless, regardless of how 'civic religion' is defined, the American situation has produced some fascinating attempts to explain the cohesive effect of religion in a seemingly pluralistic social context. One of the more influential of these is the so-called 'three-generations hypothesis' adopted by Herberg (1960) which, though it has been severely criticized on empirical grounds (Lazewitz and Rowitz 1964), is an impressive attempt to explain the *process* by which the contemporary American religious situation developed.

Herberg points to a number of features of the religious situation which need to be explained—the 'unknown God' of Americans who, though widely subscribed to, lacks any particular denominational identity or dogmatic content; the existence of a type of religious pluralism incorporating the three major orientations which Herberg labels the 'triple melting pot;' and the use of religious legitimation by political leaders such as Eisenhower in a completely indiscriminate way: 'Our government makes no sense,' the former President once declared, 'unless it is founded in a deeply felt religious faith—and I don't care what it is' (Herberg 1960: 84). Herberg incorporates all these aspects of American religion into an explanation of how immigrants to the United States gradually became assimilated—not into a homogeneous culture but into one of the three major religious divisions which resulted from the dialectic between imported ethnic identities and the need to forge a new social unity.

The first-generation immigrant to America found a strong source both of security and identity within the ethnic community, protected as it was by boundaries of language, social custom, and religious observance. However, for the second generation, those born in America, the ethnic community was a source of perplexities and social conflict. Their ethnic status came to be seen as a cause of deprivation and a reason why many channels of mobility were closed to them. In particular, they experienced the religious patterns of their parents as constricting and rigid and for many, the attempt to become fully American entailed severing links with the ethnic church; as they did so it became increasingly clear that the ethnic community was a transitional phenomenon or makeshift device that could not survive permanently. Finally, the third-generation American faced no major problem of defining his 'Americanness' but in the impersonal environment of urban America he faced a critical problem of finding a firm social identity. This was eventually achieved, says Herberg, by a 'return to religion'—not to the restricted confines of the ethnic church but to one of the three major religious orientations, Protestant, Catholic or Jewish. In short, Herberg's hypothesis is concerned with the process by which religious pluralism becomes a basis for social cohesion and ethnic integration.

(4) *An integrated approach and a future prospect*

Throughout this paper emphasis has been placed on the extent to which the insights of social theorists, and especially those who are canonized with the label 'founding fathers,' have served to integrate the mass of empirical data on religion. One of the functions of a social theory is to provide as comprehensive a framework for explaining the social world as is possible without being trivial or tautologous, and a second function is to high-light 'problem areas' requiring explanation and to generate the working hypotheses that will facilitate research in these areas. In the study of religion, a clear pedigree can be traced back from the contemporary concerns of sociologists of religion, through such figures as Wach and Niebuhr, to the seminal researches of Marx, Weber, and Durkheim. It is equally evident that this pedigree has tended to bifurcate into an emphasis on the one hand of power and social change in the dialectical relationship between religion and society and on the other into an emphasis on the socially cohesive functions of religion. Is an integrated approach possible?

The work of Berger and Luckmann is a conscious attempt to combine the insights of the different theorists and to produce a phenomenological theory of religion which will explain in particular the situation of religion in contemporary Western societies. It is obvious from their writing that the integration they have achieved is only partial and that, as was shown above, disagreement exists about the definitional scope of 'religion.' Berger is more influenced by the Marxian/Weberian approach and Luckmann's work owes much to Durkheim; indeed, one of the most accessible approaches to Durkheim's thought is *The Invisible Religion* (Luckmann 1967). As a result of these divergent influences, the phenomenological approach draws attention not only to the dynamic engendered by conflicting worldviews and social contexts but also to the way in which religion can serve to integrate a social group by providing it with an overarching system of meaning—a 'sacred canopy.' Perhaps most significant for the analysis of contemporary ideologies and social movements is the fact that 'religion' is seen not as something which is encapsulated within an institutional shell but as an integral part of the wider system of knowledge and beliefs. This is the starting-point for a consideration of their work.

Luckmann draws attention to the centrality of religion for social life by showing that it occupied a key place in 'classical' sociology. For Durkheim, religion transcended the individual and was the condition for social cohesion and order: at the same time, only the internalization of an external social reality by the individual could create a genuine human being. Man is therefore *homo duplex* and we can speak both of 'man in society' and 'society in man.' Weber too, says Luckmann, examined 'the social conditions of individuation' but in the historical context of specific religions and particular societies. In common with a number of theoretically-oriented sociologists writing in the mid-1960s, Luckmann believes that in the study of religion the links with the classical tradition have been weakened by an exaggerated concern with demographic, statistical and institutional studies and that the market-research concern with what goes on inside ecclesiastical buildings has led to an increasing marginality of the sociological study of religion.

Once 'religion' and 'religious institution' become equated, a process such as secularization comes to be inadequately defined as the shrinking influence of institutional churches, which come to resemble islands in a sea of secularity. However, Luckmann contends, church-oriented religion is more appropriately treated as being on the *periphery* of modern society: church attendance is more a rural than an urban phenomenon; women attend more frequently than men only to the extent that they are non-working women; and the occupational groups which are most involved tend to be 'traditional' ones. Church-oriented religion is thus of shrinking relevance for the integration and legitimation of everyday life in modern societies and its place has been taken by a plurality of 'symbolic universes' of meaning through which individuals are able to encapsulate and interpret their social experience. In a nutshell, the ecclesiastical roof has been replaced by a more privatized umbrella of meaning, though the function of both is to shelter the individual from a deluge of meaninglessness.

The description Luckmann gives of the characteristic form of contemporary religiosity originates in Troeltsch's 'parallelism of spontaneous religious personalities' (Troeltsch 1931: vol. 2, 381): the individual 'shops around,' selecting different themes or products from a range of 'ultimate' meanings and then constructs them into a somewhat precarious private system of 'ultimate' significance. The image here is very close to that used to depict the clientele of cultic groups: conversion to a 'deviant' religious perspective requires an initial self-definition as 'seeker;' and the supernatural supermarket depicted by Luckmann is identical with Campbell's 'cultic milieu' (Campbell 1972). Perhaps most importantly, the 'invisible religion' of Luckmann differs from traditional, church-oriented forms of religion in that it does *not* seek to legitimate the whole of society. Thus in Luckmann's terms, secularization is the process by which traditional religion retreats from public social significance, but since by definition religion is a universal anthropological condition, secularization cannot mean the complete emptying of religious symbols and activities from the social world: they are instead transmuted in a religion of the 'private sphere.' For Luckmann, man will always need to construct a sacred cosmos to render his experience ultimately meaningful.

Berger works from a similar basic insight on the social construction of reality to that of Luckmann, though his emphasis on the constant dialectical interplay between man and society and his association of the externalization of social experience with the concept of alienation brings him closer to a Marxian/Weberian perspective. Individuals in society, he says, organize their experience into a meaningful pattern and thus create a *nomos* which is shared by the group. The *nomos* tends towards greater levels of generality and when its maintenance is rendered precarious by events such as death—when the problem of meaning arises in a very clear form—there will be a tendency for the *nomos* to be identified with some ultimate truths inherent in the universe and hence to merge with the *cosmos*, which gives an external source of legitimacy. Religion appeals to some stable criterion of ultimate reality, but at the same time religious legitimation always serves to maintain some socially constructed reality, either on the level of the individual (for example, by making marginal situations like death meaningful and thus re-establishing his place within the social group) or on the social level, an example of which might be the prominence of religious legitimation at a time of social crisis (for examples see Clements 1971, Ahler and Tamney 1964).

A question arises at this point. Does not the direction of Berger's argument lead to the view of religion as a social product? Berger himself strongly denies the implication that any religious system can be seen merely as the effect of or as a 'reflection' of social processes: 'Rather, the point is that the *same* human activity that produces society also produces religion, with the relation between the two products always being a dialectical one' (Berger 1969: 47). The term which links religious beliefs and activity with social context is 'plausibility structure' and the relationship within this structure is two-way, just as we saw in the section on religious organization. And so, while Berger explicitly avoids a crude sociological determinism, his position remains one of 'methodological atheism:' 'Thus sociological theory must, by its own logic, view religion as a human projection, and by the same logic can have nothing to say about the possibility that this projection may refer to something other than the being of its projector' (Berger 1969: 180).

One of the most valuable features of the phenomenological approach of Berger and Luckmann is that it is simultaneously based very firmly on the mainstream of sociological theory while indicating possible directions for future research (M. Hill 1973a: 263–266). It is likely that this research will encounter some immediate problems, especially those related to the operational definition of Berger and Luckmann's concepts, but if these can be overcome there are some attractive research prospects.

First, there is growing interest in—and a developing literature on—'new' religions, or what has been called 'the new religious consciousness' (Glock and Bellah 1976). While a number of these have features which clearly bring them within the scope of existing typologies of religious organization, others are much less amenable to analysis in these terms and seem to overflow the available categories. Hopefully, a more fluid phenomenological approach with its emphasis on the creation and maintenance of a sacred cosmos as part of an overall plausibility structure will make it possible to incorporate more facets of these movements in a sociological treatment.

Second, the phenomenological approach may—if it can be developed with greater precision—open up the interesting area of the extent to which religious and political worldviews are alternatives or can be mutually reinforcing. While we have an excellent literature on the linkage between, for example, the growth of non-conformity and liberalism in nineteenth-century Britain, it would be of great value if we could examine the importance of 'religious' as against 'political' rhetorics in the choice of membership in some of the 'new' religious groups. Research in this area would require a 'biographical' approach (Berger and Berger 1976) in order to trace those factors predisposing some categories of individuals towards membership in specific types of movement, but there are already published research findings which suggest that there are symmetries between childhood religious experience and adult conversion to certain types of religious movement (Johnson 1971).

Finally, and related to the last comment, I think we may anticipate a much greater cross-fertilization in the future between the sociology of religion and the sociology of deviance. In a glib sense, of course, religion *is* becoming a deviant area of activity with the continued erosion of conventional forms of religiosity and the growth—or at least, greater visibility—of exotic forms of religious practice both inside and outside the mainstream organizations of Christianity. In an interpretation of the contemporary situation it is likely that the concepts devised by specialists in deviance will prove extremely useful to sociologists of religion; indeed, they may well be usefully applied to historical situations, as can be seen in a recent article on the origin and social 'careers' of nineteenth-century missionaries (Potter 1975). Certainly, an article by Taylor on the study of conversion expresses some surprise that a convergence of approach has not yet occurred: '... it seems both curious that prevailing approaches to conversion have not utilized perspectives developed in other sub-areas and possible that such utilization may yield fruitful analytic potential. The areas of sociology of deviance and sociology of motives seem particularly relevant in this respect. A generalised sociology of deviance approach is useful in dealing with the mechanisms whereby converts acquire deviant identity in both interactional and cognitive senses, and in its stress upon the non-reciprocity of deviance-defining stances' (Taylor 1976: 16).

Although, with a few notable exceptions, the sociology of religion and the sociology of deviance have pursued very different interests, a convergence between the two is not entirely fortuitous. After all, one of the more prominent themes of Troeltsch was that out of the dialectical opposition of church and sect would emerge a more esoteric, individualistic, and fluid form of religiosity that would represent the end-point of Christian development and which we now associate with a deviant cultic milieu. Perhaps in this insight, as in so many others, the founders of the sociology of religion have served their present-day practitioners well.

Bibliography

General note: In order to avoid excessive detail, reference to some articles are labelled *Yearbook 1*, *Yearbook 7* etc. These all refer to *A Sociological Yearbook of Religion in Britain*, published annually by SCM Press, London, from 1968 to 1975. *Yearbooks* 1 and 2 (1968, 1969) were edited by David Martin, *Yearbook* 3 (1970) by David Martin and Michael Hill and *Yearbooks* 4 to 8 (1971–1975) by Michael Hill.

ABC Television (1964), *Television and Religion*, ABC TV, London.

Acton, H.B. (1958), 'The Marxist-Leninist Theory of Religion', *Ratio*, 1(2): 136–149.

Ahler, J.G. and Tamney, J.B. (1964), 'Some Functions of Religious Ritual in a Catastrophe', *Sociological Analysis* 25(4) Winter: 212–30.

Apter, D.E. (1968), 'Nkrumah, Charisma, and the Coup', *Daedalus*, 97, (3) Summer: 757–92.

Barkun, M. (1974), *Disaster and the Millennium*, Yale University Press, New Haven.

Baxter, J. (1974), 'The Great Yorkshire Revival 1792–6: A Study of Mass Revival among the Methodists', in *Yearbook 7*.

Becker, H. (1932), *Systematic Sociology ... of Leopold von Wiese*, Wiley, New York.

Beckford, J.A. (1975), *The Trumpet of Prophecy*, Blackwell, Oxford.

Bellah, R.N. (1967), 'Civic Religion', *Daedalus*, Winter: 1–21.

— (1970), *Beyond Belief*, Harper and Row, New York.

— (1975), *The Broken Covenant: American Civil Religion in Time of Trial*, Seabury Press, New York.

Berger, P.L. (1969), *The Sacred Canopy*, Doubleday Anchor, New York.

Berger, P.L., Berger, B. and Kellner, H. (1974), *The Homeless Mind*, Penguin Books, Harmondsworth.

Berger, P. and Berger, B. (1976), *Sociology: A Biographical Approach*, Penguin Books, Harmondsworth.

Birnbaum, N. (1955), 'Monarchs and Sociologists: A Reply to Professor Shils and Mr Young', *Sociological Review*, 3: 5–23.

Bocock, R. (1974), *Ritual in Industrial Society*, Allen and Unwin, London.

Boulard, F. (1960), *An Introduction to Religious Sociology*, Darton, Longman and Todd, London.

Campbell, C. (1972), 'The cult, the cultic milieu and secularization', in *Yearbook 5*, 119–136.

Clements, K. (1971), 'The Religious Variable: Dependent, Independent or Interdependent?' in *Yearbook 4*, 36–45.

Cohen, M.R. (1946), *The Faith of a Liberal*, Holt, New York.

Cohn, N. (1962), 'Medieval Millenarianism: its Bearing on the Comparative Study of Millenarian Movements', in Thrupp, S.L. (ed.) *Millennial Dreams in Action*, Mouton, The Hague.
Cohn, N. (1970), *The Pursuit of the Millennium*, Paladin, London.
Coles, R.W. (1975), 'Football as a "Surrogate" Religion?' in *Yearbook 8*, 61–75.

Douglas, M. (1970a), *Natural Symbols*, Barrie and Rockliffe, London.
— (1970b), *Purity and Danger*, Penguin Books, Harmondsworth.
Durkheim, E. (1976), *The Elementary Forms of the Religious Life*, Allen and Unwin, London.

Field, C.D. (1977), 'The Social Structure of English Methodism: Eighteenth–Twentieth Centures', *British Journal of Sociology* 28(2) (June): 199–225.
Fustel de Coulanges, N.D. (1874), *The Ancient City*, Lee and Shepard, Boston.

Gellner, E. (1969), *Saints of the Atlas*, Weidenfeld and Nicolson, London.
Glock, C.Y. and Stark, R. (1965), *Religion and Society in Tension*, RandMcNally, Chicago.
— (1966), *Christian Beliefs and Anti-Semitism*, Harper and Row, New York.
Glock, C. Y. and Bellah, R.N. (eds.) (1976), *The New Religious Consciousness*, University of California Press, Berkeley.
Greeley, A.M. (1963), *Religion and Career—A Study of College Graduates*, Sheed and Ward, New York.
— (1966a), *The Education of Catholic Americans*, Aldine, Chicago.
— (1966b), 'After Secularity: the Neo-Gemeinschaft Society: a Post-Christian Postscript', *Sociological Analysis* 27(3) (Fall): 119–127.

Halévy, E. (1924), *A History of the English People in 1815*, T. Fisher Unwin, London.
Hebblethwaite, P. (1975), *The Runaway Church*, Collins, London.
Herberg, W. (1960), *Protestant-Catholic-Jew*, Doubleday Anchor, New York.
Highet, J. (1950), *The Churches in Scotland Today*, Jackson, Glasgow.
Hill, C. (1968), *Puritanism and Revolution*, Panther Books, London.
Hill, M. (1973a), *A Sociology of Religion*, Heinemann, London.
— (1973b), *The Religious Order*, Heinemann, London.
Hobsbawm, E.J. (1957), 'Methodism and the Threat of Revolution in Britain', *History Today* 3: 115–24.
— (1959), *Primitive Rebels*, Manchester, Manchester University Press.

ITA (1970), *Religion in Britain and Northern Ireland*, ITA, London.

Jackson, M.J. (1974), *The Sociology of Religion*, Batsford, London.
Johnson, W.T. (1971), 'The Religious Crusade: Revival or Ritual?', *American Journal of Sociology* 76(5) March: 873–890.

Kiernan, V. (1952), 'Evangelicalism and the French Revolution', *Past and Present* 1(1) February: 44–56.

Lazerwitz, B. and Rowitz, L. (1964), 'The Three-generation Hypothesis', *American Journal of Sociology* 69(5) March: 529–538.

Le Bras, G. (1955, 1956), *Études de Sociologie Religieuse* (2 vols.), Presses Universitaires de France, Paris.

Lenski, G. (1961), *The Religious Facter*, Doubleday, New York.

Long, N. (1968), *Social Change and the Individual*, Manchester University Press, Manchester.

Luckmann, T. (1967), *The Invisible Religion*, Macmillan, New York.

MacIntyre, A. (1967), *Secularization and Moral Change*, OUP, London.

Macourt, M. (1974), 'The Nature of Religion in Ireland' in *Yearbook 7*.

Malalgoda, K. (1976), *Buddhism in Sinhalese Society 1750–1900*, University of California Press, Berkeley.

Martin, B. (1968), 'Comments on some Gallup Poll Statistics', in *Yearbook 1*, 146–197.

Martin, D.A. (1962), 'The Denomination', *British Journal of Sociology* 12(1) March: 1–14.

— (1965), *Pacifism*, Routledge and Kegan Paul, London.

— (1967), *A Sociology of English Religion*, Heinemann, London.

— (1969), *The Religious and the Secular*, Routledge and Kegan Paul, London.

Mass Observation (1948), *Puzzled People*, Gollancz, London.

Moberg, D.O. (1961), 'Potential uses of the Church—sect typology in comparative religious research', *International Journal of Comparative Sociology* 2(1) March: 47–58.

Mol, H. (1972), 'New Zealand' in H. Mol (ed.) *Western Religion*, 365–379, Mouton, The Hague.

Moore, R. (1974), *Pit-Men, Preachers and Politics*, Cambridge University Press, London.

Nelson, G.K. (1969), *Spiritualism and Society*, Routledge and Kegan Paul, London.

Niebuhr, H.R. (1929), *The Social Sources of Denominationalism*, Holt, New York.

North, M. (1975), *The Mind Market*, Allen and Unwin, London.

Nottingham, E.K. (1971), *Religion: A Sociological View*, Random House, New York.

Oromaner, M.J. (1970), 'Comparison of influentials in contemporary American and British sociology: a study in the internationalization of sociology', *British Journal of Sociology*, 21(3) September: 324–332.

Pickering, W.S.F. (1967), 'The 1851 Religious Census—a Useless Experiment?', *British Journal of Sociology* 23 (4) December: 382–407.

Potter, S. (1975), 'The Making of Missionaries in the Nineteenth Century: Conversion and Convention', *Yearbook 8*, 103–124.

Radcliffe-Brown, A.R. (1922), *The Andaman Islanders*, Cambridge, Cambridge University Press.

Robertson R. (ed.) (1969), *Sociology of Religion*, Penguin Books, Harmondsworth.

Robertson, R. (1970), *The Sociological Interpretation of Religion*, Blackwell, Oxford.

Robertson, R. & Campbell, C. (1972), 'Religion in Britain: the Need for New Research Strategies', *Social Compass* 19(2): 185–197.

Sharot, S. (1975), *Modern Judaism: A Sociology*, David and Charles, Newton Abbot.

Shils, E. and Young, M. (1953), 'The Meaning of the Coronation', *Sociological Review* 2: 63–81.

Spiro, M.E. (1967), *Burmese Supernaturalism*, Prentice-Hall, Englewood Cliffs.

— (1970), *Buddhism and Society: A Great Tradition and its Burmese Vicissitudes*, Harper and Row, New York.

Stark, R. and Glock, C.Y. (1968), *American Piety: The Nature of Religious Commitment*, University of California Press, Berkeley.

Stark, W. (1966, 1967), *The Sociology of Religion. A Study of Christendom*, Routledge and Kegan Paul, London. *Volume 1. Established Religion*, 1966. *Volume 2. Sectarian Religion*, 1967a. *Volume 3. The Universal Church*, 1967b.

Swanson, G.E. (1960), *The Birth of the Gods*, University of Michigan Press, Ann Arbor.

Taylor, B. (1976), 'Conversion and Cognition: an Area for Empirical Study in the Microsociology of Religious Knowledge', *Social Compass* 23(1): 5–22.

Thompson, E.P. (1968), *The Making of the English Working Class*, Pelican Books, Harmondsworth.

Towler, R. and Chamberlain, A. (1973), 'Common Religion' in *Yearbook 6*, 1–28.

Towler, R. (1974a), *Homo Religiosus*, Constable, London.

— (1974b), *A Sociological Analysis of the 'Honest to God' Correspondence*, Dept. of Sociology, Leeds University.

Troeltsch, E. (1931), *The Social Teaching of the Christian Churches*, 2 vols. (translated by Olive Wyon), Allen and Unwin, London.

Turner, B.R. (1974), *Weber and Islam*, Routledge and Kegan Paul, London.

Wach, J. (1947), *Sociology of Religion*, Kegan Paul, London.

Wallis, R. (1976), *The Road to Total Freedom*, Heinemann, London.

Weber, M. (1976), *The Protestant Ethic and the Spirit of Capitalism*, (Introduction by Anthony Giddens), Allen and Unwin, London.

Whitworth, J.M. (1975), *God's Blueprints*, Routledge and Kegan Paul, London.

Wickham, E.R. (1957), *Church and People in an Industrial City*, Lutterworth, London.

Wilson, B.R. (1959), 'An Analysis of Sect Development', *American Sociological Review*, 24(1) February: 3–15.

— (1961), *Sects and Society*, Heinemann, London.

Wilson, B.R. (1964), 'The Paradox of the Exclusive Brethren', *New Society*, 20 August, No. 99: 9–11.

— (1966), *Religion in Secular Society*, Watts, London.

Wilson, B.R. (ed.) (1967), *Patterns of Sectarianism*, Heinemann, London.

Wilson, B.R. (1967), 'Establishment, Sectarianism and Partisanship', *Sociological Review*, 15(2) July: 213–220.

Wilson, B.R. (ed.) (1970), *Rationality*, Blackwell, Oxford.

Wilson, B.R. (1973), *Magic and the Millennium*, Heinemann, London.

— (1975), *The Noble Savage*, University of California Press, Berkeley.

Wilson, J. (1978), *Religion in American Society: the Effective Presence*, Prentice-Hall, Englewood Cliffs.

Worsley, P. (1968), *The Trumpet Shell Sound*, MacGibbon and Kee, London.

Yinger, J.M. (1946), *Religion in the Struggle for Power*, Duke University Press, Durham N.C.

— (1957), *Religion, Society and the Individual*, Macmillan, New York.

4

Sociological Approaches (2)

GÜNTER KEHRER AND BERT HARDIN

Tübingen

The Founding Fathers

The sociological theories of religion that were typical of the discussion after World War II cannot be reduced to any one dominant approach. In 1964 Talcott Parsons wrote that the main theoretical developments in the sociology of religion had been due to the work of Pareto, Durkheim, Weber, and Malinowski (1964: 197–211). Although, with the exception of Malinowski, the contributions from these authors had occurred before 1918, it can be said without exaggeration that their writings dominated the changes in sociological thinking that took place in the period between the two world wars. It was not only Parsons's 'voluntaristic bias' that led to a high estimation of post-positivistic (or post-Spencerian) sociology. There was also a general shift in the moral, political, religious, and philosophical reasoning that served as a frame of reference for modern sociology. Modern sociology was less interested in the so-called objective trends in the evolution of society and culture, and more interested in the subjective motives and aims of the actors. *Lebensphilosophie* and existentialism were the philosophical expressions of this development, the roots of which dated back to the end of the nineteenth century (cf. Simmel 1912). In this context a very different understanding of religion from that of the 'classical' fathers of sociology became necessary. Comte, Spencer, and Marx had paralleled religion more or less with the past and science with the future although they did have a more favourable attitude toward religion than, for instance, Voltaire, Condorcet, or Holbach. Thus, in some respects, they were not the direct successors of the radical Enlightenment. The generation that included Durkheim, Weber, Pareto, and Malinowski was even less influenced by the philosophy of the Enlightenment. It is not our task to speculate about the social origins of voluntaristic thinking, it is more important for our purpose of describing the present situation of the sociology of religion to draw attention to the fact that there is at least one point that the two generations had in common. It was the problem of order, or to state it in different terms: how can societies be integrated? The same problem (which can, of course, be traced back to the thinking of Machiavelli and Hobbes—if not Aristotle) has become the most prominent theoretical issue for the modern sociology of religion.

It is a very rarely discussed fact that the most important scholars in the field of the sociology of religion—Pareto, Durkheim, Weber, and Malinowski—did not spend their time in systematically exploring the situation of religion in modern societies. They were interested either in the religious life of existing tribal societies (Durkheim, Malinowski), in the role of religion in the history of European societies (Weber), or in the non-logical components of social action (Pareto). Essentially the same limitations had been found in the work of the founders of sociology (Comte, Spencer) but the conclusions their successors drew were totally different. Whereas Comte and Spencer had sought 'functional equivalents' for religion which could fulfil the same integrating functions that religion had had in less differentiated societies, Durkheim postulated that this function is always fulfilled by religion, although the religion of modern societies will have some new features compared with the religion of the past. Pareto and Malinowski (with Weber it is not clear) seemed to believe that religion cannot be replaced at all. Despite these differences it is evident that the founders of modern sociological thinking about religion formulated their theories out of generalizations drawn from non-modern societies. This cannot be explained exclusively by the role of historical thinking before 1918; it seems to be a consequence of an underlying belief that religion had its best time in the past. This belief corresponds to the fact that all four of these men were personally agnostics (cf. Savramis 1968: 39).

Thus it is at least questionable whether the theoretical findings of Durkheim or Malinowski can be used as explanations for the role of religion in modern societies. It is, in any case, impossible to make use of their concepts for theological thinking. The Christian religion which had served as an integrating factor had lost this function by the process of what can be called an 'intellectual' secularisation. The Christian explanations of the world and of life were no longer valid for the majority of the populations in modern societies. There was no doubt for Durkheim and others that the religion necessary for the society of the future was not the Christian religion, indeed Durkheim believed that 'memorial days' celebrating great national events would replace Christian holidays. However, our primary interest is not with the sociology of religion of the famous 1890 to 1920 generation. Instead, some of its features have been mentioned in order to point out a logical problem which prevails even up to the most recent sociological reasonings about religion. On the one hand, sociology (in itself a recent science) is mainly interested in theories about modern societies. In fact, general theory is only useful when it helps towards an understanding of the conditions of modern society. On the other hand, in the attempt to be as broad as possible sociologists must contend with phenomena which also existed in earlier societies, often in other forms. In the case of religion this means that general theory must annihilate important traits of modern self-understanding in regard to religion. This is due, at least in part, to problems with the universe of discourse in the sociology of religion. Concepts which are shared in the general universe of discourse in a linguistic sense are not shared in the ideational sense (see Hardin 1977: 113–116). Although this will occur in every science, in sociology it leads to many misunderstandings because, in general, sociologists are not inclined to use words in a strictly nominalistic sense. We shall show later that a good deal of discussion in the sociology of religion can be reduced to this problem.

After 1945 it seemed evident that the sociology of religion could not be done in the Spencerian way. As Parsons put it, in a famous sentence, 'Spencer is dead' (1942). The dominance of the so-called voluntaristic sociology was not debated. This means that—given the situation of the supremacy of American sociology—the European traditions of Weber,

Durkheim, etc. came back to Europe disguised in Parsonsian sociology. There can be no doubt that after 1945 European sociologists, for the most part, looked to America. However, there were at least two European developments in the sociology of religion of consequence for this time which date back to the pre-war period. The first of these was the phenomenological approach, and the second was *la sociologie religieuse*.

The phenomenological sociology of religion can be analyzed as a combination of the phenomenology of religion and formal sociology. In fact, it is sometimes difficult to distinguish between the sociological approach and that of the religious-phenomenological. The main traditions are to be found in Dutch and German liberal theology. The most prominent theologians who developed a phenomenology of religion are G. van der Leeuw (1933, enlarged 1956, translated 1938) and Rudolf Otto (1919, original 1917). In formal sociology the works of Georg Simmel (1923) and Leopold von Wiese (1955) serve as excellent examples.

The combination of these two traditions is most clearly expressed in Joachim Wach's *Sociology of Religion*. Although it was originally published in America and only later translated into German, it is a thoroughly continental book (1944, German translation 1951). Its German counterpart is Gustav Mensching's *Religionssoziologie* first published in 1947. Wach and Mensching, who were, of course, influenced by Weber, were mostly interested in general patterns of religion. The material from which they drew their conclusions was found in the history of religion, mostly of Greek and Roman origin, and in the descriptions of ethnographers. As far as we can see this kind of sociology of religion did not find any successors in Europe or America. There are, however, many ways in which the modern sociological analysis of religion is influenced by these authors. There are also connections between the phenomenological study of religion and the beginning of voluntaristic sociology. Thus discussion of the typologies of religious bodies (the famous church-sect typology which up to recent times was one of the most debated issues in the sociology of religion) can be found in the works of Max Weber and Ernst Troeltsch (1912) and later in the works of Joachim Wach and Gustav Mensching.

The increased interest in small religious groups (which has never ceased in Great Britain—see Wilson, 1961, 1963) has presented occasions to make use of some of the concepts developed by scholars of the 'phenomenological school.'

Sociologie religieuse was only partly guided by academic interests. It has become common to date this kind of sociology of religion back to Gabriel Le Bras and Fernand Boulard (cf. Le Bras 1955/56 and 1956). Even if this is correct in some respects, it must be noted that there were some predecessors in the nineteenth and twentieth centuries, e.g., Godin and Daniel (1943) and Boulard, Achard, and Emerard (1945). Church organizations were always interested in collecting data about the religious life of their adherents, and about the effectiveness of the mission of the church. Gabriel Le Bras tried to give these ecclesiastical interests a more scientific basis. This meant, first of all, using a historical perspective in analyzing the data about church attendance, baptisms, etc. Before Le Bras it was very common to use concepts such as industrialization, secularization, and urbanization in a simple way to explain the low figures in ecclesiastical statistics. Despite some shortcomings in *sociologie religieuse* it should be mentioned that it was Le Bras who drew attention to the fact that differences in religious behaviour between the regions of France were very old and could in some cases be traced back to the time of Louis XIV. Although Le Bras did little to connect his findings with theoretical approaches in the sociology of religion, it is not difficult to see a resemblance in his work to Max Weber's 'sociology of religion' in the well known seventh paragraph of chapter 5 in *Wirtschaft und Gesellschaft* (1956). Le Bras was more interested in scientific historical research and was less occupied with equipping the ecclesiastical administrations with data.

The reason why church officials—Catholic and Protestant—were suddenly eager to have sociological support in doing their jobs lay only partly in the characteristics of *sociologie religieuse*. To a much greater extent it was due to the general change in the relationship between administrations and the social sciences. The most interesting case is that of industrial sociology. This change was caused by the apolitical attitude of post-war sociology, and the attempts of administrative élites (political, economic, and ecclesiastical) to make use of the techniques and data of the social sciences to aid in decision-making or to legitimate decisions. It can easily be shown that *sociologie religieuse* had its strongholds in the Catholic countries of Europe. This is due to two reasons. First, religious behaviour is better defined in the Catholic church than in the Protestant churches, thus it is easier to develop research techniques for exploring the religiosity of Catholics, or at least it seems to be easier. Second, the authorities of the Catholic church are in a better position to use sociological findings than their Protestant colleagues because normally the legitimation for their authority is independent of the effectiveness of their work. Nowadays no sociologist would admit that he or she belongs to the school of *sociologie religieuse*.

Whereas the phenomenological sociology of religion was only of academic interest, *sociologie religieuse* did have political and ecclesiastical relevance. The situation of the modern sociological analysis of religion can only be understood as a reaction against this *sociologie religieuse*. However, there are limitations which must be placed on the preceding statement, i.e., it holds true for continental Europe, it is only partly true for Great Britain, and it is even less true for the USA. We shall see that one of the few authors who has become prominent in Europe *and* America, Thomas Luckmann, developed his theory of religion, in the beginning, as a critique of *sociologie religieuse*.

Structural-Functionalism

We said earlier that American sociology of religion in the 1950s was Parsonsian sociology. This is particularly true if one regards the great theoretical approaches. However, empirical research work was only partly directed by structural-functional theory. In many cases the old discussion of church-sect typology prevailed, and there were various attempts to prove or to refute the Weber-thesis. The relevance of the structural-functional understanding of religion cannot be denied, because this approach became one of the most important theoretical schemes for the sociological discussion of religion. Therefore it must be presented here at some length.

During Parsons's whole academic life he was interested in religious phenomena. He wrote many papers which fall into the field of religion, yet the space reserved for the discussion of religion in his main contribution to sociology, the *Social System* (1951), is very limited. Only in chapters 5 and 8 did Parsons write in any detail about the functions of religion for the social system. The contribution in chapter 8 is a more systematic discussion of what he had said in the paper 'The Role of Ideas in Social Action' (1938). According to Parsons, religion has two main functions for the maintenance of the social system. First, it gives cognitive meaning to the moral-evaluative sentiments and norms of an action system; second, religion serves to balance out the frustrating discrepancies between the results of action which can be legitimately expected, and the results which can be observed in reality. These two functions are not independent of each other.

There seem to be at least two main problems involved in the structural-functional approach to the sociology of religion. The first problem concerns the role of older approaches within this theory. The second problem concerns the question: what kind(s) of society, and consequently what kind(s) of religion, must be supposed in order to formulate such a theory? We shall present Parsons's theory of religion in such a way that it enables us to discuss these problems.

With Parsons's first function mentioned above, the point in question is 'the cognitive definition of the situation for action as a whole, including the catechetic and evaluative levels of interest in the situation.' Parsons discusses this point with reference to a supernatural order distinguished in some sense from the natural and moral orders of things. Although this supernatural order is separated from the more empirical and moral orders, it is by no means meaningless for them. On the contrary, it serves as a point of reference when such questions are to be answered as why the natural order is what it is, and why we should obey the moral obligations of the moral order. Thus, the concept of order on earth seems understandable when there is also a heavenly order. Parsons cannot overlook the fact that there are only a few societies and a few religions which have developed an order of the supernatural. There may even be cases where the difference between natural and supernatural order cannot be found (Parsons mentions the case of communist societies). In other words: the problem of the universality of religion—

in a logical, not a purely empirical sense—is under discussion. Since Parsons intends to work out a general frame of reference for the understanding of all possible societies, and since religion plays an important role in this frame of reference, he must insist on the logical universality of religion, and, consequently, on the logical universality of the difference between the two orders of things. The possibility of doing this lies for Parsons in the conviction that one can distinguish between things that are scientifically knowable and things that are not knowable in this sense. It is not very difficult to show that Parsons follows here the standards of positivistic epistemology which were only rarely attacked in the first half of this century (1951: 359–63; Adorno et al. 1969). As we stated above, Parsons wanted to overcome the shortcomings of a positivistic sociology that could see in religion only residuals of pre-scientific thinking. However, Parsons is in one important respect a successor to this positivistic thinking, at least in methodology.

The second function of religion, as discussed by Parsons, is that of 'explaining' the discrepancies between what an actor can expect from doing 'good,' e.g., well-being, and the actual result of action. Parsons points to two perennial problems in this context, namely the problem of (premature) death, and the problem of undeserved suffering. These problems refer to the age-old theological and philosophical issue of theodicy. Parsons appears to believe that these problems are universal in a twofold sense: First, that the phenomena of premature death and suffering, though not usually explainable in terms of immoral behaviour, nevertheless exist; and second, that these phenomena need an explanation that goes beyond the realm of scientific and empirical thought. Since Parsons defines religious belief systems as being non-empirical and evaluative, it is evident that every explanation which transcends empirical *and* cognitive (descriptive) thinking is by definition a religious one. The question is, however, whether the problems of this kind of theodicy are universal in the sense of Parsons's theory. We would suggest that it is helpful to relate these problems to a particular stage in the development of religion. The question of theodicy can only occur when there is a very close connection between religion and ethics. It is by no means sure that this connection is universal. It seems more plausible to assume that this kind of 'moral religion' is a very recent product in the history of religion. Events need explanation, some events need more explanation than others, but not every explanation that transcends the average amount of 'theory' is a religious one. But even when the concept of religion is very broad, it is unlikely that the problem of undeserved suffering will be articulated without the frame of reference of an ethical religion. Rather, it is more likely that the problems of suffering and death will be solved by seeking the person who is responsible for them, for example in terms of witchcraft. Parsons relies too much upon the belief systems of the great world religions, particularly upon the Christian belief system in its Protestant form. Within this belief system the moral problem of undeserved suffering (including that of premature death) is very crucial.

It is interesting to see that Parsons' view of religion can also be upheld when the general theory of society moves to evolutionary concepts. In *Societies: Evolutionary and Comparative Perspectives* (1966) Parsons wrote that the legitimation system of every society is 'always related to, and meaningfully dependent on, a grounding in ordered relations to ultimate reality. That is, its grounding is always in some sense religious.' The legitimation system defines the interrelations between a society and a cultural system. Further, even in primitive societies there are at least four analytically defined components of the societal system: religion, kinship, technology, and symbolic communication—the so-called evolutionary universals in society.

It is impossible in this context to refer to every author who has formulated his sociology of religion in accordance with Parsons. We shall mention only two examples: Kingsley Davis's *Human Society* (1948) and Elisabeth K. Nottingham's *Religion and Society* (1954). (See also Nottingham 1971, Goode 1951, Hoult 1958, Schreuder 1962, Lundberg et al. 1963, Goldschmidt and Matthes 1962). Kingsley Davis states frankly: 'So universal, permanent, and pervasive is religion in human society that unless we understand it thoroughly we shall fail to understand society.' Davis postulates at the very beginning of his discussion what should be the result of a careful investigation, i.e., that there is only one theory of religion which is not outmoded, the functional one. 'In making scientific sense of nonscientific belief and practice in explaining religion, myth, magic, and ritual, there has been one trend of social

theory more successful than the rest. This is the functional-structural type of sociological analysis....' The main function of religion is its unique and indispensable contribution to social integration. Four things are most important in this respect. Religion provides:
(1) a justification of the primacy of a group's ends; (2) a constant renewal of common sentiments; (3) a concrete reference for a group's values; and, (4) a source of reward and punishment for conduct.

This theory was very much influenced by Émile Durkheim, whom Davis considers to be one of the most prominent authors in structural-functional sociology. Integration means for Davis the dominance of common ends over private ends, or to state it in another way: how is it that individuals with competing ends and wishes are able to work together and fulfil tasks necessary for the achievement of group ends? This is the problem of order which was the starting-point for the sociological thinking of Auguste Comte. It is the same problem that Thomas Hobbes tried to solve in purely political terms. It can be shown that there is a close relationship between the concept of politics and that of religion in social theory. This relationship is as follows: the more the coercion aspect or the power aspect in politics is dominant, the less important is the role ascribed to religion. Since every consensus-theory of politics needs a field where the consensus must be fixed, it is more than plausible to seek this field in a realm that transcends the empirical world. Although measurement of the degrees of integration seems to be difficult, one can assume that societies have different degrees of integration. However integration is necessary, i.e., a group (a society) must share certain values in common. The sharedness of values and goals needs a non-rationalistic explanation, a religious one. Only a society that had no shared values and goals would need no religion, but such a society could not exist. Davis seems to suppose that, despite the fact of the logical universality of religion, the process of social development from small isolated societies to complex urbanized ones (Davis cannot speak of evolution as the structural-functional theorists did some 15 years later) will weaken the role of religion though it can never disappear. This process of weakening the function of religion is called secularization. The question for Davis is 'how far can secularization go?'. The extreme end of the secularization process would be social disorder. In this state of affairs it is likely that new religious sects will arise. It can happen that one of these sects will prevail and give rise to a new religiously legitimated order or integration. Davis draws our attention to the origin of early Christianity. It would seem, according to Davis, that there is merely a circulation of religion and that secularization could only mean the decline of one religious synthesis and the rise of another one. Usually, however, secularization implies a much broader field of debate, particularly the decline of supernatural thinking in the modern world. Therefore, the question is whether 'the religion of the future may dispense with the supernatural.' Davis answers this question by differentiating the concept of the 'supernatural' into two. The first conceives of a spiritual world peopled by anthropomorphic imagination, and the second consists of beliefs which transcend experience. The second case of the 'supernatural' will never disappear. Davis refers to concepts such as the master race, manifest destiny, progress, democracy, the classless state, etc., as being ideas, whereas Parsons would prefer to classify these ideas as ideologies which can serve as functional equivalents for religion. Thus, Kingsley Davis seems more inclined to have a broader theory of religion.

Elisabeth K. Nottingham discusses the problem of whether or not the modern movements of nationalism, socialism, fascism, and communism should be included in the category of religion. Nottingham stresses the fact that the answer to this question is dependent on one's definition of religion. She uses a very broad—or inclusive—definition and classifies these movements as non-supernatural or secular religions. One can question whether it makes much sense to coin such a concept as 'non-supernatural religion.' This apparent contradiction seems to be reasonable if one considers that the structural-functional theorists do not use the concepts in the old scholastic manner. Words are defined in a 'functional' way; this means that all phenomena that fulfil the same function can be classified under the same heading. It is arbitrary what name is given to it. This procedure seems rather plausible, if the words are used in a purely nominalistic sense. Although most functionalists would pretend to do this, it is questionable whether a nominalistic usage of words can be successful in sociology where every object of research is named by words which have descriptive and prescriptive meanings in ordinary language (see Hare 1967). The unfruitful discussions about 'the' definition of religion, namely the debate between the adherents of an inclusive and an exclusive definition, can never be decided, because both parties have a totally different starting point. Whereas an inclusive definition makes sense only in a functional frame of reference, an exclusive definition is interesting in the comparative analysis of religious phenomena. It is not possible to decide one way or the other which is heuristically more fruitful for the sociology of religion. The main problem with an inclusive definition of religion is that one must label very different things with the same word when these things fulfil the same function. To do this is not a necessary condition for a functional analysis of society.

Conflict theory and evolutionary schemes

As Ralf Dahrendorf (1957, 1967) and later on—in the field of sociology of religion—J. Milton Yinger said (1970), functionalism is very much interested in harmony (integration), but only to a very small degree in conflict. One might speculate whether functionalist sociology laid so much stress on religion because religion integrates society, or whether the functionalist theory leads to a view of religion as an integrative power. Yinger is right when he says, 'there is little by way of research based on a conflict perspective' (1970: 92; see also 1946). Some sociologists see a difference in the sociological theory of religion between theories of integration and theories of change. We believe, however, that this difference is only a minor one, though, of course, theories which emphasize the normality of change place less stress upon the importance of integration. Though social conflict is seen by Dahrendorf as the main cause of social change, there is no necessary connection between theories of change and those of conflict. The famous Weber-thesis explains social and cultural change, but nevertheless it is one of the main witnesses for functional theory. Talcott Parsons demonstrates, by use of the Weber-thesis, the importance of the role of ideas in social action.

The main difference is between an integration theory of religion and a possible theory based on conflict. Although it might seem that Marxian sociology would produce a conflict theory of religion, the very few remarks of Marx relating to religion point to integration rather than to conflict. The reason for religion is to comfort those who live under inhuman conditions. Although religion is for Marx in some way 'protest' against misery, it is first of all the destruction of religion (or the critique of religion) that enables the oppressed to revolt against the real cause of their situation. Genuine Marxism is not interested in religion, because the task of criticizing religion had been done by the philosophers of the radical enlightenment (see Marx and Engels 1958, Marx 1958: 378ff). We shall see later that the so-called neo-Marxist interest in religion is more influenced by existentialism than by Marxism. Thus the question is still open. Is a sociological theory of religion possible which is based on the concept of conflict?

Another point which is no less important is the problem of development, or the concept of evolution. In the years between the two world wars, evolutionary sociology seemed to be completely dead. Parsons's statement in 1937 that 'Spencer is dead' meant also the end of evolutionary thinking. The breakdown of conceptions of evolution in social thinking is without any reasonable doubt a result of the loss of faith in the supremacy of European culture. Whereas in the nineteenth century this faith had prevailed, the emergence of existential beliefs in the twentieth century led to a kind of philosophical and political thinking which saw every culture as unique and not simply a stage in an inevitable process of evolution. Some fifteen years after the second world war we can see the rebirth of evolutionary approaches in the social sciences. The reasons for the emergence of this neo-evolutionism are complex and cannot be reduced to one cause. Keeping this reservation in mind, we believe that interest in the problems of the so-called underdeveloped countries led to reflections about the reasons for underdevelopment, and the forces that are favourable to modernization. Robert N. Bellah was the first prominent sociologist to speak of 'religious evolution' (in 1964, we cite from Birnbaum and Lenzer, 1969: 67–83). Bellah started his career as a sociologist with an analysis of the role of Japanese religion in the modernization process of Japan during the Tokugawa period (1957). At first glance this seems nothing else than a transfer of the

Weber-thesis to the Far East, but this view implies also the conception of an autonomous development of religion (see also 1970, 1975).

The main feature that serves as a key to Bellah's evolutionary scheme is the emergence of religious rejection of the world. Interestingly enough, this emergence is observed not only in the formation of the great empires of Asia but also in the smaller one of Greece. Bellah points out the role of literacy and the role of religious organization at the stage of the 'historic religions' which are the carriers of world rejection. This had not been found earlier in 'primitive religion' or in 'archaic religion,' nor can it be found in the so-called 'modern religion' of the present. The stage of 'early modern religion' serves as a 'missing-link' between historic and modern religion. Bellah draws a line from the stage where 'church and society are one' (primitive religion) through the stage where religion denied the world and in some form society, to the modern world where, despite the fact of religious pluralism, religions offer the opportunity for 'creative innovations in every sphere of human action.' Thus modern culture and modern society, which do not rest on rejection of the world, could only come into existence when the original identity of religion and society was dissolved by the world-rejection of the historic religions. It is nearly impossible to prove the adequacy of Bellah's evolutionary scheme with data from the history of religions. We believe that one of the major problems with Bellah's approach lies in his theoretical insistence on the rather elaborate belief systems of religions. It cannot be denied that in the first millenium BC theological and philosophical thinking—as far as it has been transferred to us—is highly world-rejecting. It must be seen, however, that we possess only the works of religious and/or philosophical specialists who elaborated ideas about the relationship of soul and body, and the possible salvation of the soul. These ideas have in many cases a very real basis in the role of intellectuals in societies. The exclusion of intellectuals from political power and economic wealth—as can easily be shown in the cases of Plato and the priests of ancient Israel during and partly after the exile—leads very often to the path of other-worldly fulfilment.

This perspective is a sociological one, because it links belief systems with the social conditions of the élites who produce the beliefs. We do not want to deny the possibility that religious belief systems have an autonomous power for development. We want to say, however, that a belief system—whether religious, political, or aesthetic—cannot exist without a social carrier (see Borhek and Curtis 1975). It may be possible that in tribal societies the whole society functions as a carrier for a religious belief system, though some elementary forms of religious specialization can be observed in many primitive societies. Since the emergence of religious specialists can be seen as a part of a process of division of labour, it seems necessary to regard developments in religion as being in close relationship with the development of other parts of the societal system. Bellah lays too much stress on religion as such. The reason for this strategy of isolating religion from society as a whole lies in over-emphasizing some ideas of Durkheim and Weber, and neglecting some principles of Marxian social thought, namely that man produces his religion, and that first of all, before producing religion, man has to eat, etc. Thus the way that man obtains food, clothing, shelter, etc., will be of some importance for his religion. This aspect was not new and was never contested. Durkheim and Weber were more interested in another aspect of religion. Whereas Durkheim emphasized the role of religion in integrating society, Weber seemed to develop a theory which showed that religion is a phenomenon *sui generis* which influenced economic and social evolution rather than being influenced by the general development. We would point out, however, that this understanding of Weber is too narrow, and it is too much based on his famous essay on the 'Protestant Ethic.' Some paragraphs of his more systematic sociology of religion in *Wirtschaft und Gesellschaft* look more like a Marxist sociology. This holds true particularly for his conception of the affinity between social classes and some kinds of religious belief systems. Although shifts in religious thinking can occur very easily, the main question remains open: why are some new religious ideas successful and some not? It may be expected that Marxist sociologists will try to find answers to this question.

Marxism, Neo-Marxism, and the Frankfurt-shool

The main contribution of Marxists to a sociology of religion should lie in an analysis of existing religious belief systems in order to find out which social groups express their social needs in these belief systems. To some extent there could be a convergence with the findings of the sociology of religion regarding all kinds of crisis-cults. As far as we can see Marxist sociologists are only very rarely interested in the phenomena of religion. In the German Democratic Republic there have been a few attempts to develop a Marxist sociology of religion. These attempts are rather orthodox and primarily try to explain why religion can still be found in socialist countries (Klohr, ed., 1966; Klohr and Klügl 1966). At the same time the so-called neo-Marxism in Czechoslovakia, and in some countries of Western Europe, started a 'dialogue' with left-wing Catholics and Protestants (Kellner, ed., 1966; Stöhr, ed., 1966, Gardavsky 1968, Metz and Rahner, eds., 1966, etc.). This dialogue is, on the one hand, a result of the 'opening' of the Catholic church and communist regimes. On the other hand, it was the common experience of communists and revolutionary theologians in South America that led to a revision of the mutual anathemas. Despite the partial political success of this dialogue, its results for a sociology of religion were poor. Even the most prominent neo-Marxist author in the field of religion, V. Gardavsky, speaks, more or less, about the fundamental functions which religion fulfils and which are dependent on the inherent nature of man. It is quite understandable that this kind of thinking about religion was of great importance for the socialist countries, because the factual denial of all problems of personal suffering was thus attacked. To point out the relevance of religion for human existence means at the same time to lay stress on neglected phenomena of life. The outcome for a more sophisticated sociology of religion in western countries cannot be appreciated in this way. Most of what the neo-Marxists say about religion is not very different from that which is now common-place in functional sociology. Thus the scientific contribution of Marxist sociology is still to be made.

Even the conceptions of religion of the so-called 'Frankfurt-school' of sociology are not of any great interest (Horkheimer in Schatz, ed., 1971: 113–19; Habermas and Negt in Bahr, ed., 1975, Geyer et al. 1970). After 1965 Max Horkheimer became more and more involved in debates about religion and the possible future of religion, but his remarks reflect a more or less pessimistic view of the future development of society and mankind. Since Horkheimer believed that the importance of the individual will diminish, and since he saw the main article of Christian faith as being the importance of the individual as an *imago Dei*, he argued for an alliance between religion and humanist forces in the western world. It is not so much the conception of the counselling function of religion in regard to suffering and death that Horkheimer pointed out, but the promise of a future without suffering, without power, without injustice. This promise is the eschatological part of the Judeo-Christian religious tradition that became politically relevant in the years after 1965 when certain factions of the Christian Churches allied with rebellious youth. In these years some attempts were made to overcome the 'conservative' bias of the functionalist theory of religion. It is interesting to see that the most important theorist of the Frankfurt School, Jürgen Habermas, speaks only very rarely about religion. Many theologians, however, believe that 'dialectical' sociology has some affinity to the kind of theological thinking they prefer. Whereas Adorno saw in the Christian religion of the twentieth century a form of totally neutralized religion that serves primarily as an agent in the process of building false consciousness (1950: 728–38), Habermas said in 1971 that he could imagine that it might be possible for us not to do away with theologians, in that the necessity for theologians lies in their contribution to reflection about the conditions that are necessary for the dignity of man. Habermas thinks primarily of the relevance of exemplary actions, which can often be found in small religious groups, and which have something to do with a kind of witnessing by doing. This conception is, of course, a political one; but the differentiation between sociological, political, and philosophical conceptions is an illegitimate distinction for the adherents of the Frankfurt School.

As far as we can see there has been only one attempt to use the conceptions of the Frankfurt School for a study in the field of the sociology of religion. Even this attempt is only to a certain degree typical of dialectical sociology. In 1973 Rainer Döbert published an essay about 'The Development of Religious Systems:—The Limits of the Frame of Reference of System-Theory.' This can only be understood as part of the controversy between Jürgen Habermas and Niklas Luhmann about 'system-theory' or 'critical theory of society' (Habermas and Luhmann 1971; Maciejewski, ed., 1973, 1974). Döbert wants to show that Luhmann's system-theory cannot adequately explain the stages of religious evolution. Although Döbert is not primarily interested in developing a theory of religious evolution, he points out some reasons for this evolution. He believes that religious development can be understood as a 'manifestation of the unfolding of the competence of communication.' This idea is in line with the general conception of Habermas that communication free of power implications (*herrschaftsfreie Kommunikation*) is the only way of proving scientific and/or moral assumptions. Thus the situation of modern religion, where ethics prevail over dogmatics, and where individuals communicate in an atmosphere of guaranteed freedom of religion, is a model for the desired state in all fields of human action. Since the evolution of religion with its most important stages (which are essentially the same as Bellah's stages) is nothing other than an 'augmentation of a more reflexive form of control of behaviour,' there must be a trend in universal history towards a diminishing of authoritarian control in favour of control by communication and reflection. This trend could only be fulfilled when societies were successful in solving the problems of basic needs. Thus we can see in Döbert's essay a very interesting combination of Marxist thought with some thinking in American sociology. More interesting, however, is the combination of Marxist thought with ideas of moral philosophy, which, however, cannot be discussed in this context.

System Theory

The influence of American sociology can be seen in another sociological theory of religion that has been discussed at least in Germany. Niklas Luhmann's general sociology, the so-called system theory, is in many aspects influenced by structural-functional sociology. Whereas structural-functional thought is part of a general theory of action, Luhmann's general thought belongs to theories that try to explain the emergence or maintenance of system within given environments. Luhmann believes that the categories he introduces in his analysis are able to explain all kinds of social phenomena, including religion (1977). The function of religion is mainly to transform the indeterminable world (environment and system) into a determinable one. Parsons defined religion as a system within the social system that relates society to its ultimate reality. Luhmann's concept is even 'more' functional. According to Luhmann, religion is not necessarily a social system. In many societies (particularly in tribal ones) there is not enough differentiation for a religious system. However, the function of religion is universal. This function is not primarily to stabilize the order of society, but to make it possible for society, as a system, to exist. To explain this approach it is necessary to unfold the basic ideas of Luhmann at some length. One of his central categories is that of complexity. Every environment is complex, this means that many choices—at least more than one—are possible. Vis-à-vis this kind of amorphous environment the act of choosing one possibility and neglecting others is of crucial importance, for this means that complexity is reduced. In terms of Luhmann's theory it is more correct to say that the function of systems is to reduce complexity. Without systems there is no reduction of complexity. This reduction, however, has its own problems, because the choice of alternatives is by no means evident, i.e., it is always possible to choose otherwise. This is the problem of contingency, as it is called by Luhmann. The degree of contingency is itself dependent upon the degree of internal complexity in a society. Societies which are simply segmented may offer only one possibility. Thus the reduction of complexity produces an increasing of contingency which must be determined. Therefore, it is possible to state that the transformation of the indeterminable world into a determinable one is the same as the transformation of indetermined complexity into determined complexity, i.e., to find a formula for ever-existing contingency. 'God' is such a formula of contingency. The problem of contingency is, in some respects, identical with the older problems of undeserved suffering which were discussed by the sociologists of the structural-functional school.

It is also possible to incorporate evolutionary approaches within Luhmann's system theory. He defined evolution, in accordance with Spencer's conception, as a process of differentiation. This means, first of all, that new systems emerge within society. One of these systems is the religious one. Although the function of religion is universal and independent from the stages of evolutionary process, some special problems theologians—and Berger—attacked the societal basis of modern Christian religion. Modern Christianity, they said, was not founded on the teachings of the New Testament, but on the teachings of a secularized social gospel. Sociology of religion serves as a critique of religion; the same function that theology has. The beginning of Berger's sociology of religion is a critique of the church rather than an analysis of the churches. The conceptions used in this critique are theological ones. On the other hand, Luckmann was not influenced by theological thinking. He started his 'career' as a sociologist of religion with a critique of the sociology of religion as it existed in the two decades after 1945, particularly *sociologie religieuse*. Luckmann confronted this school with the great traditions of the sociology of religion of Max Weber and Émile Durkheim. Whereas these authors saw in religion the core of society itself, so that sociology of religion was general sociology, modern *sociologie religieuse* used a very narrow conception of religion which was in fact reduced to some easily observable religious practices, such as church-going, which cannot be regarded as the relevant religious phenomena. Berger's and Luckmann's essays in sociology of religion have been used sometimes as specimens for a sociological critique of the theory of secularization. This usage is superficial, because both authors are very much interested in the change that religion undergoes in modern industrial society. Berger makes use of the word 'secularization' without any hesitation, whereas Luckmann is cautious to avoid any identification with the meaning of 'secularization' as a loss of religion (cf. Lübbe 1965; Martin 1969, 1978). Luckmann is one of the first sociologists to have such a broad definition of religion that many phenomena fall under this category. The point is not whether the so-called secular 'religions,' namely ideologies, particularly political ones, should be summarized as religions, but to find a definition of religion that enables one to have a common name for things that seem to be different, but are really the same. It is evident that this definition can only be a functional one. Thus Luckmann is the most radical fighter for a purely functional definition of religion. His definition is rather simple. Religion is the process of transcending the individual existence of man in a structural meaning, which is, in most cases, a culturally given system of meaning. It can hardly be denied that in every society human existence is shaped by giving transcendent meaning to a mass of 'isolated' facts. In other words, religion can be handled as being equivalent to socialization. Luckmann says that this definition is a direct consequence of Durkheim's sociology of religion, and in some respects this seems to be true. One might think of Durkheim's notions about the future of religion in modern societies. We believe, however, that Luckmann's definition is even broader than Durkheim's. What then are the reasons for such a broad definition of religion? Partly it can be explained by the shortcomings of *sociologie religieuse*. In concentrating on the observable facts of religious behaviour as they were shaped by the norms of the churches and other religious bodies, the authors of this school overlooked the possibility that new forms of religious life might arise in modern society. *Sociologie religieuse* confronted the traditional forms of religious life with so-called secular trends. Thus interests focussed on individualism, or sexuality, or familism were considered not only to be opposed to certain Christian teachings, but also to be against religion in general. The consequence was that modern society was labelled irreligious. It is not difficult to disclaim the procedures chosen by the sociologists of *sociologie religieuse*. They identified one form of religion with religion in general, the result being that the decline of this form was identical with the decline of all religion. This narrow definition of religion was guided by ecclesiastical interests rather than by sociological intentions. If one compares the situation of sociology in the fifties with the works of Max Weber and Émile Durkheim, it is quite understandable that Luckmann demanded a reorientation of the sociology of religion which would start with a more adequate definition of religion. *Sociologie religieuse* narrowed religion to some features of religious practice; Luckmann widened religion to include the constituent phenomena of society in general. Thus sociology of religion could only move between the Scylla of the loss of religion in modern society, and the Charybdis of a state where there is nothing more important than religion. There is no time now to continue discussing Luckmann's concept of religion at length. However it must be admitted that Luckmann's definition proved its usefulness in at least one case, namely in explaining the shifts in the relationship between society and religion. Although Luckmann does not elaborate an evolutionary scheme, he is able to show that some stages in societal development—archaic societies, great civilizations, modern societies—correspond very closely with specific forms of the institutionalization of religion. In archaic societies, the structured cosmos of meaning is very closely knit with the biographies of the individuals living in these societies, and societies in the stage of the great civilizations tend to be differentiated in such a way that religion became an institution and sometimes an organization on its own. The existing churches of our own age are residuals of this period. In modern societies the specialized forms of religion that were typical of the period of great civilizations still exist, but they must compete with emerging religions which can have political forms (ideologies), or a more private form (cults of the individual, and subjectivistic philosophies), etc. These systems of meaning are normally not organized or specialized in distinguishable bodies or organizations. The difference between the situation of religion in modern societies and that in archaic societies is to be found primarily in the fact that the new belief systems are extremely pluralistic. This has the consequence that systems of meanings are not obligatory for every member of society or for every situation. This pluralistic situation leads to an attitude vis-à-vis systems of meaning which is comparable to the situation of a buyer in a supermarket. He or she can choose between different offerings of merchandise, and the goods, once chosen, have no compulsory consequences for the next choice. If this analysis holds true, it is indeed not a very good prospect to do research in the field of ecclesiastically defined religious activities in order to find out what the state of religion in modern societies may be. Although Luckmann believes that some forms of specialized religion will survive in the future and consequently the importance of the churches will only very slowly diminish, one may expect elements of the new religions to amalgamate with elements of specialized religion. This process of amalgamation can be understood as secularization when one is ready to limit the concept of secularization to what happens to specialized religion.

Peter Berger's approach to the sociology of religion is not very different from Luckmann's. As mentioned above Berger prefers a more exclusive definition of religion. In addition to this, Berger seems to have a concept that identifies religion with *sacralized* nomos and this is not fully identical with the system of meaning which constitutes religion according to Luckmann. 'Nomos' is the attempt of man to struggle against the meaninglessness of the world. Because man tends to establish the meaning crystallized in nomos for the entire world, there is always the tendency to connect nomos and cosmos into one entity. It seems evident that Berger could test this approach with examples from tribal societies. It is less likely for modern societies to have such a sacralized nomos linked with a meaningful cosmos. Thus the category of secularization can be adequate for an understanding of the religious situation in modern societies. A more exclusive definition of religion, that would understand religion as the cosmos to which meaning is ascribed by the nomos, prevents a view that sees religion everywhere in society. The 'plausibility structure' which connects cosmos and nomos is not easily found in modern society. Religion is not the core of society itself, but one side of the dialectic between society and religion. It follows from this view that religion can lose its importance in the course of societal evolution. This loss of importance can take place in several ways. One of the most common forms is the total adaptation of religion to society. The earlier books of Berger laid stress on this point. Another very important way in which religion can lose its relevance is by the segregation of religion into discrete institutions within which religion becomes encapsulated. The possibility of influencing the world (including society) outside religious institutions thereby becomes diminished. It would seem that Berger is pessimistic about the future of religion in modern societies. But he believes that the supernatural—which is in some way identical to religion—cannot entirely vanish from the earth. Traces of the supernatural can be found in phenomena that at first glance seem to have little in common with religion in its more traditional understanding. For example the shelter a mother gives to her child when it awakes in the night, the laughter of a clown, etc., are all phenomena which show that man is not completely a victim of the outer world, but that he can overcome this world by his action. It seems to us that Berger enlarges his understanding of religion by these remarks, and that it goes in the direction of Luckmann's definition.

Most recent development and final theses

One of the most recent sociological approaches to religion is the attempt to use the concept of identity for the understanding of religion. The concept of identity has been of great use to psychologists and sociologists, and has served in some cases even for analyzing the individual religious career of some "hero" in the history of religion. An attempt to bring together all these scattered sketches was done by Hans Mol in 1976 (see also 1978). Mol starts with the dialectic between differentiation and identity. Identity is necessary for every kind of existence (individual, group, and societal), and it is always challenged by the likewise inevitable process of differentiation and adaptation. Mol relates religion to the identity side of this dialectic. This does not mean that religion is always on the 'conservative' side of the struggle, because the religiously defined identity of groups can be a source of great societal changes. The most important aspect is, in our opinion, Mol's differentiation between the foci of identity. It can be questioned whether the differentiation between individuals, groups, and societies is sufficient, but even if this were not the case Mol can show that some problems in the field of the sociology of religion may be solved when one considers that the foci of identity are not the same. Thus sacralized group identity can be disfunctional in regard to the identity of a society as a whole. The discussion between the adherents of different definitions of religion could also be ended by Mol's approach. The advantages of Mol's conception lie primarily in the possibility of reinterpreting the findings of studies which were guided by other theories of religion. It is still an open question as to whether it will be possible to inaugurate research following the outline of an identity theory of religion. Because Mol intends to incorporate a sociological understanding of sacralized identity into a much broader frame of reference that can serve as a formula for understanding nearly all the phenomena of life, it is difficult for him to avoid the the pitfall of explaining too much by one theory.

This attempt to give an impression of modern sociological approaches to religion is, of course, subjective, and we do not claim that everybody will accept it. We feel, however, that the most important approaches are mentioned and briefly discussed. We have not tried to give a survey of the findings of empirical research, even though the more sophisticated approaches are not independent of this research. Likewise we have neglected the whole field of anthropological approaches which, particularly in Great Britain and the USA, cannot be separated from sociological theories without difficulty. We have discussed only briefly the problem of secularization which was nevertheless one of the most fruitful and also one of the most important concepts about religion in this century. Further we do not think that the old problem of the typology of religious organizations earns much interest at present, although we do not deny that very much intelligent work has been done in this field. It is primarily shortage of space that has led to the omission of theories which try to explain the several waves of religious 'revival.' The most recent event in this area is the emergence of new cults in the Western hemisphere.

Keeping in mind all of these reservations, one might ask if there are any final fruits in the sociology of religion emerging in the post-1945 period. What is the contribution that sociologists have made toward a better understanding of religion? We believe that these questions can be answered by some theses with which most sociologists of religion might agree:

(1) Modern sociological approaches to the study of religion have shown that religion cannot be understood as an extra-social phenomenon which will diminish in the course of societal evolution.

(2) It has become evident that there must be differentiation between the social function of religion on the one hand and religious belief systems and religious institutions on the other. This differentiation which was sometimes neglected is very important because the two aspects relate to very different social phenomena which must be explained by theories of different ranges.

(3) The question of whether religion is an inevitable part of social life is still open. Since this question belongs to the problem of the definition of religion, the answer will always be arbitrary.

(4) Some old problems have not been solved; it can be shown, however, that they must be redefined in order to obtain a more scientific perspective. For example, this holds true for the question of secularization. After the structural-functional approach it became very

common to ask the old—sometimes theological—questions in a new manner.

(5) Attempts are being made to incorporate the sociology of religion into general sociology. The reason for these attempts lies partly in the situation of the sociology of religion immediately after 1945. As this situation no longer exists, it is unnecessary to fight for a scientific independence which is not seriously denied.

(6) At this time there is no dominating sociological theory of religion. This reflects the situation of sociology in general.

Bibliography

Adorno, Theodor W. et al. *The Authoritarian Personality*, Harper, New York, 1950.

Adorno, Theodor W. et al. *Der Positivismusstreit in der deutschen Soziologie*, Luchterhand, Neuwied-Berlin, 1969.

Bahr, Hans-Eckehard ed. *Religionsgespräche. Zur gesellschaftlichen Rolle der Religion*, Luchterhand, Darmstadt-Neuwied, 1975.

Bellah, Robert N. *Tokugawa Religion*, Free Press, Glencoe, 1957.

— *Beyond Belief. Essays on Religion in a Post-traditional World*, Harper and Row, New York, 1970.

— *The Broken Covenant: American Civil Religion in Time of Trial*, Seabury Press, New York, 1975.

Berger, Peter L. *The Noise of Solemn Assemblies*, Doubleday, Garden City, 1961.

— *The Precarious Vision*, Doubleday, Garden City, 1961.

— *The Sacred Canopy: Elements of a Sociological Theory of Religion*, Doubleday, Garden City, 1967.

— *A Rumor of Angels: Modern Society and the Rediscovery of the Supernatural, Doubleday*, Garden City, 1969.

Berger, Peter L. and Thomas Luckmann *The Social Construction of Reality: A Treatise in the Sociology of Knowledge*, Doubleday, Garden City, 1969.

Birnbaum, Norman and Gertrud Lenzer *Sociology of Religion. A Book of Readings* Prentice-Hall, Englewood Cliffs, N.J., 1969.

Borhek, James T. and Richard F. Curtis *A Sociology of Belief*, Wiley, New York, 1975.

Boulard, F., A. Achard, and H.J. Emerard *Problemes Missionnaires de la France Rurale*, 2 vols., Paris 1945.

Dahrendorf, Ralf *Soziale Klassen und Klassenkonflikt in der industriellen Gesellschaft*, Enke, Stuttgart, 1957.

— *Pfade aus Utopia. Arbeiten zur Theorie und Methode der Soziologie*, Piper, Munich, 1967.

Davis, Kingsley *Human Society*, Macmillan, New York, 1948.

Döbert, Rainer *Systemtheorie und die Entwicklung religiöser Deutungssysteme*, Suhrkamp, Frankfurt, 1973.

Durkheim, Émile *Les Formes Elémentaires de la Vie* Religieuse, Alcan Paris, 1912.

Dux, Günter 'Ursprung, Funktion und Gehalt der Religion', in *International Yearbook for the Sociology of Religion*, Westdeutscher, Opladen, 1973, 7–62.

Gardavsky, Vitezslav *Gott ist nicht ganz tot. Betrachtungen eines Marxisten über Bibel, Religion und Atheismus*, Kaiser, München, 1968.

Geyer, H.G., H.N. Janowski, and A. Schmidt *Theologie und Soziologie*, Kreuz, Stuttgart, 1970.

Godin, H., Y. Daniel *La France, Pays de Mission?*, Lyon, 1943.

Goldschmidt, D. and J. Matthes (eds.) *Probleme der Religionssoziologie*, West-deutscher, Köln und Opladen, 1962.

Goode, William J. *Religion among the Primitives*, Free Press, Glencoe, 1951.

Habermas, Jürgen and Niklas Luhmann *Theorie der Gesellschaft oder Sozialtechnologie*, Suhrkamp, Frankfurt, 1971.

Hahn, Alois *Religion und der Verlust der Sinngebung. Identitätsprobleme in der modernen Gesellschaft*, Herder and Herder, Frankfurt/New York, 1974.

Hardin, Bert *The Professionalization of Sociology. A Comparative Study: Germany -U.S.A.*, Campus, Frankfurt/New York, 1977.

Hare, Richard M. *The Language of Morals*, Oxford University Press, Oxford, 1967.

Hill, Michael *A Sociology of Religion*, Heinemann, London, 1973.

Hoult, Thomas F. *The Sociology of Religion*, Dryden, New York, 1958.

Kellner, Erich ed. *Christentum und Marxismus—heute. Gespräche der Paulusgesellschaft*, Europa, Vienna, 1966.

Klohr, Olaf ed. *Religion und Atheismus heute. Ergebnisse und Aufgaben marxistischer Religionssoziologie*, VEB Deutscher Verlag der Wissenschaft, Berlin, 1966.

Klohr, Olaf and J. Klügl *Grundriss der marxistischen Soziologie der Religion*, VEB Deutscher Verlag der Wissenschaft, Berlin, 1966.

Le Bras, Gabriel *Études de Sociologie Religieuse* 2 vol., Presse Univ. de Paris, Paris 1955/56.

— "Sociologie Religieuse et Science des Religions", in: *Archives de Sociologie des Religions*, 1956, (1): 3–18.

Leeuw, Gerardus van der *Phänomenologie der Religion*, Mohr, Tübingen, 1956.

— *Religion in Essence and Manifestation. A Study in Phenomenology*, Turner, London, 1938.

Lenski, Gerhard *The Religious Factor*, New York, 1963 (3d ed.).

Luckmann, Thomas *Das Problem der Religion in der modernen Gesellschaft*, Rombach, Freiburg, 1963.

— *The Invisible Religion*, Macmillan, New York, 1967.

— "Sammelbesprechung zur Religionszoziologie", in: *Kölner Zeitschrift für Soziologie und Sozialpsychologie*, 1960 (12): 315–326.

Lübbe, Hermann *Säkularisierung. Geschichte eines ideenpolitischen Begriffs*, Freiburg-München, 1965.

Luhmann, Niklas *Funktion der Religion*, Suhrkamp, Frankfurt, 1977.

Lundberg, George A. Clarence C. Schrag, and Otto N. Larsen, *Sociology*, Harper and Row, New York, Evanston, London, 1963 (3d ed.).

Maciejewski, Franz ed. *Theorie der Gesellschaft oder Sozialtechnologie Supplement 1 und 2*, Suhrkamp, Frankfurt, 1973 und 1974.

Martin, David *The Religious and the Secular*, Routledge and Kegan Paul, London, 1969.

— *A General Theory of Secularization*, Blackwell, Oxford, 1978.

Marx, Karl 'Zur Kritik der Hegelschen Rechtsphilosophie', in *Marx-Engels-Werke (MEW)*, Bd. 1, Berlin, 1958.

Marx, Karl and Friedrich Engels *Über Religion*, Dietz, Berlin, 1958.

Mensching, Gustav *Soziologie der Religion*, Ludwig Röhrscheid, Bonn, 1947.

Metz, Johann Baptist and Karl Rahner, eds. *Der Dialog oder ändert sich das Verhältnis zwischen Katholizismus und Marxismus?*, Rowohlt, Reinbek, 1966.

Mol, Hans *Identity and the Sacred*, Blackwell, Oxford, 1976.

Mol, Hans ed. *Identity and Religion*, Sage Publications, London, 1978.

Nottingham, Elizabeth K. *Religion and Society*, Random House, New York, 1954.

— *Religion. A Sociological View*, Random House, New York, 1971.

Otto, Rudolph *Das Heilige*, Trewendt und Granier, Breslau, 1919 (3d ed.).

Parsons, Talcott *The Structure of Social Action*, Free Press, Glencoe, 1949 (2d ed.).

— *The Social System*, Free Press, Glencoe, 1951.

— *Essays in Sociological Theory*, Free Press, Glencoe, 1964.

— *Societies. Evolutionary and Comparative Perspective*, Prentice-Hall, Englewood Cliffs, N.J., 1966.

Savramis, Demosthenes *Religionssoziologie*, Nymphenburger Verlagshandlung, München, 1968.

Schatz, Oskar ed. *Hat die Religion Zukunft?*, Verlag Styria, Graz, Wien, Köln, 1971.

Schreuder, Osmund *Kirche im Vorort*, Herder, Freiburg, 1962.

Simmel, Georg *Die Religion*, Hütten und Löning, Frankfurt, 1912 (2d ed.).

— *Soziologie. Untersuchungen über die Formen der Vergesellschaftung*, Duncker und Humblot, München und Leipzig, 1923 (3d ed.).

Stark, Rodney and Charles Y. Glock *The American Piety: The Nature of Religious Commitment*, Univ. of Calif, Press, Berkeley, Los Angeles, London, 1970 (2d ed.).

Stöhr, Martin ed. *Disputation zwischen Christen und Marxisten*, Kaiser, München, 1966.

Troeltsch, Ernst *Die Soziallehren der christlichen Kirchen und Gruppen*, Mohr, Tübingen, 1912.

Wach, Joachim *Sociology of Religion*, Univ. of Chicago Press, Chicago, 1944.

Weber, Max *Wirtschaft und Gesellschaft*, 2 vol., Mohr, Tübingen, 1956 (3d ed.).

Wiese, Leopold von *System der allgemeinen Soziologie als Lehre von den sozialen Prozessen und den sozialen Gebilden der Menschen*, Duncker and Humblot, Berlin, 1955 (3d ed.).

Wilson, Bryan R. *Sects and Society*, Heinemann, London, 1961.

— "Typologie des Sectes dans une Perspective Dynamique et Comparative", in: *Archives de Sociologie des Religions*, 1963 (16): 49–63.
Yinger, J. Milton *The Scientific Study of Religion*, Macmillan, Toronto, London, 1970.
— *Religion, Society, and the Individual*, Macmillan, New York, 1957.
— *Religion in the Struggle for Power. A Study in the Sociology of Religion*, Duke Univ. Press, Durham, 1946.

5

Social Anthropological Approaches

ANTHONY JACKSON

Edinburgh

1. Introduction

It is a fair generalization that many anthropological studies of religion are not concerned with the *explanation* of religion but with the *role* of religion in the explanation of society (Spiro 1966: 122). In other words, we do not find today the kind of theories on religion which were put forward before 1945 and, indeed, it has been suggested that we have made no theoretical advances of major importance since the days of Durkheim, Weber, Freud, and Malinowski (Geertz 1966: 1). While this is now too harsh a criticism to level at all the anthropological studies written in the last three decades it does make a valid point—anthropologists are not constructing grand theories on religion. It is also true to say that anthropologists are indeed wary of grand theories nowadays and they usually content themselves with fairly specific models of particular societies. As a result we cannot speak of any integrated approach to the study of religion since it has not been, until recently, the object of much interest among social anthropologists generally but whether this is due to the lack of a satisfactory theory or whether the subject is too broad and intrinsically difficult, it is hard to determine. At all events, research in this field has covered a number of topics which may be broadly subsumed under the heading of religion but which are not necessarily linked together by any common theoretical approach to religion.

Another way of considering the above-mentioned state of affairs is that quite simply, social anthropologists do not and could not specialize in religion as a special study. In the first place, social anthropologists generally study exotic societies by going to live among them for a few years during which time they have to find out everything they can about their particular society. They may eventually learn something about the religion of that society but they have to learn quite a lot else besides. Thus religion is only one aspect of the society that they study. In the second place, if they then go to another society again it will take a few more years to understand that religion, and so on. Hence there will be a limit to the number of societies and the number of religions that can be investigated by a single anthropologist, for it takes a genius like Malinowski to generalize from a single society and yet have anything significant to say. Most anthropologists cannot obtain first-hand knowledge of more than a few religions and this is insufficient to make a speciality of such a study. Instead, they concentrate either on a specific theme or a specific society but not on building a theory of religion. Even with the published monographs on religion to hand it is rare that sufficient data are available for constructing a theory of religion on a cross-cultural basis. While this may not altogether account for the lack of theories on religion in anthropology it indicates some of the limitations imposed upon anthropologists and why the contributions are so diffuse and varied. It follows that any trends that may be discernible in the anthropological study of religion are more likely to be manifested in particular topics of investigation rather than in any broad theoretical advance.

There is no best way of presenting the research that has been undertaken in social anthropology on the subject of religion over the last three decades. As investigations have taken place on a broad front and under changing theoretical banners it would be too confusing to adopt a strictly chronological approach.

Neither is it easy to adopt any logically progressive development of thematic materials since the debates on one topic invariably spill over into other areas. The following order of presentation has no particular theoretical significance and does not imply that the initial topics are more basic or have any priority. It is simply a matter of convenience, guided by the anthropologists' own weighting, that these works have been gathered thus together into topic areas. As will be seen by the dates of publication there have been periods when certain topics have attracted great interest for a time. These periodic waves of interest may themselves be of some significance although it should be borne in mind that world politics play a considerable role in where and when anthropologists may operate. However, it can be no part of this review to rehearse the history of social anthropology nor to attempt to describe the aims and methods of the discipline. Readers who wish to acquaint themselves with these matters are referred to the bibliography for this section where a few introductory texts are mentioned.

A few more disclaimers must be made. No review can be exhaustive or comprehensive and the limits of this one are set by works in English (or works translated into English). There are many other omissions since one cannot include every reference to 'things religious' in such a summary review, and, like the writers quoted, this writer is also idiosyncratic in his views. The main aim has been to direct attention to those areas where worthwhile debate has taken place. It has not been the intention to summarize the outcomes of these debates (if there were any) but to bring together relevant references so that the reader can pursue his own particular interests by further reading.

In brief, this review is a selection of works that I consider to have made a contribution to the study of religion. Rather than imposing my particular interpretation of what these anthropologists are saying by quoting passages in support of a sustained argument I would wish the reader to make his own judgements. To repeat, this is not a critique of social anthropology but a review of work published in the field of religion.

The topics that follow are unequal in length but this, in itself, is no guide to their relative importance but only an indication of the amount of material published. As mentioned previously this is partly a reflection of the wave of interest expressed in the particular topic. What is significant is the point in time when that topic ceased to attract attention. This switch of interest may occur when no theoretical progress is being made in that area and when a new paradigm seems more attractive. Such a change can be seen, e.g., when the structural-functional model was abandoned for the structural-linguistic approach in the 1960s.

Finally in regard to bibliographies I have restricted myself to a couple of hundred references only. However, by just consulting these the enquiring reader will discover several thousand books and articles on the topics discussed below. It is to be hoped that I have given sufficient lead to the reader to follow up the clues provided by the necessarily brief accounts of some of the contributions made to the study of religion by the anthropologist.

A brief word is necessary on the rationale of setting out the topics in the order given. The topics are roughly grouped into four equal sections:

I. *Primitive modes of thought* (topics 2–3)
—where the problems of belief, rationality, and classification systems are discussed.

II. *The communication of thought and feeling* (topics 4–6)
—where symbols, myths and meaning are considered.

III. *The theory and practice of religion* (topics 7–8)
— where monographs on religion and accounts of ritual behaviour are examined—this being the central topic.

IV. *Ancillary ritual practices* (topics 9–10)
—where such activities as magic, ecstasy, possession, and spirit mediumship are treated.

This grouping is merely convenient and implies neither logical nor empirical priority of importance. The aim has been to guide the reader to that topic he is interested in as quickly as possible since this is basically a work of reference and not a sustained account of religion. However, a straight-through reading should show how closely related are many of the topics, so that by the end one can return to the beginning with fresh questions about primitive modes of thought. The study of religion is, as Lévi-Strauss (1970: 5) remarked on the analysis of myths, an endless task, for there is no hidden unity waiting to be grasped once the analysis is completed.

2. *Primitive thinking*

An elementary example of the sort of puzzle that exercises anthropologists is the statement by some 'primitive' people that certain things can be both themselves and something else. A famous debate was provoked by Firth (1966) in his examination of the Nuer assertion that 'twins are birds.' Firth holds that this is not simply an intellectual classification but a symbolic way of stating that what people *do* matters. By invoking sentiment Firth is opposing Lévi-Strauss's view that animal classification is just a mode of thought. This last view will be taken up again in the next section on totemism.

Another puzzle was provocatively raised by Leach (1966) on the subject of virgin birth: how are we to explain this belief? A long discussion ensued including a rejoinder by Spiro (1968) and contributions from many quarters in *Man* (1968–69). In this controversy Leach takes a 'structuralist' view that all such beliefs are mythological while Spiro adopts a 'literalist' viewpoint that these beliefs have a functional explanation. Although the argument began with ethnographic reports that certain Australian natives were ignorant of physiological paternity, the real core of the dispute was on how these beliefs were to be interpreted.

These two debates exemplify the different stances that anthropologists can take with regard to 'primitive' thinking and on the question of the 'irrationality' or otherwise of these beliefs. A feature of this type of controversy is the assumption of a universal logic which, if applied to these beliefs, either renders them illogical from the 'intellectualist' standpoint since they are taken literally or, to avoid imputations of illogicality, such beliefs are to be regarded as symbolic and not factual statements at all by 'structuralists'. In an endeavour to avoid having to accept either of these two alternatives Cooper (1975) suggests that primitive thought incorporates a non-standard logic which has three truth-values: true, false, and indeterminate. While this has the merit of dissolving anomalies at one level it raises problems at the ethnographic level. But, as Needham (1973: xxxiv) remarks '... matters of logic are not decided by cultural particulars, and conversely the ordering of ethnographic evidence by logical criteria does not prove that these are intrinsic to collective representations.'

The above quotation comes from the introduction to a collection of essays on dual symbolic classification edited by Needham (1973). Taking its theme from Hertz, it is entitled *Right and Left* and the contributors discuss how various societies categorize the world in this way. These essays illustrate that this dual mode of classification is widespread; their virtue is not in proving any Durkheimian association between modes of thought and social organization but in stimulating examination of field data from a structuralist viewpoint in order to reveal unsuspected polarities which can enhance our understanding of primitive thinking.

Barnes (1974) has specifically examined the collective representations which the people themselves use. He shows that there is a general concordance throughout all phases of Kédangese conceptual order which is based on a form of dualism consisting of pairs of ranked and complementary opposites. The most irreducible conceptual distinction found is that between the form, or structure of being, and the spiritual essence which moves through it. This structual analysis of a single society exemplifies Mauss's idea of 'total social phenomena' in a convincing way.

Mauss and Hertz also inspired an even grander application of their ideas in Dumont's (1970) attempt to interpret the Indian caste system in terms of a ritual hierarchy based on an opposition between purity and pollution. Dumont maintains that 'the lack of progress in this field, as in others, is due to the fact that the main effort has not been directed towards the proper aim of questioning our preconceived ideas' (1970: 29). In particular he singles out 'our misunderstanding of hierarchy' which arises from the fact that our society honours equality above all other values and we thus fail to recognize that in India the principle of inequality is formally recognized as governing all social relations. In other words, Dumont raises the issue of objectivity when dealing with other societies since our own fundamental assumptions are a product of *our* culture and are not universal truths that are applicable at all times and places.

Dumont suggests that in Hindu society status is determined by principles which are independent of the distribution of authority and the way in which higher or lower status is expressed is through the idiom of purity. What gives this hierarchy meaning is not political or economic superiority but religious purity. Dumont's structural analysis of the intellectual classification in Hindu society is an ambitious exercise in the sociology of knowledge along Durkheimian lines.

The concept of purity is closely linked to that of pollution and this is a topic that has been taken up and skillfully treated by Douglas (1966). Arguing that we will not understand other people's ideas of contagion, sacred or secular, until we have confronted our own, Douglas looks at our notions of dirt, which is simply matter out of place, i.e., something that must *not* be included if a pattern is to be maintained. In order to make sense of pollution rules they must be examined in the context of a total structure of thought in which boundaries, margins and internal lines are ordered by rituals of separation. Douglas makes her point by analyzing the abominations of Leviticus in terms of the Hebrew classification of animals whereby 'clean' animals are those that conform fully to their class while the 'unclean,' or abominable creatures, are imperfect members of their class or those whose class confounds the general scheme of the world. In this way anomalies are indicative of disorder and symbolize danger and power, thus attracting ritual attention. Similarly, persons in marginal states are also in an ambiguous position and precautions must be taken to avoid the contagious power or the pollution they may engender. Such pollution rules, arising from the society's rules of classification, are also connected with moral values.

Also on the subject of modes of thought and how they have changed, Goody (1977) suggests that we often cause even more problems for ourselves by the very categories we employ to study others. Thus the use of 'advanced' and 'primitive' mentalities and other such dichotomies may hinder rather than help us in understanding the changes occurring in 'traditional' societies. In particular, he looks at the influence of literacy upon man's conception of the world—a point of special significance to those societies whose religion is based upon a Book. Because many of the societies studied by anthropologists are non-literate, this aspect has not always been considered even when missionaries have been active in the area.

3. Taboo and Totemism

Both topics of taboo and totemism are peculiarly anthropological subjects and are alike in many respects, not least of which being the fact that the terms were invented to account for certain types of behaviour and belief found among primitive societies. After years of confused debate over both topics they have become the subject of closer scrutiny from a linguistic point of view due mainly to the work of Lévi-Strauss.

Steiner (1956) has carefully reviewed the history of the concept of taboo and has shown how inadequate most theories have been on the subject. He concludes that taboo is an element of all those situations in which attitudes to values are expressed in terms of danger behaviour. He dissolves the assumed unity of the concept and shows that neither sociologically nor psychologically are we dealing with a single problem. Taboo has two quite separate social functions: (1) the classification and identification of transgressions; and, (2) the institutional localization of danger.

It is precisely these two points that Douglas (1966) takes up in a discussion on how all religions have rules of purity whose neglect is punished by dangers of all kinds. Douglas avoids using 'taboo' and prefers to say rules of purity or pollution-avoiding rules when analyzing the assumptions on which such rules are based. Taking pollution as a particular class of danger that is released by human action in infringing some rule, whereby spiritual powers are involved, Douglas attempts to link these powers with the social structure. She suggests that where the social system recognizes positions of authority, such positions are endowed with explicit, controlled, conscious, external, and approved spiritual powers, e.g., to bless or to curse. Where, however, the social system requires people to hold dangerously ambiguous roles then such people are endowed with uncontrolled, unconscious, dangerous, and disapproved powers, e.g., witchcraft. Thus where there is a well-articulated social system, articulate powers are likely to be vested in the points of authority, whereas an ill-articulated social system is likely to have inarticulate powers vested in certain persons as the source of disorder. This idea was put forward earlier by Leach (1961) when he suggested that the social structure is credited with primitive powers that maintain it in being. Douglas has taken this idea a bit further so as to encompass the more ill-defined areas of a social system. Adopting a Durkheimian stance that spiritual powers are part of the social system which they express, Douglas points out the other main area of danger:

the powers of pollution that inhere in the very structure of ideas itself and which punish any symbolic breaking of those things which should be joined, or of joining together those things which should be kept separate. The significant point here is that pollution, and hence taboos, are only likely to occur where the lines of structure, cosmic or social, are clearly defined. Hence, taboos are likely to be found in conjunction with the presence of elaborate systems of classification, which is the link we have been looking for between totemism and taboo.

Leach (1964) puts forward his own theory of taboo in which he links psychological and linguistic variables. He suggests that we are taught that the world consists of 'things' distinguishable by names and therefore we impose upon our environment a kind of discriminating grid by training our perception to recognize a discontinuous environment. Such trained perception is achieved by the simultaneous use of language and taboo. Our language gives us the names to distinguish things while taboo inhibits the recognition of those parts of the continuum which separate things.

It is in this anomalous zone, between distinguishable categories, that ambiguity arises and which is subject to taboos and which causes anxiety. Leach illustrates his argument by reference to the way speakers of English classify animals and how this classification relates to the matters of killing and eating and verbal abuse. His thesis has been strongly criticized by Halverson (1976).

A common taboo in societies that classify animals totemistically is that one may not eat the totem animal. Fortes (1966) takes up this topic and reviews the theories on totem and taboo and, in particular, defends the functionalist theory of Radcliffe-Brown against the structuralist interpretation of Lévi-Strauss. He suggests the difference in approach is that functional analysis is actor-centred while structuralists ignore the actor; for the one, language is verbal custom; for the other, all custom is transposed language. Hence, they talk past each other. Fortes maintains that totemistic observances are not intelligible from the actor's point of view without taking into account their taboo or morally-binding character. Taboos constantly keep an individual aware of his enduring identity as a person, as opposed to other persons, and taboos are also regarded as moral imperatives. Arguing against Lévi-Strauss's dictum that natural species are 'good to think' and not just 'good to eat,' Fortes suggests they can be both, in the following way. Natural species and animals, in particular, are apposite for symbolizing kinship connections, but they are also ideal for totemistic observances or taboos because they are 'good to forbid.' Animals, especially, lend themselves to moral constraint because, being alive, they are 'good to kill' and 'good to eat' for, without such properties such taboos would be meaningless. Thus taboos formulated in this way, prohibiting the eating of totemic animals, reinforce the actors' perception of themselves as having a special identity.

Following on from this use of animals as classifying devices there is another aspect, referred to by Leach (1964), in that the man-animal involvement touches on an emotional level whereby animals are attributed qualities that may affect persons. Buxton (1968) examines some of these factors that lead to the ascription of a special 'identity' to certain animals and to the idea that a violation of this animal identity can lead to ritual peril. Such ideas are intimately linked to various assumptions about the nature of particular animals and how they relate to man.

Bulmer (1967) poses the taxonomic question about why the cassowary is not a bird and why the dog has a unique place among the Karam of New Guinea. The short answer, in both cases, is that both animals are thought to have a unique relationship with man: they are quasi-human. However, to understand the status of these animals and the rules governing the treatment of them one has to take into account an extensive body of ethnography and one cannot just rest content with simple generalizations about dietary status and taxonomy.

Morris (1976) also found difficulties in relating the taxonomy of a hunting and gathering society to the animals which they are prohibited to eat. This finding goes against the Durkheimian notion that cultures with a low division of labour are characterized by integrated symbolic classifications that unite their various taxonomies into one totality. It would thus appear that certain simple societies live in a 'totemic void'—just like modern industrial societies do. This view also contradicts Lévi-Strauss's suggestion that tribal cultures have no sharp division between their various levels of classification because they are part of an organized whole. Morris contends that this explanation of totemism confuses folk taxonomies over particular domains with symbolic classificatory schemes that embrace several domains.

Much of our current views on totemism, it must now be clear, are greatly influenced by Lévi-Strauss and so it is necessary to have a look at what he says. However, it is impossible to do justice to his contribution in such a short review for his ideas are not confined to the narrow field of totemism and myth. The works that are central to this discussion are the two linked analyses: *Totemism* (1963) and *The Savage Mind* (1966). Although these works are ostensibly about totemism they are more of a demonstration of the structuralist method that Lévi-Strauss has been using for a long time. Readers who wish to know more about the method are referred to Leach (1970) where they are given a typically idiosyncratic account of Lévi-Strauss's theories.

The significant difference with Lévi-Strauss's treatment of totemism as opposed to other writers is the point of departure: he does not seek to define it, or explain it but, instead, he enquires how totemic phenomena are arranged. To Lévi-Strauss, totemism is an illusion, an artificial unity, existing solely in the mind of the anthropologist and which corresponds to nothing in reality. The reason, he explains, is that we confuse two problems when we talk of totemism: the first problem concerns the frequent identification of human beings with plants and animals (which is only part of the general relations between man and nature) and the second problem concerns the designation of kinship groups (which may be done with animal or vegetable terms). It is only when these two orders of classification coincide that we can talk of totemism. In other words, totemism covers relations between two series, one *natural*, the other *cultural* in which the former comprises categories and particulars while the latter series comprises groups and persons. Lévi-Strauss argues that any combination of these terms could be chosen to illustrate the relation between the natural and cultural series viz. (1) category and group, (2) category and person, (3) particular and person, and (4) particular and group. All four combinations are logically equivalent but only the first two combinations have ever been counted as totemism, and it is this distorted usage that gave rise to the totemic illusion that there is something mysterious about the phenomena. In fact, Lévi-Strauss declares, we have failed to see that these transformations are only part of an integral system of communication. His objective is to decode these communications and, to this end, he systematically destroys the totemic illusion by pointing out the errors of previous writers on totemism.

Having cleared away the problem of totemism in his first book, Lévi-Strauss goes on to explain how to decode totemic classifications in his second work on the savage mind. He offers us four linked concepts: 'bricolage', totemic logic, transformations, and the totemic operator which, together, are used to explain how the primitive mind works. Only a brief indication can be given of how Lévi-Strauss deals with this problem. Bricolage is the science of the concrete and a precondition of the logic of totemic classification which shares in that creativity that gives rise to myth. Lévi-Strauss pictures a mythical artist, a *bricoleur*, who codes and recodes the totemic messages. Using whatever is to hand and with the simplest of materials the bricoleur arranges images (really signs) in strikingly new ways to get a novel pattern, a new totemic code. The point that Lévi-Strauss is making is that it is a mistake to assume that each element in a totemic code *means* something. Neither can we discover the principles underlying a classification in advance but only afterwards by experience and ethnographic investigation. As far as transformations are concerned, these are something we observe when we examine social and mythical classifications e.g. where all the significant terms are reversed in a system. The most startling example that Lévi-Strauss gives of a transformation is when he suggests that the Indian caste system and the Australian Aboriginal totemic system can be reduced to a common but inverted model. Thus transformations are always variations in the code. Finally, we come to the totemic operator which is Lévi-Strauss's attempt to explain how primitive man can move from the idea of himself as an individual to the idea of a species and also how he can move back again. This logical operator is, of course, only a model that allows us to comprehend specific sets of classification made by particular peoples. One begins with the simplest type of system based upon binary opposition and proceeds to elaborate this by adding new terms that are chosen because of their opposition or correlation with the original. The logic employed is not necessarily homogeneous throughout but may contain sets of local logic and it is the rules of transformation that allow one to pass from one set to another.

The structuralist method that Lévi-Strauss employs enables him to bring together a wide range of phenomena in his discussion of how totemic classifications work—everything, in fact, that comes under the topics previously discussed here, besides many that follow later. His breadth of treatment is so vast that it is difficult even to summarize a few of his findings. What he has achieved is a complete re-appraisal of primitive thought and this has obvious implications for the study of religion. Needless to say, his ideas have provoked a great deal of controversy especially from the British anthropologists. It is not that they are saying he is wrong but that he tends to oversimplify in many cases and that, perhaps, binary opposition is not the most satisfactory way of dealing with complex facts, cf. Worsley (1967). We need not go all the way with Leach (1967) in his remark that Lévi-Strauss gives him ideas, even when he does not know what Lévi-Strauss is saying. It is true that Lévi-Strauss can be difficult, but he also can put forward ideas in a novel and stimulating way that does make one think over problems afresh. This is his importance to the study of religion.

4. Symbols

For the reader still puzzled by structural analysis, Leach (1976) has written an introductory text, *Culture and Communication*, subtitled 'The logic by which symbols are connected.' He first contrasts the two major attitudes that anthropologists can adopt: the empiricist and the rationalist viewpoints. This is a useful point to bear in mind when reading the differing accounts of religion. The empiricist position represented, say, by Barth is a development of the functionalist tradition of Malinowski and Firth and close to the structural-functionalism of Radcliffe-Brown, Fortes, and Gluckman. The rationalist or structuralist view is a development of the later writings of Evans-Pritchard besides Lévi-Strauss and would include Leach himself and Douglas. The difference between the two approaches (and it should be noted that anthropologists may adopt either or both) is that the empiricists assume that their basic task is to record directly-observed, face-to-face behaviour of people in their everyday tasks whereas rationalists are more concerned with what is *said* than what is done and hence they are interested in mythology and what informants say ought to be the case. Put succinctly, empiricists are interested in the structure of society while rationalists are interested in the structure of ideas.

The above distinction is relevant to the study of symbols by the two sets of anthropologists since it helps to explain their different approaches. Empiricists take symbols (and rituals) to be mainly instrumental whereas structuralists regard them as expressive and communicative. The former are interested in symbols for the light they will cast upon the society in question while the latter consider their task to be to decode the meaning of the symbols. Although this is a simplistic differentiation, it should suffice to keep one aware of the fact that anthropologists may be operating with very different schemes of interpretation in mind when they discuss religion.

Leach (1976) himself distinguishes signs from symbols in terms of metonymy and metaphor: signs are contiguous relationships while symbols are assertions of similarity. This distinction is the key to his structuralist analysis of a variety of topics in the book ranging from myths, magic, ritual, cosmology, and symbolism to sacrifice. His thesis is that the various modes of communication must be transformations of each other and must employ a common code. In order to decode these messages one has to realize that signs and symbols convey meaning in combination, indeed, the meaning depends on a transformation from the metaphoric to the metonymic code and back again. This is why Leach insists on this prior differentiation of signs and symbols as essential to his method.

However, distinguishing sign and symbol is necessary for other types of analysis as well, including empiricist anthropologists like Cohen (1974) who is interested in the instrumental value of symbols with regard to the distribution, maintenance and exercize of power. Cohen suggests that symbols are 'objects, acts, relationships or linguistic formations that stand *ambiguously* for a multiplicity of meanings, evoke emotions, and impel men to action.' Signs, on the other hand, need not agitate emotions but symbols do; hence signs are contrasted to symbols in their degree of potency in this regard. Symbols are grouped together within ideologies or worldviews which are carried by specific groupings of people. Cohen argues that the symbolic complexes of kinship and ritual support each other and are used to express and validate the political organization of such groupings. He distinguishes symbolic forms from symbolic functions and suggests that what we mean by cultural differences is simply that societies adopt different symbolic forms to achieve the same kind of symbolic functions. Cohen maintains that although social anthropologists have differed individually in their approach and explanations of symbolic forms and functions, they have been collectively concerned with the interdependence between symbolism and power relationships.

In a detailed review of symbolism, Firth (1973) stresses the instrumental character of symbols with regard to expression, communication, knowledge, and control and he rejects Lévi-Strauss's concern with the primary character of the symbolic function in human thought. Firth outlines the development of anthropological interest in symbols from the time of Adam Ferguson to the present and shows how modern social anthropology has given explicit recognition to the symbolic nature of the phenomena studied. This is exemplified by Leach's statement (1954) that ritual action and belief were alike to be understood as forms of symbolic statement about the social order. Having examined a number of modern studies Firth concludes that there are still two major questions: Is the statement that symbol systems have an existence of their own more than a metaphorical statement? What is the nature of collective symbols in relation to the symbolization of individuals?

The second problem that Firth raises is essentially concerned with how social anthropologists are to deal with psychology since the question revolves around the relation between public and private symbols. One book that sets out to explore this relation is a collection of papers edited by Lewis (1977) which resulted from a seminar between social anthropologists, psychiatrists, and psychoanalysts on the topic of symbols and sentiment. As Lewis points out, in a lightly ironic manner, despite the austere Durkheimian rejection of psychology by social anthropology, nevertheless, most of the leading anthropologists have employed implicit psychological concepts while strenuously denying that they are doing so! These papers provide a corrective to the rigidly held view that anthropology has nothing to learn from psychology and they show how symbols, seen in a cross-cultural perspective, may be analysed anthropologically and psychologically. Other psychoanalytic interpretations of symbolism are to be found in Beidelman (1966) and Hayley (1968).

Douglas (1970) begins her book dealing with the human body as a symbolic mode by stating that a grave problem today is the lack of commitment to common symbols. In trying to explain the present turning-away from ritual she is led to account for an individual's inner experience. However, she eschews psychological explanations and turns to sociology instead by using Bernstein's work (1965) on how speech systems transform the experience of speakers, in order that she can analyze ritual as a form of communication. Elaborating Bernstein's distinction between elaborate and restricted codes, Douglas regards ritual as a restricted code that is simultaneously a means of communication and a system of control. She puts forward the idea that one method for classifying social relations may be to see them as structured according to two independently varying criteria she calls grid and group. Group is the experience of the bounded social unit while grid refers to the rules which relate one person to others on an ego-centred basis. Using this method Douglas explores how various societies employ their symbolic codes.

One anthropologist who has specialized in studying symbols is Turner (1957, 1967, 1968) and he has recently summarized the work in this field (1975). He differentiates between sign and symbol, pointing out that signs tend to be univocal whereas symbols are multivocal—having many meanings. These meanings also depend on their context, and have exegetical, operational and positional meanings as well. Some symbols may be dominant or key symbols which constitute semantic systems in their own right. Turner has developed an elaborate vocabulary for discussing symbols and illustrates this with a wealth of detail from the Ndembu society. Pointing out that symbols are triggers of social action, that they have a dynamic quality, Turner analyses these in a processual way employing the situational analysis method.

An attack on the current idea that symbols can have meanings, much like words do, has come from Sperber (1975) in a provocative book simply entitled, *Rethinking Symbolism*. Arguing that the most interesting cultural knowledge is tacit or implicit knowledge and that it is the task of the ethnographer to explicate this sort of knowledge, Sperber suggests that this is typical of symbolism itself. Explicit forms of symbolism are unintelligible without the existence of an underlying tacit knowledge, so how are we to proceed? Sperber rejects the prevailing semiological view that the explicit forms of symbolism are just signifiers associated with tacit signifieds, like sound and meaning in language. He takes a cognitive view that symbolic interpretation is not a matter of decoding but it is an improvisation based on tacit knowledge which obeys unconscious rules. In addition, he does not see symbolism as simply an instrument of social communication as semiologists do. The principles on which symbolism, as a cognitive mechanism, works is not induced from experience but is part of the mental structure that makes experience itself possible.

What Sperber questions is whether one can usefully say what symbols *mean*. He examines the contributions of Turner, Freud, and Lévi-Strauss to the semiological debate on symbols and concludes they are labouring under an illusion, for if symbols did have meanings it would by now be obvious enough! Furthermore, interpretations of symbols are not meanings. Sperber goes on to outline a theory of symbolism in which symbols represent knowledge, but of a different kind to our ordinary encyclopaedic knowledge about the world. Symbolic knowledge is about our memory of words and things; it is about our conceptual representations of words and things. The process involved is one of displacement of attention and of evocation that takes place in an improvised and unconscious way, cf. Lienhardt's discussion of Dinka ritual in topic 7.

5. Myths

Just as symbols have been thought of as modes of communication so have myths and hence it is not surprising that what is sauce for the goose is also sauce for the gander—in this case, the structural method of Lévi-Strauss. Recent work on myths is so heavily influenced by his writings that one cannot avoid bringing his contribution into the centre of the discussion. Nevertheless, one should not be persuaded that all other theories on myth are therefore superseded and Cohen (1969) outlines seven main types of theory that have been put forward: those that treat myth as explanation, as mythopoeic thought, as expressing the unconscious, as functioning to create social solidarity, as legitimating social institutions, as symbolic statements about social structure, and as mediating contradictions in society. Typical representatives of these theories are, respectively, Frazer, Cassirer, Jung, Durkheim, Malinowski, Leach, and Lévi-Strauss. These theories are still used by various anthropologists, depending on their own particular view of myth. A good selection of these different approaches is given in Middleton (1967) and Maranda (1972a). Other reviews of recent work on myth are given in Maranda (1972b) and Dorson (1973). The former review is ostensibly about structuralism, but, in fact, is a useful summary of the way that myth has been treated by structuralists, especially Lévi-Strauss.

Although not an anthropologist, but a classicist, Kirk (1970) has used anthropological insights in his study of myth in ancient cultures and has some useful things to say about the relation of myths to folktales and to ritual. He chides anthropologists for only writing short papers on myths and suggests that this error of scale prevents them from adequately considering the essential preliminaries of classification and definition. While welcoming the fertile imagination of Lévi-Strauss and his detailed treatment of myth, Kirk considers that he is wrong in implying that all myths in all cultures have a similar function viz. to mediate contradictions, for there is no *one* definition of myth. Kirk also rejects the notion that myths are exclusively concerned with gods, ritual or religion. Instead, he considers investigating the relation of myths to folktales as being more profitable since both are governed by the laws of story-telling, though to different degrees.

Kirk, then, examines Lévi-Strauss' theory and suggests some modifications which he feels will enable him to employ more successfully the structural method upon myths from ancient cultures in which he is interested. Indeed, Kirk does reveal some interesting contrasts between Akkadian and Greek myths, e.g., that the former contain a nature culture awareness that is wholly lacking from Greek myths. He shows that while there is no single type of myth, one can typify the function of myths according to three categories: (1) narrative and entertaining—which are rare; (2) operative, iterative and validatory—which are repeated at rituals, either because they are thought to be efficacious or because they act as charters; and (3) speculative and explanatory—which may offer solutions to problems. It is, of course, the latter type that excites the modern mind and to which Kirk himself makes a contribution. Clearly, one writer above all others has played the major role in our present study of myth and that is Lévi-Strauss. Interestingly enough, Lévi-Strauss's first essay on the structural study of myth was published in the *Journal of American Folklore* in 1955. This famous analysis, which not only demonstrated the method but formed part of his explanatory theory, concerned the myth of Oedipus. Lévi-Strauss breaks the myth down into four component parts which he shows have a structural, not a chronological, relation with each other. The myth sets up these contradictions but also mediates them, according to Lévi-Strauss—a point which has worried many of his commentators.

Another acclaimed piece of analysis was Lévi-Strauss' treatment of 'The story of Asdiwal' and this was the subject of a sustained commentary in Leach (1967). It should be noted that these commentators were mainly British and hence displayed a sceptical, empirical but sympathetic attitude towards Lévi-Strauss's analysis. This myth comes from the Northwest Coast Indians and Lévi-Strauss shows us its internal structure by using the same method as before. As it happens, the themes are similar to that of the Oedipus myth and concern kinship, sex and murder—or as T.S. Eliot aptly put it: 'That's all the facts when you come to brass tacks: birth, and copulation, and death.' However, Lévi-Strauss goes on to ask the question how this myth relates to life and answers it by saying that not only is the structure of myth dialectical but so is reality and, more importantly, so are the relations between the two as well. What worries Douglas (1967) about such analyses is that in reducing mythical themes to 'brass tacks' may one not be losing some of the richness and majesty of these themes? She raises Ricoeur's objection that Lévi-Strauss has confined his analyses to certain areas of totemism and never uses examples from Semitic, pre-Hellenic or Indo-European areas. Is Lévi-Strauss' claim that he has selected *typical* areas correct or has he chosen only extreme examples by taking totemic cultures?

Although Lévi-Strauss himself has not ventured to analyze myths from non-totemic areas, other people have. As mentioned above, Kirk has looked at Akkadian, Greek, Germanic, Egyptian and Hindu myths while Leach (1962, 1966) has applied a structural analysis to accounts from the Old and New Testaments. However, while these analyses have revealed unsuspected structures and are informative, they have not established that mythic thinking proceeds along the universal lines suggested by Lévi-Strauss.

Without doubt, Lévi-Strauss' masterpiece is the four-volumed *Mythologiques* (1964, 1967, 1968, 1971) in which he examines some thousand Amerindian myths from South and North America. He claims that this is an experiment of possibly universal significance in which he hopes to prove that there is a kind of logic in tangible qualities and, moreover, the experiment will demonstrate the operation of this logic and reveal its laws. The aim is to show how empirical categories in the form of pairs of opposites like cooked/raw, moistened/burnt, infra-culinary/super-culinary are used as conceptual tools to elaborate abstract ideas and to combine them in the form of propositions. Lévi-Strauss does this by showing how a key myth is simply a transformation of other myths—a demonstration that he admits is endless. He chose mythology for the experiment because it apparently has no obvious function and so if he can show that the seeming arbitrariness of myth-making is nevertheless governed by rules at a deeper level then he can also establish that the human mind itself is determined in all its spheres of activity. The aim is not simply to show how men think but how myths operate in men's minds without them being aware of it. He, somewhat disingenuously, remarks that his own work itself could even be regarded as a myth—the myth of mythology!

Fortunately it is not necessary to attempt to account for Lévi-Strauss' work here (it is being treated separately in this work) since the undertaking would be too vast for this section, and it would distort the presentation. What is obvious is the great influence that this anthropologist has made to our view of primitive man and the way he thinks. One can judge the importance of Lévi-Strauss by the numerous articles that his works have called forth c.f. Hayes and Hayes (1970), Freilich (1975), and others already mentioned.

6. Cosmology and culture

One way of looking at culture is to regard it as a system of ideas and this has implications for all the previous sections as well as for cosmology, which is the most all-embracing category we have, since the latter is often taken to be equivalent to world-view. In any anthropological discussion there must be either an explicit or implicit reference to culture and cosmology. It is therefore of some importance to consider the various ways in which anthropologists have approached cosmology and culture since this affects their analyses of religion.

In a wide-ranging review of theories of culture Keesing (1974) distinguishes two broadly opposed approaches: one views cultures as adaptive systems while the other views cultures as systems of ideas. The adaptive view takes an evolutionary and/or ecological perspective towards culture. Some of the assumptions on which this view rests are that ways of life function to relate communities to their ecological setting, that culture change is an adaptive process, that the economy is primary and religion is secondary, but that religion may have adaptive consequences. This last point is well-demonstrated by Rappaport (1967) where he shows how ritual prestations form part of an adaptive system; cf. also Reichel-Dolmatoff (1976).

Keesing points out three differing approaches to culture viewed as a system of ideas. The first is the so-called 'new ethnography' approach which has concerned itself with folk taxonomies, or 'ethnoscience', in which culture is seen as a system of knowledge. One example is Frake's (1964) attempt to describe religious behaviour but, on the whole, this approach has yielded little. The second approach outlined is Lévi-Strauss's structural view of cultures as shared symbolic systems. Lévi-Strauss has sought to discover the processes of mind which generate such cultural elaborations as myth, kinship and language. The third approach treats cultures as systems of shared symbols and meanings. Exemplars of this last approach are Dumont (1970), Geertz (1973), and Schneider (1972). Keesing discusses the theoretical contributions of the last two writers and the paradoxes and problems that such an ideational approach raises.

Another relevant review article is Kearney's (1975) on world-view theory in which he discusses the contributions of Jones (1972), Douglas (1973), and Wilson (1971) in particular. Kearney detects a much more systematic approach to the study of worldview at the moment as is shown by the holistic approach of Douglas. A recent collection of essays by Douglas herself (1975) makes the Durkheimian point that knowledge is a product of social behaviour and therefore all questions of meaning ultimately depend on interpreting the social context first.

In a sense Geertz (1973) also stresses that anthropology is essentially interpretation (*pace* the decipherment of Lévi-Strauss)—a 'thick description' of a context. He argues that an understanding of symbolic systems or culture is only gained by inspection and not by arranging abstracted entities into unified patterns. In other words, coherence alone cannot be a major test of validity for a cultural description especially if the interpretation is divorced from concrete reality. Culture is public because meaning is and hence to study a culture is to study shared codes of meaning. Geertz thus adopts a semiotic approach to culture which he hopes will aid us to gain access to the conceptual worlds within which the people we study live. The aim of anthropology is not to answer *our* deepest questions but to make available the answers that other peoples have given.

An example of such systematic studies of a people's cosmological ideas in the context of the environment and social organization is found in Forde (1954), where nine African societies are examined. Where these studies differ from conventional accounts of ritual and belief is that they are not written in the context of a particular problem of the social structure or of cultural change. They present the religious ideas in a social context and show some of the variations found in cultural values and social organization. Two studies can be singled out: Douglas on the Lele (1954), and Griaule and Dieterlen on the Dogon (1954). This early study by Douglas laid the basis of her later reflections on symbolism (1970, 1975). The study of the Dogon by Griaule and Dieterlen is remarkable, not simply for the intricate cosmological ideas of the Dogon themselves but for the years of patient ethnography that were involved in dealing with this one society.

Another comprehensive collection of studies is given in Fortes and Dieterlen (1965) where British and French ethnographers present material covering a wide range of topics dealing with African systems of thought. As already mentioned, French anthropologists give priority to studying the *connaissance* (the total body of knowledge and belief) which is expressed in mythology, symbolism, and cosmological ideas, and which they see as a totality. The question this raises is whether the elaborate and complex cosmologies described by the French as being found among some West African peoples is common knowledge or esoteric? A further question is to what extent such complex cosmologies are indeed common—are they just a product of the observer? The point being that either the French are lucky and the British are unlucky, since the British never seem to find them, or whether such cosmologies emerge more readily from the French approach. In either case, there is plenty of evidence that cosmological ideas penetrate the social organization of a people, and that they themselves can influence these ideas. Such cosmological systems are not, then, purely reflections of the social structure but tend to form coherent bodies of belief which have all-embracing interpretative powers. Indeed, the very ambiguity inherent in symbols and their use in rituals may even exert a synthesizing influence, such that the conflict and disorder in secular life is reinterpreted while the discrepancies between the cosmological and social order are diminished.

Kuper (1973) discusses the cosmological ideas of the Swazi with special reference to their animal symbolism, not in any totemic sense but with reference to their use of animal costumes. She points out that Swazi cosmology is not binary but has many interacting components in which the dominant concept is of 'powers' and it is around this concept that the animal symbolism is arranged.

To conclude this section reference is again given to Leach (1976) in which he discusses a basic cosmological problem about how the power of a deity, located in another world, can be transmitted to men? This and similar problems Leach deals with in a structural manner on the premiss that culture communicates. He cites Geertz's injunction that ethnography should have 'thick description' rather than be a simple inventory of custom, but he feels that too much detail, the essence of fieldwork, can also be stultifying to understanding. However, it is open to question whether such a structural key will open the door of our understanding by decoding the variety of symbols that culture and cosmology possess. The method tries to make sense of symbolic forms only in terms of their internal structure and not how symbols actually function in real life to organize people's perceptions of the world.

7. Some monographs on religion

A loose distinction is made here between religion and ritual since they are treated separately in this and the following section. The difference lies mainly in the minds of the anthropologists who, for one reason or other, use either 'religion' or 'ritual' in the titles of their works. There is no great consistency of usage but 'religion' implies treating the religious beliefs and actions of a people as an independent enquiry whereas 'ritual' often indicates treating of ritual actions in conjunction with some other aspect of the social structure. While this difference is not one of substance it can indicate that a particular view has been taken with regard to the analysis.

One of the first monographs to be written on religion after 1945 also dealt with West Africa and that was Nadel's study (1954) of the Nupe in which the concepts of luck and fate also play a central role. It should always be remembered with any monograph that the fieldwork preceding it may have taken place considerably earlier and that as far as the theoretical presuppositions underlying the work are concerned these may belong to quite another era than that in which the book was eventually published. Generally speaking with regard to monographs specifically on religion, and these are often the last to be written on any particular society, they may be published some fifteen to twenty years after the fieldwork was begun. In the present case, Nadel's field work was conducted in 1934–36 when he was a student at the London School of Economics during Malinowski's time. It is also important to note, besides the date of fieldwork, the university that the anthropologist comes from, as this can indicate the kind of theoretical treatment he is likely to employ. These points need to be stressed since it must always be remembered that monographs on religion are *interpretations* of particular societies at a certain point of time and are made by individual anthropologists. These ethnographic accounts do not necessarily reflect the situation today and they may even have appeared quite differently had another anthropologist undertaken the study—as has already been discussed regarding the French and British approaches to cosmologies.

This last issue raises the problem of truth and relativity which is a common theme of debate in the social sciences but which cannot be resolved here—cf. Wilson (1974) and Douglas (1975). The best measure of the truthfulness in these accounts of religion is internal coherence of interpretation in the light of what else we know of that society. This means that monographs especially devoted to religion should not be read as complete works in themselves but that they should be read in conjunction with the author's other publications. In order not to overload the bibliography here these works are not included but reference should be made to the originals for further information.

Nadel sets himself a difficult task for the religion he wishes to describe is the traditional one of the Nupe people, despite the fact that they are largely Islamicised nowadays. Not surprisingly he opts for a wide definition of religion especially as the Nupe conceive of their universe as being ruled by chance and without having any clear guidelines about how one ought to act. He begins by outlining the Nupe creed and cosmology, followed by a technical description of their divinatory techniques, which are very important because divination is the key to all contemplated action. Next there is a discussion of the various types of ritual and then he gives an account of medicine and witchcraft. He concludes by discussing imported beliefs and the general problem of 'what is religion?'.

Religion, Nadel declares, is what we call that complex of beliefs and practices which is made up from three inseparable elements: (1) a doctrine formulating the content of ideas; (2) a congregation or an organized collection of believers and officiants; and (3) a set of observances—actions that are more or less ritualized. It is roughly along these lines that Nadel actually conducts his analysis, but with a stress on the observances.

The Nupe have little doctrine, practically no mythology and no coherently formulated set of beliefs. Nadel makes the significant observation that this does not mean that their beliefs are not therefore abstract, for it is precisely because they avoid the *concreteness* of myth that the Nupe can sustain a high level of abstractness—a point with which Lévi-Strauss might concur!

The Nupe have an otiose High God who is responsible for both good *and* evil but He can only be approached through the intermediary of ritual which is conceived to be an object that may be owned by a community and through which the people may tap His sacred power. In counterpart to this divine gift there is the manmade power of 'medicine' which is antisocial and linked to the worst of evils—witchcraft. The most clearly conceived spirit to the Nupe is that of the spirit-double who may be good or evil, weak or strong and who is responsible for the luck or fate of its human twin, but not their character. Not surprisingly twins are thought to be lucky among the Nupe although this is an uncommon attitude in Africa. They also believe that the disembodied souls of the ancestors are reincarnated in their descendants, which means they thus act like some principle of descent.

The various explanatory conceptions of fate parallel the organization of society: the fate of the community is controllable by means of ritual, the fate of the kinship group by sacrifice to the souls of the ancestors, and the fate of the individual may be affected by his use of 'medicine.' Nevertheless, the very uncertainty of the Nupe world demands some extra aid, and this is found in the widespread and compulsive use of divination.

After discussing the fixed and movable rites of different communities Nadel discusses 'medicine' and how it is learned and practised. This leads on to the problem of witchcraft which is seen as a covert battle of 'medicines,' for witches reputedly used secret medicines. In fact, no such secret information existed but, paradoxically, it was this very belief that maintained the belief in witchcraft. Nadel shows that the commonly-held view in the West that witchcraft is a means of explaining evil does not hold among the Nupe since they already admit evil as part of creation. He suggests instead that witches provide a certain enemy to grapple with in an uncertain world.

Finally, Nadel considers what religion does in terms of what he calls its 'competences' viz.: (1) its explanation of the universe; (2) its announcement of moral values; (3) its support of the social structure; and, (4) its provision of religious experience. He then links this scheme up with the three basic elements: doctrine, congregation and ritual actions. Summarizing Nupe religion, Nadel thinks it is as rational a religion as can be, but this view may be a result of Nadel's abstraction of time-past and his reconstructing a now non-existent religion which has been overlaid by the dynamism of Islam.

It can be seen that this account of Nupe religion bears close comparison with the beliefs of another kingdom just south of the Sahara viz. the Azande who were made famous by that classical description of their witchcraft beliefs by Evans-Pritchard (1937). As this work falls outside our timespan it cannot be included for review but it is only fair to say that this masterpiece was not fully recognized at the time and that it is only during the postwar period that its importance was given due credit, as will be seen later.

Instead we will turn to Evans-Pritchard's (1956) account of Nuer religion which, like Nadel's, took twenty years to mature. Evans-Pritchard's name is closely associated both with Oxford and with his predecessor Radcliffe-Brown, who strongly influenced his theoretical outlook. It is also not insignificant to note that when he conducted his fieldwork Evans-Pritchard was an atheist but that when he wrote his book on religion he had turned to Catholicism. This observation receives added point when one recalls his remark (also made in his review of theories of primitive religion) that 'those who give assent to the religious beliefs of their own people feel and think, and therefore also write, differently about the beliefs of other peoples from those who do not give assent to them' (1965: vii). In this account of Nuer religion, Evans-Pritchard states he is studying religion as an entity *sui generis* and he adopts an anti-rationalist stance of decrying those people who, he says, describe rites simply as examples of irrational behaviour. This study, he declares, is a study of what the Nuer consider to be the nature of Spirit and man's relation to it.

The Nuer constantly talk of *kwoth* (Spirit) and Evans-Pritchard considered that a full understanding of that word would give him the key to their philosophy and this is precisely what the book focuses on—the meanings of *kwoth* as God, Spirit, or spirits. Thus, at different levels, the Nuer may be thought of as being monotheistic, polytheistic, or even totemistic. Evans-Pritchard shows how this relativity in the conceptualization of *kwoth* bears close parallels to the social organization of the Nuer, thus indirectly supporting Swanson's thesis that particular kinds of spirit spring from the experiences with certain persisting sovereign groups. The first third of the book is concerned with the structural aspects of *kwoth* as God, spirits of the above (the sky) and spirits of the below (the earth).

Briefly, *kwoth* as God or Spirit is the creator and protector of mankind in general and the founder of morality. The two other types of spirit are not separate but simply emanations of Spirit itself. The air spirits are held to be responsible for misfortune by possessing people as punishment for their neglect; this fault may be corrected by sacrificing an animal to the spirit in question, whose identity is discovered by divination. Any person who should happen to become permanently possessed by such a spirit may become a prophet. The structural importance of this belief in sky spirits is that all agnatic kinsmen of the afflicted person are expected to attend the ritual sacrifice on terms of amity. Thus a particular air spirit afflicting a given lineage then acts as a focus of agnatic loyality at this level, yet being at the same time a refraction of *kwoth*, the Spirit of the Nuer; this particular belief thus unites all Nuer within a common framework. The earth spirits are totemistic and thus relate natural phenomena to social groupings and individuals. The respect that totems engender is not towards the things in themselves but to things as representations of Spirit. The actual choice of totemic objects is not made on utilitarian grounds but simply because these objects call to mind the ideal relationship of man to Spirit, which is often explained in myths of twin births of man and totem. Such beliefs are thought to have been introduced by their neighbours, the Dinka—about whom more will be mentioned later. The significance of these material totems possessed by certain lineages is that, again, they relate the total social order to *kwoth* via one of His manifestations.

In the central section of the book Evans-Pritchard discusses the concept *kwoth* in structural terms and in terms of meanings, for he sees religion as being the reciprocal relation between man and God. This leads on to a discussion of death, sin and suffering in which a vital part is played by the notion of spiritual purity. Evans-Pritchard concludes with a discussion of sacrifice which he divides into two types: (1) piacular rites, to do with personal misfortune; and (2) collective rites, to do with *rites de passages* and which thus have a confirmatory character. In a sense, all sacrifices are to *kwoth* and the ideal sacrifice is an ox—the Nuer, it should be remembered, are pastoralists—and, in fact, their entire herds are destined for eventual sacrifice. The difference between these two sets of sacrificial rites is that in piacular rites Spirit has come too close (i.e., by possession) and must be driven away, while in collective rites Spirit is asked to come to bless and confirm the new statuses that have been announced.

It is not possible to go into further details of this analysis here but it provides a crown to all the work that Evans-Pritchard has done on this particular people. There is added salience to this work since it affords comparison to one of his pupil's analysis of the Dinka, who are close neighbours of the Nuer. Lienhardt (1961) conducted this research after the war in 1947–50. That the Dinka have a remarkable similarity of belief to the Nuer is not so surprising since the two peoples practise a similar economy and are very closely linked. Indeed, some anthropologists like Southall (1976) suggest that the distinctions we generally draw between Nuer and Dinka are erroneous and that perhaps it is only a matter of emphasis that we can draw any line whatever in this case. Southall's interpretation should be looked at when considering both these 'tribes.' Lienhardt divides his book in two: one half dealing with the spirits and the other half dealing with the Dinka ritual specialist—the spearmaster. There is surprisingly little reference to the Nuer despite the similarity of belief and, indeed, Lienhardt even goes out of his way to avoid Evans-Pritchard's own terminology. Just as *kwoth* is a keyword for the Nuer, *nhialic* expresses the same idea for the Dinka. Lienhardt calls the corresponding various aspects: Divinity (= Nuer God), free divinities (= Nuer spirits of the air) and clan divinities (= Nuer spirits of the below) and collectively he refers to them as Powers. This usage he claims avoids the usual connotations and ambiguities of the English terms: God and spirit. The scope of these Powers is very similar to the corresponding ones among the Nuer but it might be noted that the Dinka refer to these Powers in a kinship idiom in quite a literal manner. Thus we get, for example, the equation Divinity: Man : father : child, which thus reinforces the authority of the human father. The only clan divinity worth singling out is 'flesh' since this is the one that informs the spearmasters and makes them quasi-divine.

Lienhardt's chief theoretical contribution lies in his central discussion on the nature of the relationship between these Powers and the experiences of the Dinka. For if these Powers are not objectively real what do they represent? Lienhardt replies that the Powers are not a description of sense-data but are an *interpretation of events*. Briefly, this can be explained by dividing experience into an active and passive half and considering the problem of illness. A sick man suffers the action of the Powers and the treatment is to separate the suffering from the man by purifying the offended and possessing divinity with sacrifices. This attitude arises because the Dinka lack a concept of 'mind' with which to bridge the gap between the self as a passive receiver of experiences and the actions made on the self. For example, memories or dreams are not regarded as activities of the self but as forces acting upon it, i.e., man is a passive object acted upon from without. Their world is not so much an object of study but an active subject—what was formerly called 'animistic.' The second part of the book concerns the spearmasters, the chief ritual specialists of the Dinka, who are thought to have transcended the separation of divinity and man and hence are believed to transcend death itself when they are buried alive. The spearmasters are considered to have superabundance of life, as witnessed by their special divinity 'flesh,' and they are thought to sustain the lives of their people which is why they are not supposed to die like other men. Spearmasters combine several roles (priest, mediator, prophet) that are performed by different ritual specialists among the Nuer.

In a brief discussion on symbolism in sacrifice, Lienhardt makes the important point that symbolic actions re-create and dramatize situations which they aim to control and thus they change the Dinka's experience (i.e., their perceptions) of those events even although the situation (e.g., sickness) remains unchanged, cf. Sperber's suggested theory in topic 4.

It is of interest to note that Douglas (1970) uses the Nuer and Dinka as a test case of her theory on natural symbols and also draws attention to the differences in treatment by the two anthropologists. However, her own analysis is flawed by over-selective quotation and, if they are not two separate tribes, then her case is weaker still. The fascinating aspect of the Nuer/Dinka controversy is that this may be perhaps the nearest we will get to having two interpretations of religion of a single people by two different ethnographers.

Before leaving Africa, mention should be made of the study by Middleton (1960) of the Lugbara group of people that, like the Nuer and Dinka, are acephalous, i.e., having no centralized authority structure. Middleton also came from Oxford and did his fieldwork between 1949 and 1952. Although Middleton entitles his book 'Lugbara religion' it is not a complete account and strictly it falls into the next section for consideration as suggested by its subtitle 'Ritual and authority among an East African people.' He is particularly interested in the interplay between ritual and the struggle for power within the lineage because this approach makes sense of some apparently contradictory ritual behaviour. He demonstrates, by case studies, how men of a single lineage group manipulate the cult of the dead to acquire and retain authority. Elders are in charge of ghost shrines and as the society lacks any central authority the main sanctions on behaviour are mystical in which sins are punished by an elder invoking a ghost to send sickness upon an errant kinsman.

The shrines the ancestors occupy are normally closely related according to the lineage genealogy but when the lineage is subject to segmentation, conflicts of authority manifest themselves, firstly as accusations of witchcraft against the elders, and later as a repudiation of the kinship links between the ghost shrines. In the latter stage the segmented lineage itself separates, with a consequent reordering of the genealogies and a redistribution of authority. Middleton gives extensive case studies to support his thesis that this process is a cyclical one.

Lastly, in an interesting conclusion, Middleton discusses the moral community in terms of myth, witchcraft, God, prophets and change which is the way that the Lugbara see their world and the structure of their society. He suggests that many of the ideological aspects display an implicit dualism whereby one set of moral values are counterposed by their inversions. This distinction is also found in the Lugbara categories of social space and time in which normal members of society live in the centre surrounded by a fringe of quasi-members of society who have superhuman powers (sorcerers) and beyond them the rest of the world, peopled with inverted asocial beings.

The above unsophisticated categorization of the world is what Leach (1968) means by 'practical' in the collection of papers entitled *Dialectic in Practical Religion*. The main focus is on Buddhism and, in particular, on pointing out the difference between philosophical religion and practical religion that studies of comparative religion have often failed to make. Western studies of Buddhism have tended to concentrate on the canonical texts and have neglected the way that Buddhism is actually practised in the villages, or they have dismissed any religious practice that is not in accord with the philosophical religion as being debased or a 'survival.'

In this volume Obeyesekere is concerned to show that in Ceylon the lay practitioner of Buddhism is faced with a series of irresolvable contradictions, posed by his doctrine, which have to be resolved. He shows how in Buddhism, theodicy, sin, and salvation are closely linked with the problem of suffering. These doctrines underlie the various precepts of behaviour that lay people and monks should follow. However, the laity are not expected to become ascetics or to withdraw from the world, for their aim is not salvation but the control of desires and an orderly conduct of life. The monks, on the other hand, are expected to be pious and other-worldly but they too are caught up in the worldly social system. Their function is, by their very existence, to act as a reminder to the laity of an ideal but unattainable model of behaviour.

Tambiah takes up in the same book this problem of how a lay public rooted in this world can adhere to a religion committed to the renunciation of the world. He discusses this in terms of the ideology of merit as practised in a Thai Buddhist village but points out that the major village preoccupation is really with death. This is because meritorious conduct in life bears a vital relation to one's fate after death and the nature of one's rebirth. This polarity between life and death may be seen in many dichotomies e.g. this world/other world, humans/ancestors, body/soul and is most clearly seen in the concepts of merit/demerit. Tambiah shows how in popular Buddhism both laity and the monks interact ritually in a reciprocal way so that the theological doctrine becomes practically meaningful. This analysis has been extended and developed by Tambiah (1970) where he describes religion in terms of four village ritual complexes which he sees as linked together in a single total field. He argues that we should perceive ritual as consisting of both 'word and deed.' He also attempts to examine the dialectical relationship between myth and ritual—an area that has had little ethnographic or theoretical analysis. Tambiah also has the typical anthropological concern with the relation between ritual and social structure but he extends this to include the relation between observed religious practices and the written canonical Buddhist texts.

On this theme, mention should be made again of the two main contributors to the volume on anthropological approaches to religion edited by Banton (1966) viz.: Spiro and Geertz. Both these American anthropologists have specialized in religions of the Far East. Spiro is particularly interested in Buddhism in Burma and he addresses himself first to the function of supernaturalism, i.e., beliefs in ghosts, witches and spirits (1967). The problem is how these beliefs can flourish together with Buddhism—a problem similar to Tambiah's. Spiro points out that there are two distinct systems operating, each with their own goals, and that their co-existence is mutually supportive to Burmese society. Then, in a massive volume (1970), Spiro looks at the problem from the point of view of Buddhism which he analyses as an ideological system, but starting from the indigenous Burmese categories. These two volumes, together with Tambiah's, provide a good and thorough account of practical Buddhism in action.

Geertz (1960) exemplifies his methodological prescription of 'thick description' in this work on the religion of Java which comprises a syncretism of three different traditions: animistic, Islamic, and Hinduistic. He shows how these three traditions are linked to specific groups of people: the peasants, the traders, and the bureaucrats. However, these three variants are not to be regarded as three distinct or isolated groupings for they all coexist in the same social structure. There are indeed conflicts and antagonisms between these different adherents but they also share many common values which serve to mitigate some of the differences. Geertz (1968) has also used his knowledge of Indonesian Islam well in a comparative study of Western and Eastern Islam by writing an anthropological and historical perspective on this world religion.

Another world religion, Christianity, has been looked at from a slightly different viewpoint. In Africa, there has arisen a bewildering number of religious movements that stem directly from missionary activity. Barrett (1968) has analyzed some 6,000 such movements on a cross-cultural basis and puts forward some explanations of this explosive schismatic tendency in Africa. Barrett lists some thirty elements that have contributed towards this phenomenal rise of separatist churches and suggests that these movements arise spontaneously from a well-defined common background. A case study of one particular people, the Zulu, and their separatist churches is given by Sundkler (1961). He examines the rise of the 'Ethiopian' and 'Zionist' churches and considers the relationship between leaders and followers, besides their techniques of worship and healing. In this connection it is useful to compare the functions of these churches' healing methods with traditional Zulu practice given in Ngubane (1977).

8. Ritual

The chief difference between this and the previous section is the deliberate emphasis by anthropologists on seeing ritual as part of the social process and not as a subject of independent study. This attitude is well-illustrated by Gluckman's (1962) edited book of essays on the ritual of social relations which deal with those ceremonies called *rites de passage* by van Gennep. Gluckman reviews the work in this field and puts forward a theory why rituals are more highly developed in tribal societies than in modern ones. He suggests, basically, that the greater the multiplicity of undifferentiated roles, the more ritual is required to separate them in a society. Ritual, then, is seen as functioning to integrate the society by means of role segregation. The only essay not to fall into this mould is one by Turner who seeks to analyze the symbols used in a *rite de passage*—the first of a whole series of interpretations that Turner was to produce.

One of the earliest analyses of *rites de passage* that foreshadowed Turner's symbolic analysis was Richards' (1956) examination of a girl's initiation rite in terms of its importance in social relations. In a volume of essays written in tribute of Richards and devoted to the interpretation of ritual, La Fontaine (1969) remarks that the common assumption used by the contributors has been that 'ritual' refers to all symbolic behaviour and is not just confined to religious institutions. This view maintains that ritual expresses cultural values, it says something in a non-verbal way that beliefs and myths express in words. In this approach can be seen the influence of Lévi-Strauss's thinking on the elucidation of myths. Amongst other contributions is a set-piece controversy between Bott and Leach on a psychoanalytic and a structuralist interpretation of the Polynesian *Tonga Kava* ceremony.

A selection of readings on religious beliefs is given in Middleton (1967) and provides a sampling of modern research on the topic.

One of the most thoroughgoing studies of the ritual symbolism of a single people is given by Turner (1967, 1968, 1969) who trained under Gluckman at Manchester and did his fieldwork between 1950–54. Not surprisingly in view of the stress laid on conflict analysis at Manchester, Turner began by studying the integrative functions of ritual and did so by using the case-study method. What is novel about Turner's approach was the detailed support he gave to his view that ritual is a means of storing and transmitting information down the generations by the use of symbols which reflected society's values, beliefs and sentiments. Developing a kind of information theory of symbolism, Turner stresses that symbols have many meanings depending on their ritual context which necessitates scrutinizing the various usages of symbols, the structure of the rite and the ritual roles employed. He sees ritual as the periodic restatement of the terms in which men must interact in order to have a coherent social life and that while it is expressive of the society's values it also has an important creative function. Ritual creates the categories through which men perceive reality: the axioms that underlie the structure of society. Indeed, he suggests, social life is an attempted imitation of the models portrayed and animated by ritual. Each society's ritual symbols constitute a unique code and each society provides a unique key to that code and it is Turner's aim to crack that code.

Turner's mode of analysis is to present a series of 'social dramas' in which conflict is resolved by ritual. He describes the field situation that the Ndembu people find themselves in and then analyzes the symbols used in the conflict-allaying rituals. A key element in the resolution of these conflicts of interest is the use of divination, for it is the diviner himself who identifies the social conflict and by his use of symbols can suggest who are the transgressors and also the appropriate course of action to be followed.

Ndembu ritual symbols represent universal values and the most important ones are what Turner calls dominant symbols which crystallize the flow patterns of many rituals. Taking a number of rites which are performed by cult members he analyzes how the symbols are used and the various meanings they may possess. Any unity the ritual has is a dramatic one, for it is not the case with the Ndembu that ritual reflects the unity of the social system as it does with many other societies. He tries to link social and ritual drama to Gluckman's idea of cyclical or repetitive social systems where conflicts can only be resolved within the system. In a cyclical system, he suggests, there will be social drama with rites involving the shedding of blood. Furthermore, such a system, by opting out of history, provides a stable background for the human drama of interaction and so ritual can then give security because the plot is known.

Another detailed account of the religious practices of a single people is given by Firth (1940, 1967, 1970) who began studying the Tikopia in 1928 and has returned there twice. It is of interest that Firth's trilogy of books on religion covers the period during which the people were completely converted to Christianity and he is able to plot the change from paganism to the Christian faith. He puts forward a model of Tikopia religious belief and practice that he infers from his observations. Pointing out that, for the analyst, ritual is a matter of observation and that of belief a matter of inference, he does not claim that his model is explanatory but is simply a set of statements about how the Tikopia conceive the nature of reality. He assumes that spirits are only personalized ideas and have no separate existence although for convenience he adopts the 'as if' convention of describing them as independent existing entities.

Firth adopts a rationalist, structural-functional approach to ritual and shows how it relates to social life in a number of ways: the organization of ritual, the role of spirit mediumship, the idea of totemism, the notions of *mana*, magic, and the soul. Some of his views are unorthodox but his general view is that ritual is a kind of formal symbolic mode of communication. His analysis is along traditional anthropological lines using ethnographical details to link together the various strands of ritual and belief to show their interconnection with other aspects of the social structure.

A final example of work in this field, and one which queries many of the assumptions made by the other anthropologists, is Barth's (1975) study of a small tribe in New Guinea. His main aim is a theoretical one: to develop ways of analyzing ritual as a mode of communication and a mode of thought. He wants to discover what is being communicated in ritual and how it is done. The Baktaman ritual has the character of a sacred mystery cult and it embodies a tradition of knowledge that is passed on through a series of rites. Barth takes us through the seven degrees of initiation to reveal the sacred symbols that emerged, and he then analyzes them. The rites are multi-channeled sources of messages that do not all have the same significance for the different participants. This problem of description is then compounded by the difficulty of conveying the meaning of non-verbal communication. Barth disputes Turner's (1969) view that native terms can be used as a framework for the analysis of rites and he also doubts whether native exegesis of rites (e.g., given by an informant of Turner) is at all common. Perhaps, he suggests, native explanations are simply an artefact of the anthropologist's own activity.

Barth also argues that ritual communication is cast in an analogical rather than digital code, i.e., it is built on metaphors not on classes of objects. Because ritual conveys non-verbal messages, the use of analogy is ideally suited to this form of communication. In analyzing this code, the symbols must be seen to be immanent properties and not definitive ones for otherwise one falls into the trap of treating them as a digital code. Barth goes on to point out that translating non-verbal messages into a verbal code (e.g., in a monograph) introduces a misleading schematization of symbols into dichotomies and dual classifications typical of digital coding that can carry the anthropologist away into another realm, far from the living reality of the people themselves. Another important observation is Barth's point that in non-literate societies 'real objects' persist while communication itself is ephemeral, hence there is a special importance attached to concrete symbols as uniquely durable messages.

Barth's analysis of this one small tribe is a strong corrective to the structuralist view that understanding symbols is simply 'cracking the code' of a linguistic message. His approach to ritual opens up a new perspective on how to treat symbolic codes.

9. Magic

The concept of magic has been a thorn in the flesh of anthropologists for some time as it is relegated alternately to science or to religion in an attempt to get rid of it. However, the idea of magic as primitive science is about as unhelpful an explanation as calling it an expressive symbolic rite. Little progress has been made in clarifying what we mean by magic as is shown by Wax and Wax (1963) who survey the discussion so far. They put forward the suggestion that the best way to comprehend magic is to think of it as a world view, where the emphasis is on rites. The dynamics of this magical worldview is Power (*mana*, etc.) and the rites are performed to ensure that a favourable balance of Power should exist.

Philsooph (1971) has taken up the question whether such a magical worldview is, or is not, personalistic. He argues that from the *actor's* point of view magic is concerned with conscious agents and that far from magic being an impersonal force it is personalistic. Reexamining the data from the Trobriands and the Zande he shows that a case can be made for associating primitive magic with conscious agents. However, this brings up the question of magical virtue and *mana*—the alleged power behind magic. After a close examination of *mana* he declares that it is simply a reification and a mystification—an illusion of the observer—to treat it as an impersonal power. *Mana* or supernatural power is not in opposition to personal agents but *belongs* to them, indeed it is essential to them since such agents can only be believed in if there are some phenomena which can then be interpreted as the manifestations of their power.

Tambiah (1968) has taken up this theme in discussing the magical power of words and by looking in particular at Trobriand ritual. He wishes to demonstrate that magical spells are based on the metaphorical use of language and not, as the classical theory would have it, on the belief in a real identity between word and thing. Tambiah elaborates on two devices used in language: metaphor and metonym (also used by Leach) which are based on the principles of similarity and cotiguity. He recalls that Frazer used these principles in his division of magic into 'imitative' and 'contagious' kinds but applied them to the *objects* used and not to the *words*. Spells can exploit the normal metaphorical use of words to make a verbal transfer of attributes but so does the metonymic use whereby a part can stand for the whole. In Trobriand magic, both linguistic procedures are used, metaphorical through substitution to permit abstractions, and metonymic to allow building up of details in a realistic manner, both being accompanied by action.

If ritual is addressed really to humans, using techniques to restructure and integrate the minds and emotions of the actors, then it exploits the special properties of verbal and non-verbal behaviour. The strength of language, Tambiah argues, is that it is not constrained by external reality and can thus invoke images and comparisons, by referring to the past or to the future in a way that cannot be represented in actions. Non-verbal behaviour excels in what words cannot easily do—to codify analogically (cf. Barth)—by imitating real events and reproducing technical acts. This analysis has improved our understanding of magic and its relation to practical activity better than most other explanations we have had so far.

A somewhat different look at magic is given us by a historian, Thomas (1971), who uses anthropological insights to reinterpret the relation between religion and the decline of magical beliefs in sixteenth and seventeenth century England. He shows how the main forms of magical beliefs were closely interrelated—the links between magic, astrology and witchcraft were both intellectual and practical. At the same time, the relation between these beliefs and contemporary religion was basically one of rivalry in providing help to everyday problems, yet both functioned as a means of social control by explaining misfortune in terms of guilt. Magical beliefs never offered a comprehensive view of the world like religion did and their, remedies were too diffuse and unsystematized but this in itself did not account for the eventual decline of magic. Religion itself had changed by the end of this period into *natural* theology and thus was easily reconcilable with the new mechanical philosophy of the time. Only then could a sharp distinction be drawn between religion and magic that would not have been possible at the beginning of this period. Magic simply went out of the newly-discovered *natural* world, for it had no justifiable place there.

Another cross-disciplinary investigation on the subject of magic is Wilson's (1973) sociological analysis into the rise of millenary cults. He uses the term thaumaturgical as being synonymous with magical in this context and considers such miracle working in connection with the new religious movements that have sprung up around the world.

In many ways, then, the concept of magic is a bridge to other worlds—a linking device—that brings together heterogeneous activities into a semblance of coherence. Because so much ritual behaviour contains both words and deeds of a stereotyped nature and because it can refer to verbally discriminable objects (seen and unseen) as well as to literally undescribable emotions (that are felt but cannot be put in words) our simply calling this activity 'magical' is perhaps more confusing than enlightening. Not surprisingly, then, we find magic everywhere when we first consider ritual behaviour, but the harder we look at it the more transparent it becomes as it recedes like a ghost of an excuse for what people do in rituals.

10. Spirit mediumship and possession

While one of the most comprehensive accounts of spirit mediumship and possession is Eliade's (1964) volume on Shamanism, he does not approach the subject anthropologically but, then, few people have ever attempted to relate spirit mediumship to the social structure. A start was made by Beattie and Middleton (1969) to do this for African ethnography. They followed Firth's (1959) distinction between possession as a trance, in which actions are believed to be controlled by a spirit, and mediumship where the person possessed acts as an intermediary and a communication link between spirits and men. The main emphasis of their book is upon the communicative aspect of possession cults, looked at in terms of their ideological aspect, what is done, and how they relate to their social and cultural context.

The spirits that possess people fall into two categories: they are either ghosts (representing social forces) or spirits (representing natural forces) and either may be evil or well-disposed, but since men and spirits are mutually dependent upon each other the spirit medium becomes basically an exchange mechanism. Spirit medium cults are generally thought to be beneficent while the mediums themselves may receive powers of divination and even become prophets. However, most such cults are conservative and tend to be supportive of the social order.

The actual state of trance of a person possessed is so convincing a change of personality to the observer that much of the description of such cults has been devoted to the social roles performed and the psychological status of the persons in trance. The actual mechanism involved in inducing trance is mentioned in Jackson's (1968) discussion of sound and ritual. But while such descriptive accounts may well be fascinating, they do not explain why it is certain categories of people that succumb to spirit possession. According to Lewis (1966), by adopting a more sceptical approach like that used in examining witchcraft, and by looking for the social tensions involved, a more illuminating approach to possession may be given. Lewis points out how widespread the use of spirit possession is by women in particular and other depressed categories, in order to exert mystical pressure on their superiors.

Lewis (1971) develops his thesis on a comparative study of religious ecstasy as a social phenomenon. He distinguishes between central and peripheral possession cults. Central cults involve possession by either the ancestors or deities in which the inspired priest has access to these powers and thus functions to uphold the morality of the group; peripheral cults on the other hand have no part in maintaining the moral code, the spirits originate outside the society whose women they possess and it is only a gesture of hopeless defiance. Basically, Lewis is saying that possession is a phenomenon arising from the innate conflict between men and women in those societies where men dominate the social structure—it is part of the war between the sexes.

This latter thesis is disputed by Wilson (1967) who sees the 'sex war' and spirit possession as two quite different phenomena. While the two sexes are involved in possession, the males usually act as agents of the female actors in the drama who, in fact, are contending with each other. Wilson's point is that the act and subsequent rites of spirit possession are a form of *rite de passage* whereby social identity may be changed and social status defined.

Another twist to Lewis's thesis that possession is a device whereby the deprived may claim attention and reward is given by Gomm (1975) who argues that in adopting such a bargaining position, women only reinforce the social control system that keeps them subservient to men.

These accounts, it should be stressed, are dealing with *cults* of possession, which naturally shade off into ritual cults of affliction as described by Turner (1968).

11. Conclusions and prospects

The above account of the trends in the study of religion has deliberately avoided oversimplification in terms of 'old' and 'new' paradigms by firmly focusing on the topics investigated by anthropologists. It is thereby hoped that the strengths and weaknesses of these various approaches will be made more apparent. If we were to interpret trends to mean simply styles of analysis then it would be necessary to place them in the broader framework of anthropological analysis in general because the study of religion is simply one aspect among many and not a discrete speciality. We could say that the employment of a particular mode of analysis on a religious topic is dictated more by the general approach in vogue than the subject matter itself. Hence our topical division cuts across these approaches and presents a variety of interpretations of the same phenomena.

Now, of course, these topics are not separated in practice and hence they may all figure in any one religion, but it is desirable to keep these distinctions for analytical purposes, as is done by the investigators themselves. Because of strong empirical connections between certain topics there is, inevitably, an overlapping of references given here and thus certain authors reappear several times under different headings.

Although this survey of published material only extends thirty years back, it encompasses fieldwork undertaken up to fifty years ago—for reasons already given—thus it can be said to cover half a century of anthropological endeavour. Hence it is always important to note the date at which fieldwork was undertaken and the date of publication, since this may indicate why the analysis was undertaken in the fashion it took.

Much of the anthropology conducted before 1945 was heavily influenced by the functionalism of Malinowski and its empirical bent did not incline it to investigate religion at all, since it was difficult to see exactly what religion 'did.' Developing out of, and alongside this approach, was the structural-functional method advocated by Radcliffe-Brown which sought to place every institution in its social context. This mode of analysis eventually came to dominate social anthropology until the 1960s and as it had to find a place for religion in the total scheme of things, it did not discourage research. All the same, this interest in religion was still largely empirical in that investigation into religious matters was undertaken mainly in order to learn about the society as a whole. Hence, the concern was more with ritual *and* politics, ritual *and* economy, ritual *and* kinship—not with religion *per se* This instrumental view of ritual arose quite naturally from viewing religion in terms of the actions of the participants and its general contribution to the maintenance of the society. If nothing else, ritual had the social purpose or function of a homeostatic control mechanism. This holistic view was the hallmark of structural-functionalism which, itself, was part of the world view of the anthropologists of that time. The many examples quoted reflect this viewpoint, not surprisingly.

More recent approaches to anthropological topics, including that of religion, display an increased sensitivity towards language. This change derives partly from linguistics and partly from philosophy. Structural linguistics in the hands of Lévi-Strauss effected a minor revolution in our attitudes towards kinship and myths—eventually undermining previously held attitudes towards their study. From the philosophers of language in particular such as Wittgenstein, and also from other philosophers, greater attention was focused on the meanings of words and on meaning itself. The outstanding feature of these newer approches is the emphasis on communication and a concern with symbols. This cognitive approach can be seen in all fields of anthropology from kinship to economics and from politics to religion. Language has become a key theme and not a few of the analyses reported here have this bias. As a result of this emphasis on the expressive side of behaviour it is not surprising that religion has come into its own again.

Thus the prospects for the future study of religion seem quite bright, now that we have moved away from the strictly functional view. This does not imply that there are not still merits in the structural-functional approach but its powers of explanation seem now to be very limited. There are, also, drawbacks to the communication-type approaches currently being employed but they do have potential—if only as heuristic models. What is apparent, today, is a greater awareness of what is going on in the related fields of linguistics and the philosophy of language which is stimulating, to say the least. With greater sophistication in our appreciation of language and language use, future anthropologists should bring us closer to realizing what the world views of our subjects mean to them themselves. Even more importantly, anthropologists may be better able to convey to their readers what the religions of exotic societies are all about.

As it is not supposed that the ordinary reader of this book will be an anthropologist since they will be generally familiar with the topic anyway, a few words need to be said about the discipline. In most other areas of study there are no inherent reasons why such disciplines should not be pursued by scholars from any country. Indeed, there seems no reason on the face of it why the same should not apply to anthropology. However, at the risk of offending every anthropologist, there are differences which need to be pointed out. While anthropology can embrace the total spectrum of man's social and natural behaviour, for our purposes it reduces to two varieties only—cultural and social anthropology—for only these two deal with religion. Without wishing to appear to be too chauvinistic, this actually embraces three styles of anthropology, which can very *loosely* be called American, British, and French anthropology, partly because these nationals have provided the bulk of the data and theory which is available. Although this may sound like cultural imperialism, it has yet to be demonstrated that any other widely accepted forms of anthropology exist. I am here discounting Catholic anthropology, Marxist anthropology (the Soviet version), and German museum-type ethnography as being marginal to the main body of anthropological data on religion and as being too *parti-pris*. This does not of course mean that sound anthropological work does not come from say, Norway, Holland or India but the approaches they employ tend to derive from one (or some) of the three major types suggested. To elaborate: by American style I mean to indicate a stress on culture, by British a stress on social, and by French a stress on structural and holistic studies resembling cultural anthropology. These differences are simplistic, of course, because nationals do not behave in identical ways and there is nothing to prevent an American using British or French styles of analysis. While this characterization may seem grossly unfair, all I wish to establish is that there is that same sort of difference in anthropology that we readily and unquestioningly accept as distinguishing German, French, and British philosophy, or German and American psychology, or French and Russian novels. If this much can be granted that such a typification is not prejudicial to others, then our understanding of anthropological styles takes on added meaning for we can begin to see why religion is treated in the way it is. To simplify again, American cultural anthropology is indebted to German philosophy (especially Kant), British social anthropology is influenced by British empirical analytical philosophy (Mill, Ayer, and Wittgenstein), and French holistic anthropology is influenced by French philosophy (Descartes and Rousseau). In a word, American anthropology is interested in what man produces, British anthropology in how man relates in society, and French anthropology in how man thinks and is. Of course, such simplifications distort but they indicate that the study of man is not uniform and that our often unspoken biases affect what we look for. At this level of generality it can be seen why communication (in the form of language) appeals to all three approaches—but in different ways. Americans see language as a product, a tool of communication that has dialectical possibilities, the British see language as a social device which is expressive, the French see language as the potentiality of the mind which has structural connotations. When we come to religion, Americans are looking for sociological and psychological explanations, the British are looking for the social and expressive correlates, while the French seek the complete vision of man in the cosmologies of society. This sketchy and much exaggerated account of the objectives of the different styles of anthropology should highlight some of the variations that may be found in the preceding accounts.

The above observations are starkly presented for the sake of emphasis and so what the novice reader must do is to acquaint himself with the history and development of the discipline. The introductory texts mentioned in the Introduction will provide a more sober guide.

Bibliography

NOTE: Because of the nature of this survey it is neither possible to give a comprehensive list of all major publications in the field of anthropological studies of religion nor is it judged to be a productive exercise to do so. By consulting the bibliographies in the books mentioned the reader should discover most of the relevant references. Much of the current debate is, of course, published in the journals and this is vast. The reader is advised to consult back numbers of the leading journals such as: *Man*, *American Anthropologist*, *Current Anthropology*, *Ethnology*, *Southwest Journal of Anthropology*, *Bijdragen*, *Africa*, etc. Also recommended are the *Biennial Reivew* (1959–1971) and *Annual Review* (1972–) *of Anthropology* edited by B. Siegel and which contain reviews of all aspects of anthropology.

1. Introduction

M. Spiro (1966), 'Religion: Problems of definition and explanation' in M. Banton (ed): *Anthropological Approaches to the Study of Religion*. London: Tavistock.

C. Geertz (1966), 'Religion as a cultural system' in M. Banton (ed): *Anthropological Approaches to the Study of Religion*.

J. van Baal (1971), *Symbols for Communication*; *Religion in Anthropological Theory*. Assen: Van Gorcum.

E. Norbeck (1974), *Religion in Human Life*. New York: Holt, Rinehart and Winston.

A. de Waal Malefijt (1966), *Religion and Culture*. New York: MacMillan.

A.F.C. Wallace (1966), *Religion; An Anthropological View*. New York: Random House.

W.R. Comstock, *The Study of Religion and Primitive Religions*. New York: Harper and Row.

Introductory texts to Social Anthropology include:
J. Beattie (1964), *Other cultures*. London: Cohen and West.
I. Lewis (1976), *Social Anthropology in Perspective*. Harmondsworth: Penguin.
A. Kuper (1973), *Anthropologists and Anthropology*. London: Allen Lane.
R.M. Kessing (1981), *Cultural Anthropology; A Contemporary Perspective*. New York: Holt, Rinehart and Winston.
V. Barnouw (1982), *An Introduction to Anthropology* (2 vols.). Homewood: Dorsey Press.
H. Selby and L. Garretson (1981), *Cultural Anthropology*. Dubuque: Brown.
O. Pi-Sunyer and Z. Salzmann (1978), *Humanity and Culture; An Introduction to Anthropology*. Boston: Houghton, Miffin.

2. *Primitive thinking*
R. Firth (1966), 'Twins, birds and vegetables—problems of identification in primitive religious thought.' *Man* 1(1): 1–17.
E. Leach (1966), 'Virgin birth,' in *Proc.* R. *Anthrop. Inst.* 39–50.
R. Horton (1967), 'African Traditional Thought and Western Science. *Africa* 37: 50–71, 135–187.
— (1971), 'African Conversion,' *Africa* 41: 85–108.
E. Durkheim and M. Mauss (1903), 'De quelques formes primitives de classification,' *L'Année Sociologique* 6: 1–71.
C.R. Hallpike (1980), *The Foundations of Primitive Thought*. Oxford: Clarendon Press.
P. Diener and E.E. Robin (1979), 'Ecology, Evolution and the Search for Cultural Origins: The Question of the Islamic Pig Prohibition,' *Current Anthropology* 19: 535–564.
M. Spiro (1968), 'Virgin birth, parthenogenesis and physiological paternity.' *Man* 3(2): 242–261.
Various authors, *Man* 3(1), 3(2), 3(4), 4(1), 4(2), 4(3).
D. Cooper (1975), 'Alternative Logic in "Primitive Thought".' *Man* 10(2): 238–256.
R. Needham (ed) (1973), *Right and Left*. Chicago: University of Chicago Press.
R. Barnes (1974), *Kédang*. Oxford: Oxford University Press.
L. Dumont (1970), *Homo hierarchicus*. Chicago: University of Chicago Press.
M. Douglas (1966), *Purity and Danger*. London: Routledge, Paul and Kegan.
M. Douglas (ed) (1973), *Rules and Meanings*. Harmondsworth: Penguin.
M. Fortes and G. Dieterlen (eds) (1965), *African Systems of Thought*. Oxford: Oxford University Press.
A. Richards (1967), 'African Systems of Thought.' *Man* 2(2): 286–288.
C. Lévi-Strauss (1966), *The Savage Mind*. London: Weidenfeld and Nicolson.
R. Needham (1976), 'Skulls and Causality.' *Man* 11(1): 71–88.
R. Needham (1975), 'Polythetic Classification: Convergence and Consequences'. *Man* 10(3): 349–369.
J. Goody (1977), *The Domestication of the Savage Mind*. Cambridge: Cambridge University Press.

3. Taboo and totemism

F. Steiner (1956), *Taboo*. London: Cohen and West.

M. Douglas (1966), *Purity and Danger*.

E. Leach (1961), *Rethinking Anthropology*. London: University of London Press.

E. Leach (1964), 'Anthropological Aspects of Language: Animal Categories and Verbal Abuse,' in E. Lenneberg (ed): *New Directions in the Study of Language* Cambridge: M.I.T. Press. also in P. Maranda (ed): *Mythology*. Harmondsworth: Penguin 1972.

J. Halverson (1976), 'Animal Categories and Terms of Abuse.' *Man* 11(4): 505–515.

M. Fortes (1966), 'Totem and Taboo,' in *Proc. R. Anthrop. Soc.*, 5–22.

J. Buxton (1968), 'Animal Identity and Human Peril'. *Man* 3(1): 35–49.

R. Bulmer (1967), 'Why is a Cassowary Not a Bird?' *Man* 2(1): 5–25.

B. Morris (1976), -Whither the Savage Mind?' *Man* 11(4): 542–557.

C. Lévi-Strauss (1963), *Totemism*. Boston: Beacon Press.

C. Lévi-Strauss (1966), *The Savage Mind*.

E. Leach (1970), *Lévi-Strauss*. London: Fontana.

P. Worsley (1967), 'Groote Eylandt Totemism and *Le Totémisme aujourd' hui*,' in E. Leach (ed): *The Structural Study of Myth and Totemism*. London: Tavistock.

E. Leach (1967), *The Structural Study of Myth and Totemism*. London: Tavistock.

4. Symbols

E. Leach (1976), *Culture and Communication*. Cambridge: Cambridge University Press.

A. Cohen (1974), *Two-dimensional Man*. London: Routledge, Kegan and Paul.

R. Firth (1973), *Symbols*. London: Allen and Unwin.

E. Leach (1954), *Political Systems of Highland Burma*. London: University of London Press.

I. Lewis (ed) (1977), *Symbols and Sentiments*. New York: Academic Press.

T. Beidelman (1966), 'The Ox and Nuer Sacrifice,' *Man* 1(4): 453–467.

A. Hayley (1968), 'Symbolic Equations: The Ox and the Cucumber., *Man* 3(2): 262–271.

M. Douglas (1970), *Natural Symbols*. New York: Pantheon.

B. Bernstein (1965), 'A Socio-linguistic Approach to Social Learning,' in J. Gould (ed): *Penguin Survey of the Social Sciences*. Harmondsworth: Penguin.

V. Turner (1957), *Schism and Continuity in an African Society*. Manchester: Manchester University Press.

— (1967), *The Forest of Symbols*. Ithaca: Cornell University Press.

— (1968), *The Drums of Afflication*. Oxford: Oxford University Press.

— (1975), 'Symbolic Studies,' *Annual Review of Anthropology*.

D. Sperber (1975), *Rethinking Symbolism*. Cambridge: Cambridge University Press.

5. Myths

P. Cohen (1969), 'Theories of Myth.' *Man* 4(3): 337–353.

J. Middleton (ed) (1967), *Myth and Cosmos*. New York: Natural History Press.

P. Maranda (ed) (1972a), *Mythology*. Harmondsworth: Penguin.

— (1972b), 'Structuralism in Cultural Anthropology,' *Annual Review of Anthropology*.

R. Dorson (1973), 'Mythology and Folklore,' *Annual Review of Anthropology*.
G. Kirk (1970), *Myth*. Cambridge: Cambridge University Press.
C. Lévi-Strauss (1955), 'The Structural Study of Myth'. *J. Am. Folklore LXXV*: 428–44. Also in *Structural Anthropology*. New York: Basic Books (1963).
— (1967), 'The story of Asdiwal,' in E. Leach (ed): *The Structural Study of Myth and Totemism*.
M. Douglas (1967), 'The Meaning of Myth, with Special Reference to 'La Geste d'Asdiwal,' in Leach, *op. cit*.
E. Leach (1962), 'Genesis as Myth'. *Discovery*, (May). Also in J. Middleton (ed) *Myth and Cosmos, op cit*.
— (1970), 'The Legitimacy of Solomon'. *European J. Sci*. VII, 1966. Also in M. Lane (ed): *Structuralism: A Reader*. London: Cape.
C. Lévi-Strauss (1964–71), *Mythologiques I–IV* Paris: Plon.
E. Hayes and T. Hayes (1970), *Claude Lévi-Strauss*. Cambridge: M.I.T.
M. Freilich (1975), 'Myth, Method and Madness'. *Current Anthropology* 16(2): 201–226.

6. Cosmology and Culture
R. Keesing (1974), 'Theories of Culture,' *Annual Review of Anthropology*.
R. Rappaport (1967), *Pigs for the Ancestors*. New Haven: Yale University Press.
G. Reichel-Dolmatoff (1976), 'Cosmology as Ecological Analysis,' *Man* 11(3): 307–318.
C. Frake (1964), 'A Structural Description of Subanam "religious behaviour"' in. W. Goodenough (ed), *Explorations in Cultural Anthropology*. New York: McGraw Hill.
L. Dumont (1970), *Homo hierarchicus*. Chicago: University of Chicago Press.
C. Geertz (1973), *The Interpretation of Cultures*. New York: Basic Books.
D. Schneider (1972), 'What is Kinship All About?' in P. Reing (ed), *Kinship Studies in the Morgan Memorial Year*. Anthrop. Soc. Washington.
M. Kearney (1975), 'World-view theory and study,' *Annual Review of Anthropology*.
W. Jones (1972), 'World views,' *Current Anthropology* 13(1): 79–109.
M. Douglas (ed) (1973), *Rules and Meanings*. Harmondsworth: Penguin.
B. Wilson (ed) (1971), *Rationality*. Oxford: Blackwell.
M. Douglas (1975), *Implicit Meanings*. London: Routledge, Kegan and Paul.
D. Forde (ed) (1954), *African Worlds*. Oxford: Oxford University Press.
M. Douglas (1954), 'The Lele of the Kasai' in D. Forde, *op. cit*.
M. Griaule and G. Dieterlen (1954), 'The Dogon of the French Sudan,' in D. Forde, *op. cit*.
M. Fortes and G. Dieterlen (eds.) (1965), *African Systems of Thought*. Oxford: Oxford University Press.
H. Kuper (1973), 'Costume and Cosmology,' *Man* 8(4): 613–630.
E. Leach (1976), *Culture and Communication*.

7. Some monographs on religion
E. Evans-Pritchard (1965), *Theories of Primitive Religion*. Oxford: Oxford University Press.

J. Skorupski (1976), *Symbol and Theory*. Cambridge: Cambridge University Press.

A. Bharati (1971), 'Anthropological Approaches to the Study of Religion,' *Biennial Review of Anthropology*.

G. Swanson (1960), *The Birth of the Gods*. Ann Arbor, Michigan: University of Wisconsin Press.

R. Berger (1967), *The Sacred Canopy*. New York: Doubleday.

P. Berger and T. Luckmann (1967), *The Social Construction of Reality*. Harmondsworth: Penguin.

J. Van Baal (1981), *Man's Quest for Partnership. The Anthropological Foundations of Ethics and Religion*. Assen: Van Gorcum.

W.E.A. Van Beek and J.H. Scherer (eds) (1975), *Explorations in the Anthropology of Religion*. The Hague: Nijhof.

T. Luckmann (1967), *The Invisible Religion*. London: Macmillan.

W. Goode (1951), *Religion Among the Primitives*. New York: Free Press.

W. Lessa and E. Vogt (eds) (1965), *Reader in Comparative Religion*. New York: Harper and Row.

C. Leslie (ed) (1960), *Anthropology of Folk Religion*. New York: Random House.

R. Robertson (ed) (1969), *Sociology of Religion*. Harmondsworth: Penguin.

R. Robertson (1970), *The Sociological Interpretation of Religion*. Oxford: Blackwell.

M. Fortes (1959), *Oedipus and Job in West African Religion*. Cambridge: Cambridge University Press.

S. Nadel (1954), *Nupe Religion*. London: Routledge, and Kegan Paul.

B. Wilson (ed) (1974), *Rationality*. Oxford: Blackwell.

M. Douglas (1975), *Implicit Meanings*.

E. Evans-Pritchard (1937), *Witchcraft, Oracles and Magic among the Azande*. Oxford: Oxford University Press.

— (1956), *Nuer Religion*. Oxford: Oxford University Press.

G. Lienhardt (1961), *Divinity and Experience*. Oxford: Oxford University Press.

A. Southall (1976), 'Nuer and Dinka are people,' *Man* 11(4): 463–491.

M. Douglas (1970), *Natural Symbols*.

J. Middleton (1960), *Lugbara Religion*. Oxford: Oxford University Press.

E. Leach (ed) (1968), *Dialectic in Practical Religion*. Cambridge: Cambridge University Press.

G. Obeyesekere (1968), 'Theodicy, Sin and Salvation in a Sociology of Buddhism,' in E. Leach, *op. cit.*

S. Tambiah (1968), 'The Ideology of Merit and the Social Correlates of Buddhism in a Thai Village,' in E. Leach, *op. cit.*

— (1970), *Buddhism and the Spirit Cults of North-east Thailand*. Cambridge: Cambridge University Press.

M. Banton (ed) (1966), *Anthropological Approaches to the Study of Religion*. London: Tavistock.

M. Spiro (1967), *Burmese Supernaturalism*. New York: Prentice-Hall.

— (1970), *Buddhism and Society*. New York: Harper and Row.

C. Geertz (1960), *The religion of Java*. Chicago: University of Chicago Press.
— (1968), *Islam Observed*. New Haven: Yale University Press.
D. Barrett (1968), *Schism and Renewal in Africa*. Oxford: Oxford University Press.
B. Sundkler (1961), *Bantu Prophets in South Africa*. Oxford: Oxford University Press.
H. Ngubane (1977), *Body and Mind in Zulu medicine*. New York: Academic Press.

8. Ritual
M. Gluckman (ed) (1962), *Essays on the Ritual of Social Relations*. Manchester: Manchester University Press.
V. Turner (1962), 'Three Symbols of Passage in Ndembu Circumcision Ritual: An Interpretation,' in M. Gluckman, *op. cit*.
A. Richards (1956), *Chisungu*. London: Faber and Faber.
J. La Fontaine (ed) (1969), *The Ritual Process*. London: Routledge, and Kegan Paul.
J. Middleton (ed.) (1967), *Gods and Rituals*.
V. Turner (1967), *The Forest of Symbols*.
— (1968), *The Drums of Affliction*.
— (1969), *The Ritual Process*. London: Routledge, and Kegan Paul.
R. Firth (1940), *The Work of the Gods in Tikopia*. London: University of London Press.
— (1967), *Tikopia Ritual and Belief*. London: Allen and Unwin.
— (1970), *Rank and Religion in Tikopia*. London: Allen and Unwin.
F. Barth (1975), *Ritual and Knowledge among the Baktaman of New Guinea*. New Haven: Yale University Press.
J. Skorupski (1976), *Symbol and Theory. A philosophical study of theories of religion in social anthropology*.
C. Geertz (1968), *Islam Observed*, New Haven Yale U.P.
H. Hubert and M. Mauss (1960), *Sacrifice, its Nature and Function* (1st. ed. 1899, French.) Chicago: University of Chicago Press.
R. Jaulin (1965), *La mort Sara*, PUF, Paris.

9. Magic
M. Wax and R. Wax (1963), 'The Notion of Magic,' *Current Anthropology* 4(5): 495–518.
H. Philsooph (1971), 'Primitive Magic and Mana,' *Man* 6(2): 182–203.
S. Tambiah (1968), 'The Magical Power of Words' *Man* 3(2): 175–208.
K. Thomas (1971), *Religion and the Decline of Magic*. London: Weidenfeld and Nicolson.
B. Wilson (1973), *Magic and the Millenium*. London: Heinemann.
Malinowski, B. (1948), *Magic, Science and Religion*. Boston: Beacon Press.

10. Spirit mediumship and possession
M. Eliade (1964), *Shamanism*. London: Routledge, and Kegan Paul.
J. Beattie and J. Middleton (eds) (1969), *Spirit Mediumship and Society in Africa*. London: Routledge, and Kegan Paul.
R. Firth (1959), 'Problems and Assumptions in an Anthropological Study of Religion,' *J.R. Anth. Inst.* 89(2): 129–148.

A. Jackson (1968), 'Sound and Ritual,' *Man* 3(2): 293–299.
I. Lewis (1966), 'Spirit Possession and Deprivation Cults,' *Man* 1(3): 307–329.
— (1971), *Ecstatic Religion*. Harmondsworth: Penguin.
P. Wilson (1967), 'Status Ambiguity and Spirit Possession,' *Man* 2(3): 366–378.
R. Gomm (1975), 'Bargaining from Weakness; *Man* 10(4): 530–543.
V. Turner (1968), *Drums of Affliction*.
F.D. Goodman (1972), *Speaking in Tongues. A cross-cultural study of glossolalia*. Chicago: University of Chicago Press.
H. Findeisen (1957), *Shamanentum*. Stuttgart: Kohlhammer.
A. Metraux (1959), *Voodoo in Haiti*. Oxford: Oxford University Press.
R. Underhill (1965), *Mysticism; a Study in the Development of Man's Spiritual Consciousness*. New York: Noonday.
S.S. Walker (1972), *Spirit Possession in Africa and Afro-America*. Leiden: Brill.
P. Lawrence (1964), *Road Belong Cargo*. Manchester: Manchester University Press.
B. Sundkler (1961), *Bantu Prophets in South Africa*.
D. Barrett (1968), *Schism and Renewal in Africa*.
W.M.J. van Binsbergen (1979), *Religious Change in Zambia*. Amsterdam: North-Holland.
J.D. Daneel (1971), *Old and New in Southern Shona Independent Churches*. 2 vols. The Hague: Mouton.
H. Turner (1968), A Typology for African Religious Movements, *Journal of Religion in Africa*, 15–48
F.E. Williams (1934), 'The Vailala Madness in Retrospect,' in *Essays Presented to C. Seligman*, E.E. Evans-Pritchard (ed). London: Kegan Paul.

6

Cultural Anthropological Approaches

JARICH OOSTEN

Leiden

Overcoming ethnocentrism

The word religion is part of our common vocabulary and as a consequence most people assume that they know fairly well what religion is about. They use the word in their conversation and when someone else uses the word they usually understand what it means. Many people have even developed private theories about the nature and origin of religion and a variety of these private theories exists in western culture. Some people think that religion consists of a mistaken belief in beings that do not exist, while other people believe that all religions are essentially the same. Then we have people who think that all religions are inspired by divine beings while others think that they were invented by primitive man to protect himself from fear. These and similar notions are not very helpful for the development of the anthropological study of religion. They are usually not based on empirical research, but on a rather ethnocentric perspective of religion. Since Christianity is the dominant religion of western culture it is not surprising that these notions are very much determined by this religion.

Christianity, however, is not an average religion. It is one of the great religions of the world with a highly developed literary tradition. It has also a strong missionary sense that was correlated to a negative appreciation of other religions. At first all other religions were considered as inferior superstitions that had to be exterminated. In Europe

Christianity attained a monopoly position and only Jewish religion was to some extent allowed to exist. In the sixteenth and seventeenth century missionary activities contributed very much to the spread of European economic and political interests over the world. It was only in the eighteenth and nineteenth century that a serious interest in the great religions of the world began to awaken. The religions of non-literate people, however, were still considered as crude and primitive and this view was maintained by many students of religion until the middle of this century (cf. Frazer, Lévy-Bruhl, van der Leeuw, and others). In the course of this century the appreciation of these religions gradually changed and primitive religions were assessed as religions of non-literate peoples (Van Baaren 1964).

Thus it took western researchers a long time to overcome their ethnocentric biasses and to attain an attitude of basic respect for other religions. But we should take into account that these biasses are not only religious, but that they are deeply embedded in western culture as a whole. The superiority of western religion, western political institutions, western arts, etc. was never seriously doubted by most researchers and even now a majority of western people is deeply convinced of the immanent superiority of this civilisation and the ideological export of western religion, values, and knowledge is still a major issue in the relations between western countries and the third world.

The anthropologist is at the same time a member of his own culture and thus subject to its conditioning, and a scientist who attempts to transcend its limitations and to escape its conditionings. Ethnocentrism is not just a problem of the past but a structural impediment to our understanding of other cultures. We can only study other religions adequately if we are prepared to consider the limitations of our own perspective. Since the meaning of the word religion is very much determined by the significance of Christianity in western culture we have to examine this concept more closely before we can apply it to other cultures.

Christianity developed from Jewry and expanded in the Roman empire. While Jewish religion (like Islam) implied a social and political order of society, Christianity was in no position to challenge the social and political structures of the empire. A fundamental change in the order of the world was only to be expected at the end of time when the kingdom of heaven would descend. In the meantime, Christianity adapted to the social and political conditions of existence and developed a powerful organisation in the church. The Roman Catholic Church was an unique institution. No other religious organisation exercised so much power for such a long time. Although it could not prevent the rise of many new churches it maintained its powerful religious and political position until modern times.

The clear distinction between the religious and the political domain, the church and the state, was developed in the crucial stage of the formation of the Christian tradition. It was elaborated theologically (cf. St. Augustine, *De civitate dei*) and it has continued to dominate western culture until the present day. The notion that religion is an autonomous domain that should be separated from the political organisation of the state is generally accepted in western culture. As a consequence many researchers expected a similar situation in other cultures. Anthropological research, however, demonstrated that this is not the case. Both in the great religions of the world (cf. the *sharī'ah* in Islam, the caste system in India, for example) and in non-literate religions a strict distinction between the religious domain and other cultural domains is arbitrary and forced. But even in western culture it is predominantly an ideological value that does not prevent a close connection between both domains. Although the history of the churches or of the Christian dogmas was often presented as an autonomous development relatively independent of other cultural processes, it is quite clear that the history of these institutions was not only determined by their internal dynamics but also by economic and political interests.

The Christian church was the repository of classical culture in western culture until the Risorgimento, and for a long time scientific research and institutions were largely controlled by the church, which opposed all research that contradicted its religious traditions (consider the famous case of Galileo). But it could not prevent itself gradually losing control of scientific developments. Religious studies were a different matter. Here the churches maintained their control much longer. The Christian religion was usually taught in theological departments, faculties of divinity, etc. that were predominantly controlled by the churches.

When the study of other religions developed it was usually integrated into those theological studies and taught in the same institutions. Interest in other religions was often related to missionary activities. Students of religion who did not show sufficient respect for the Christian tradition could endanger their own position (cf. the case of Robertson Smith).

It was often maintained that only people who were religious themselves had sufficient affinity with their subject to study it adequately and this assumption was then often a means to maintain a monopoly of Christian scholars in these institutions. It was not surprising that a critical approach to religion could not flourish very well in these conditions.

These approaches developed in other departments like philosophy (Feuerbach, Marx, and others) and they also developed in the context of the study of social sciences like ethnology, sociology, psychology, etc. (cf. Freud, Durkheim, and many others).

Christian scholars usually considered Christianity as the highest of all religions and tended to measure all other religions by Christian standards, while psychologists, ethnologists, etc, tended to reduce religion to psychological or sociological categories implicitly or explicitly denying its divine origin (cf. Evans-Pritchard's discussion (1965) of those theories and Adam Kuper's assessment (1981) of Evans-Pritchard's own position in this respect).

Both positive and negative assessments of Christian religion deeply influenced the anthropological approach to religion. As long as religion is a crucial and controversial issue in western culture and in its relations with other cultures emotional involvement either positively or negatively is unavoidable. The anthropologist should at least try to become clear about this involvement and try to refrain from value judgments as much as possible. He should not be concerned with the falsity or truth of religion nor with its superiority or inferiority. His main concern is with understanding and explaining.

The anthropological study of religion is in many ways similar to the study of language. No language is false or true, inferior or superior. Each language can be considered as an independent design of the world. First of all the student of language has to learn a particular language.

Once he has a thorough knowledge of it he can attempt to translate it into his own language and to examine its structure in his own terminology. He should be aware that the terminology he uses is not an objective scientific apparatus that transcends the limits of all cultures. It is determined by the history of his own culture.

In the same way the student of religion should become familiar with the religion he is studying before he attempts to translate it into terms of his own culture. Translations easily imply distortions. When we state that the Muslims believe in Allah or the Inuit in Nuliajuk we seem to indicate a similar relation between participants and a divine being, but this is not the case. The word belief in Christianity expresses notions of faith, self surrender, love, etc. while the Inuit consider Nuliajuk as a dangerous spirit that can be controlled by able shamans. We should acknowledge that the relation between Nuliajuk and the Inuit is completely different from that between Christians and God.

The anthropological study of religion is a process of confrontation, translation, and communication. Different cultural perspectives meet in anthropological research: the perspective of the anthropologist and that of the participants. The anthropologist should examine both perspectives and the ways they determine each other. He can never escape the obstacles of ethnocentrism completely, since he is irrevocably conditioned by his own culture, but he should reflect on his own perspective as a methodical requirement of all anthropological research. This implies a careful consideration of his own terminology.

The problem of defining religion

The meaning of the word religion does not cause many problems in ordinary language, because it allows for various interpretations. Everybody can have his own ideas and association when he uses the word. The test of an adequate understanding of the concept in daily use does not consist of a definition of the concept, but of a correct use of the word in various situations. The word religion is best considered as a family resemblance in the sense that this concept was developed by the philosopher Wittgenstein. It refers to a set of complex phenomena. Each of these phenomena shares some features with some other phenomena of this set, but it is not necessary that all phenomena share one particular feature that can be considered as their common essence. No generally accepted rule exists that decides which phenomena have to be included in this set and which have to be excluded.

Wittgenstein's notion of family resemblance helps us to understand how the word religion is used. The anthropologist is not only interested in the use of the concept in his own culture, but he wants to transform it into an analytical tool that can be applied to other cultures. Many definitions of religion have been proposed and none of them is generally accepted in anthropology. Usually different definitions stress different dimensions of religion. Geertz emphasized the cognitive level of religion when he defined religion as: (1) A system of symbols which acts to (2) establish powerful and longlasting moods and motivations in men by (3) formulating conceptions of a general order of existence and (4) clothing these conceptions with such an aura of factuality that (5) the moods and motivations seem uniquely realistic' (Geertz 1965: 4). Spiro on the other hand stressed the action level of religion when he defined religion as an 'institution consisting of culturally patterned interaction with culturally postulated superhuman beings' (1965: 96). Milton Yinger emphasized the significance of religion as a means to deal with ultimate problems: 'Religion then can be defined as a system of beliefs and practices by means of which a group of people struggles with these ultimate problems of life. It expresses their refusal to capitulate to death, to give up in the face of frustration, to allow hostility to tear apart their human associations' (1970: 7).

These three examples give some idea of the variety in religious definitions. Each definition approaches religion from a different angle and stresses a different aspect. As a consequence they are not contradictory. It is the angle from which one views religion that determines the kind of definition one arrives at.

The question: 'What is religion really?' is therefore meaningless. Many approaches to religion are possible and there is no reason to select one of them as the only correct approach. Sociologists, psychologists, anthropologists, all will approach religion from different angles. Here we will be mainly concerned with the anthropological study of religion.

An anthropological approach to the study of religion should be based on the general theoretical framework of cultural anthropology. The key concept then becomes culture. Religion, social organisation, political organisation, are all considered as aspects of culture by the anthropologist and as a consequence religion should be examined in the wider context of culture.

Religion as a cultural order

Many definitions of culture exist (cf. Kroeber and Kluckhohn 1952) but no general agreement is reached about them. The word culture is used on different levels of abstraction. It refers to the ways human beings order and shape their natural world in general, but it also refers to the ways particular peoples order and shape the world. We can speak of western culture, of Greek culture, of the culture of the Athenian nobility in the fourth century BC, etc. The anthropologist selects the level of abstraction that enables him to organise his data most fruitfully in the context of his research.

No human society can exist without order. Every culture can be considered as a particular way of ordering the world. The cultural order is expressed in various ways in different cultural dimensions: religion, art, social organisation, etc. According to Lévi-Strauss all dimensions of culture are determined by the same organising principles that constitute an order of orders ('*ordre des ordres*'), but it is not quite clear why this should be the case. It may be that human beings strive for a homogeneous and consistent cultural order but they will often be subjected to foreign laws, influenced by foreign cultural traditions, etc. An homogeneous and consistent cultural order will therefore usually not exist.

The cultural order determines the life of the participants: concepts, emotions, religious experiences are all shaped by the cultural order. Loss of face can lead to suicide in some cultures while it has few consequences in other cultures. Deep religious experiences are realised through celibacy and ascetism in some cultures and through orgies in others. Different cultural experiences entail different emotional and cognitive associations. The anthropologist who is studying other cultures has to become familiar with other ways of thinking, perceiving, feeling. A culture that attaches much value to visionary experiences will usually have ritual practices that enable their participants to have these visions. The nature of these experiences is clearly determined by the cultural framework. Thus a Christian will see the Virgin Mary or Jesus in a vision while a Buddhist may see a Boddhisattva. Although the cultural order shapes the life of the participants almost completely, it is arbitrary from a logical point of view. There are no intrinsic reasons why a monotheistic religion should be preferable to a polytheistic religion or a matrilineal social organisation to a patrilineal one. The participants are aware of this. They can think of alternative orders and they are often confronted with other people who behave differently and think differently without any serious consequences for themselves or their kinsmen. Therefore the participants need an adequate foundation for their cultural order to protect it from disorder. The rules of the cultural order should be respected by the participants and they should not be changed at random.

In every culture we find a set of beliefs, practices, institutions, that explains the origin and nature of the cultural order and preserves its existence. It is this set of beliefs, practices, institutions, that is usually qualified as religion by the anthropologist.

Religions usually involve belief in personal beings, but this is not necessarily the case (cf. classical Buddhism). It is the cultural domain that is considered to be most fundamental by the participants themselves. It gives significance to their existence and their world and it cannot be reduced to any other cultural order. Thus the nature and organisation of social organisation, political institutions and economic prerogative can be explained in myths, expressed in rituals and maintained by religious institutions. Gods, spirits, ancestors, or cosmic laws are thought to guard the cultural order, and transgressors of its rules are punished in this world or the next.

In many cases the notion of an all encompassing order is clearly expressed in a central religious concept (e.g., Indian Ṛta or Egyptian Maat). In other cases it is reflected in a system of religious laws (cf. Judaism and Islam). Religion does not only constitute the most fundamental order of the world in the perspective of the participants, but it deals also with discrepancies between ideal and reality. Myths explain the origin of suffering and evil, rituals provide means to restore the cosmic order, religious professionals admonish people to maintain the cosmic order. Thus religion is both the last and final order of the world and the means of overcoming transgressions of its rules.

The anthropologist does not have the same perspective concerning a cultural order as do participants in it. He may be convinced that economic or ecological conditions determine a cultural order, but he has to acknowledge that for participants their religion is fundamental. The anthropologist has interests and priorities other than those of the participants. He examines religious beliefs, practices, and institutions, and he will discover many different versions of the religion among the participants. Religion has often been identified with its interpretation by a religious or political élite, but each religion is constituted by a great variety of beliefs, practices, and institutions. Different versions are sometimes contradictory. What is considered as tenets of faith by one group of participants may be considered as superstition by another one. Different versions of a religion are usually related to other cultural differences such as power, status, wealth. These correlations are of great importance to the anthropologist in the explanation of different religious forms and variants. Unlike the participants he is not primarily interested in the truth of a particular interpretation, but he considers all forms of religion as variants that inform him about its structure. He examines these variants and he attempts to construct models that enable him to discover the rules that determine the relations between different variants of a religion in time and space.

Thus the anthropologist arrives at an order that is different from that of the participants. Although the perspective of the participants constitutes the point of departure of his analyses the anthropologist finally attempts to construct models that explain its order in terms of his own anthropological theory.

The division of culture into separate domains is a theoretical construction by the researcher. Most cultures do not have expressions for our concepts of religion, or politics. These words have significance in our own culture and in the context of anthropological theory.

The notion that religion can be considered as a cultural order implies a strategy of research that is directed towards the discovery of that order. Many sociologists and anthropologists have applied this approach to religion (Berger, Douglas, Geertz, Lévi-Strauss, for example). Religion is considered as a complex whole and no particular feature is selected as the most important distinguishing one (e.g., belief in gods, religious (inter) action).

The qualification of religion as a cultural order also implies that its nature is determined by its relative position towards other cultural orders. But although religion is related to these orders it can never be explained completely by its relations to them, since religion is at the same time a relatively autonomous domain with its own internal structure. Both the examination of this internal structure and its dynamics and the study of its relation to other cultural orders are necessary for an adequate understanding of the significance of religion in its cultural context.

Religion and other cultural orders

While other cultural orders should be based on religion the religious order itself cannot be reduced to any other cultural order. This raises major problems. How can the religious order give an adequate foundation to its own existence and validity? From a logical point of view this problem cannot be solved. It is like Baron von Munchhausen pulling himself upwards by his hair. How can any order justify its own existence without reference to another higher order? Nothing can be solved by a process of infinite progression that postulates always higher orders of existence. The participants are aware of this and the paradox is often clearly expressed in religion itself. A good example is given in the book of Job in the Old Testament. Job wants to call God to account for his sufferings, but God is not subject to any higher authority or rules. As a consequence Job has no alternative but to acknowledge God's universal power and this proves to be a satisfactory solution since Job is again well-endowed with worldly possessions. Many variants on this problem can be found in other religions in rituals that inverse the existing order of the world and myths that give a negative proof of the existing order.

Although other cultural orders are ideally founded in the religious order they have often a different structure and origin. Many traditions have contributed to the development of western culture. Jewish religion contributed to Christian religion, Greek religion to western philosophy and science, Roman law to many western codes of law, German social and political organisation to many western social and political institutions, for example. All these traditions merged into western civilisation in a complex process of acculturation. We cannot just assume that they all share the same basic structure. We have to examine how the participants consider different cultural orders to be related and how they are related in our own anthropological perspective.

The participants usually attempt to harmonize different cultural orders on a conceptual level. In many cases theological or ideological superstructures are created to reconcile apparently contradictory principles in different cultural orders. These superstructures become important factors in the process of cultural change.

The participants also attempt to harmonize their social behaviour, status and so on, with their religious convictions. In some cases they give only rationalizations that do not inform us about their real motives, but it also happens that they sometimes cause themselves economic and political hardships for the sake of their religion. Some people forsake their possessions for their religious convictions while others forsake their religious convictions for their possessions. It is impossible to establish an absolute causal priority of one particular cultural order over another one since the relations between them continuously vary. It is clear, however, that different cultural domains are closely related. Weber demonstrated in his well-known analysis of the relation between capitalism and Calvinism how religious and economic factors interacted in the development of capitalism in western Europe (Weber 1922). We usually find correlations between religious convictions and economic and political positions. Thus the poor will be more attracted towards messianistic movements that promise a new order of the world than the rich, who will tend to suppress these movements in order to defend the existing order of the world.

As social, political, economic, and other conditions of existence change in the course of time new questions have to be formulated and answered in the context of religion. If the religious order loses its close connections with other cultural orders which it has to explain, its existence becomes precarious. It becomes an abstract and irrelevant institution for the participants and it is easily replaced by a religion that is more relevant to their conditions of existence.

Religion is in an ambiguous position in another respect. It has to give significance to other cultural orders, but at the same time it participates in these orders as a political institution, an economic institution and so on. Religion cannot escape this ambiguity. In many of the world's religions we find traditions of protest against the wealth and power of the great religious institutions, but once these movements are institutionalized they tend to become sources of political and economic power themselves. The more their members practice poverty as individuals the greater the chance that these institutions accumulate capital as was the fate of many Christian and Buddhist monasteries that practised poverty.

The anthropological study of religion should examine how religion is determined by politics, economics etc. and how at the same time it shapes these cultural orders.

We have now discussed religion as a cultural order that gives significance to other dimensions of culture. But how is religion related to other cultural orders like philosophy, ideology, science, etc. that are often thought to play a similar part in human culture? How is religion related to concepts like magic, superstition, etc. that are usually associated with religion? It is time for some terminological distinctions.

Terminological distinctions

Religion occurs in all cultures while ideology, philosophy, science, etc, are usually confined to the great civilisations. In non-literate cultures we find speculations about the nature of the world and human life that we could qualify as ideological or philosophical but as a rule they do not give rise to philosophical traditions. Oral tradition is a suitable medium for the transmission of tales, lists, proverbs, etc. but it seems to be less suitable for philosophical and ideological speculation. It is only when writing becomes important that philosophical and ideological traditions can develop. In the great civilisations philosophical traditions emerged from religion. Indian philosophy developed from the reflections on religion by the Brahmins. In these philosophical traditions divine beings could be transformed into cosmic essences and atheistic philosophical and religious systems could arise (cf. Sāṇkhya, Buddhism). Similar developments occurred in Greece, China, and other great civilisations.

These philosophical traditions could to some extent substitute for religion. This was only possible when they did not confine themselves to the cognitive level, but also developed practices and institutions similar to those of religion. Since these practises involve some belief in their efficacy the philosophical systems that substituted for religion tended to be transformed into religions again. The founders of the systems were transformed into divine beings (Confucius, Buddha) and the systems themselves could be considered as philosophical and religious systems at the same time.

While religions are based on belief in the fundamental order that was instituted by gods, ancestors and spirits, philosophies usually assume that the understanding of the final order of the world can be gained by rational thinking. Buddhism stresses the importance of meditation that is thought to transcend rational discursive thinking and to prepare the mind for enlightenment.

The word ideology usually refers to the way people conceive of an ideal organisation of their society. Ideologies are usually thought to reflect the natural order of the world and they share with philosophies the notion that true understanding of the nature of the world can be gained by rational thinking. In western societies the great ideological systems developed predominantly from philosophy. In some cases ideologies constitute coherent well-thought-out systems and in other cases ideologies consist of a complex of loosely organised notions about the nature of society. Ideologies usually imply a strategy to realise the ideal state of society. Religions usually have an ideological dimension in the sense that many religious convictions reflect economic and political interests but religion covers a much larger range of problems than that of an ideal society (problems of life and death, the origin of human beings and their world, etc.) and is predominantly based on faith, as we have seen.

Western science also developed from philosophy. The historical opposition between religion and science has induced some people to consider science as the most true perspective of reality. They think that religion explains a lot of things that can be explained more satisfactorily in scientific terms. But we should take into account that religious explanations serve a different purpose. Religion explains the significance of things for human beings while science is concerned with both theoretical knowledge for its own sake and its practical applications. Although scientific explanations help us to understand and explain the order of the world in theoretical terms they fail to explain its significance for mankind and it is therefore not surprising that science cannot replace religion—not even in Aldous Huxley's 'brave new world,' where science can only be supreme by being transformed into religion.

Religion, magic, and superstition are closely connected with each other. Religion is usually associated with positive values, while those beliefs and practices that do not seem to be compatible with these values are usually considered as magic and superstition. The term magic refers to beliefs and practices that are intended to induce certain effects by ritual means: procuring of game, making of rain, etc. Magical practices can be found in all religions. The difference between a rain ritual in Southern Africa and a prayer for rain in a European church should not be interpreted as a difference berween magic and religion. Both practices are magical and derive their meaning from their religious context. The traditional notion that magical man rules while religious man serves (cf. van der Leeuw 1933) is an ethnocentric generalisation that is based on Christian values. The general framework of magical practices is provided by the religious order and every religion has a magical dimension to the extent that it attempts to effect certain results by ritual means. Praying and cursing, curing and bewitching are usually structurally related techniques that use the same (or inverted) practices to effect opposite results. In most cultures the distinction that counts is that between black magic, directed against the interests of society and its members, and white magic, furthering their interests. Magical practices are thought to have some effect, but these effects are seldom interpreted in a simple causal model. The effectiveness of the ritual depends on the moods of the performer, the attitude and reactions of gods, spirits, ancestors, counter-magic, etc. Rain rituals will be held in periods when there is some chance of rain and game rituals when the game is approaching. Magic is not irrational. The performer of magical practices decides on a suitable time, place, and situation and he is led by many rational considerations. In many cultures we find specialists who are professionals in magical practices and often they can perform both as white and as black magicians. Some magical practices are rejected while others are accepted and practised by the religious establishment, others again are discussed (cf. the ambiguous position of exorcism in many Christian churches).

The distinction between superstition and faith is also based on religious values. In some periods of western cultural history belief in witches was quite accepted, while it was considered as superstition in other periods. The great religions usually have an élite of religious professionals who decide what is to be considered as superstition and what is not. Their judgments may differ considerably from those of the layman. Gnomes, witches, werewolves are usually considered as supersition in the Christian religion and therefore not included in descriptions of that religion by the anthropologist. This has resulted in a rather artificial distinction between religion and folklore, that is usually not applied to other cultures, where similar beliefs are included in descriptions of their religion. The term superstition is better avoided by the anthropologist, since it often only expresses the value judgments of the participants. When he examines religion as religious order the anthropologist will often have to include many beliefs and practices in that order that are considered as superstition by some participants but not by others.

Literate and non-literate religions

The transformation from a non-literate religion to a literate religion has many implications for its structure and development. In literate cultures philosophies, ideologies, and sciences can develop and the position of the religion itself is changed considerably. When the art of writing is developed it is usually applied to preserve religious knowledge and wisdom, and many of the oldest written texts are of a religious nature. The great religions of the world are literate religions and they possess sacred texts that enable them to spread out into other cultures and yet preserve their unity.

Non-literate religions once were the universal type of religion, but they have gradually been replaced by the great religions of the world. This can to some extent be explained by the differences in the relation between culture and non-literate religions on one side and culture and literate religions on the other side. In order to examine these differences more closely we will now examine the general features of literate and non-literate religions.

Non-literate religions

Since there is no sacred book, the continuity and uniformity of the religion depends on oral traditions that are much more flexible than books. Oral traditions are often sacred and the mnemotechnical skill of the participants is usually considerable, but often political, economic, and other interests cause the participants to adapt their oral traditions and once they have done that the earlier versions are lost irrevocably.

Like a culture each religion consists of a set of variants. Inuit religion consists of the religion of Western, Central and Eastern Inuit. The religion of the Central Inuit consists of different variants of the Netsilik Inuit, the Iglulik Inuit, the Caribou Inuit, etc. The religion of the Iglulik Inuit again consists of different variants: those of the Iglulingmiut, the Aivilingmiut, etc, and each local group of these groupings will have its own version of the religion. These versions will usually depend to some extent on the personalities and interests of influential people like the *angakkut* (shamans). When we take into account that these local groupings are very flexible units that vary each year in size and composition it will be clear that the local versions of religion are also subject to change and variation.

A religion can be described on each level of abstraction. Rasmussen described the religion of the Netsilik and Iglulik Inuit in separate monographs, Boas described the culture and religion of the Central Inuit, and Hultkrantz, Lantis, and others described Inuit religion in general.

The religions of neighbouring peoples like the Chuckchee in Siberia or the Athabascans in northern America are in many respects related to Inuit religion and they can be considered as variants in the wider context of the religions of the hunting and gathering peoples of northern Siberia and North America. It is in this context that the shamanistic complex is often examined (cf. Findeisen, Eliade, and others). In this way the scope can always be extended and this explains why Lévi-Strauss could pursue his mythical analysis all over the Americas. He could have continued over into Siberia and finally have arrived in western Europe. That structural relationships cannot only be found in the structural analysis of myth but also on other levels is demonstrated in many studies, cf. Kretschmar and others on the theme of the dog, or the studies of shamanism in these areas. Structural relations between religions can be explained by an examination of other relations between the cultures concerned. The examination of these relations is in practice very complicated because innumerable historical processes (e.g., migrations, processes of acculturation) influence the relation between neighbouring cultures in many ways. Even then it should be clear that the study of non-literate religions always implies a selection of the level of abstraction of the analysis. The study of a religion as an isolated unit tends to neglect the importance of its relations with other neighbouring religions which often have great value for our analysis. The examination of the relations between different neighbouring religions has too often been neglected. The cause of this neglect can be partially found in an exaggerated confidence in diffusion that proved sterile in the long run. The structural approach of Lèvi-Strauss, however, has opened new and fruitful perspectives for the examination of these relations.

Anthropologists have sometimes argued that religions without literary traditions lack a historical dimension or consciousness. This is a misunderstanding. All cultures have notions about the past that are expressed in their myths and genealogies, but it is clear that the significance of the historical perspective varies in different cultures. As a rule we find myths about the origin of the world and the first human being. Rights on status, land etc. are usually based on myths and genealogical relationships to mythical heroes. Historical traditions tend to become mythical in structure since their function is determined by the interests of the present and no literary tradition can safeguard them against mythical manipulation.

The local variant of a religion can be very much adapted to the specific conditions that determine the life of that group. A ritual transgression can specify which place cannot be passed and which river has to be avoided. While the great religions of the world tend to become rather abstract and ethical in their outlook since they are not confined to the particular conditions of specific groups, non-literate religions can be much more concrete and interwoven with the practice of daily life. This close relation has induced some anthropologists to argue that non-literate people are deeply religious but this is a misunderstanding that is based on an ethnocentric conception of religion and not on an understanding of the religious life of people in non-literate societies. The core of the problem does not rest on different degrees of spirituality but on different structural relations between religion and other domains of culture. The great religions of the world also influence the life of the believers deeply, but in completely different ways. While non-literate religions tend to give a spiritual perspective to the world as it is, many of the world religions tend to preach an alternative to the world of everyday life as a superior and more important dimension of life.

Non-literate religions are very dynamic. Since they are not limited in their development by sacred texts they can adapt more easily to historical processes. Ecological, economic, and other changes have to be accounted for. In all religions a structural field of tensions exists between the preservation of the old traditions and the need to account for and adapt to new developments. The notion that non-literate religions are static is completely false. While there is no need to reinterpret the old texts time and again, the oral traditions themselves can gradually change as need requires.

The complete adaptation of a non-literate religion to other cultural domains also constitutes its weakness. When social, political, and economic conditions change rapidly the religion becomes vulnerable. Traditional frameworks lose their meaning and the religion disintegrates. This process can often be seen when the non-literate culture comes into contact with a great civilisation. Many reactions are possible (syncretism, messianic cults etc.), but in the long run the traditional religion is usually doomed. When the culture is integrated into a great civilisation the participants usually accept the religion of the dominant culture and adapt it as much as possible to their local needs. Their local customs often constitute an essential core in the practice of the religion. Thus it can be argued that the Christmas tree and other symbols that have nothing to do with Christianity itself have constituted essential elements in Christian rituals, and in some cases they even seem to survive the religion itself when we perceive that many people, who do not consider themselves as Christians anymore, still celebrate Christmas and Easter with traditional symbols.

The literate religions

The great religions of the world have spread from their place of origin in a complex historical process; in some cases they have disappeared from it, but have maintained themselves in other areas (e.g., Christianity, Buddhism). All these religions were deeply influenced by other cultural traditions during their development. Christianity developed from the Jewish religion, was transformed by the Greek and Roman traditions, and was deeply influenced by Germanic traditions in the course of its history. Buddhism proved to be exceptionally adaptable since it tolerated the existence of other religious traditions and considered itself to be a more advanced teaching. Christianity and Islam were less tolerant and Christianity in particular succeeded in almost destroying all rival religious traditions in Europe. Islam faced many more religions with literary traditions (religions of the book) in its territory, and although it persecuted non-literate religions, religions of the book were tolerated. All great religions became related to fixed political and social interests and these determined much of their history. The expansion of Christianity and Islam was usually connected with the expansion of Christian and Islamic political powers. In all the great religions of the world a structural tension exists between the unity of the religion and the cultural diversity between different areas where the religions extend. If regional diversity is stressed the unity of the religion dissolves and when the unity of the religion is stressed it is difficult to adapt the religion to the needs of the local traditions. Within this field of tension many sects and religious variants developed that were usually connected with regional and local interests. The unity of the religion was usually preserved by the literary tradition and the social organisation of the religious professionals.

In the great religions the oldest religious texts (Vedas, Bible, Qur'ān) have most authority. They were created in the stage of formation of the religion and they are usually accepted by all later sects and denominations in that religion. Different comments and interpretations on these texts were developed and these comments gave rise to new comments and interpretations. Thus the literary tradition became more and more complex in the course of time. As a rule the oldest texts are accepted by all believers, while different sects and denominations make their own selections out of the more recent literature and develop their own comments and interpretations as a particular literary tradition. Thus the unity of the religion is preserved by the oldest texts. The great religions all dispose of an élite of religious professionals, who share and preserve the common traditions. Sometimes they are organised in a hierarchical and centralised institution (like the Roman Catholic Church), sometimes they consist of a privileged caste (like the Brahmins), sometimes they consist of specialists in the scriptures whose status depends almost completely on their learning (like the Sunnitic Ulamās).

All these professionals derive their prestige and status from their position in the religious organisation and their knowledge of the great religious traditions. As a rule we find a strong resistance among these élites against deviations from the ideal patterns. They constitute an *avant garde* of the religion against those beliefs that are considered as superstition in the great tradition. They play an important part in the continuous struggle between the great traditions that try to preserve and develop the teachings of the religion and the folk traditions (local traditions) that tend to adapt the religion to local customs.

We should not only distinguish between a great tradition and a folk tradition as two opposed entities but acknowledge the existence of different intermediate levels. The great tradition is usually constituted by rivaling traditions from different areas. Their regional variants can adapt better to the local traditions than the religion as a whole.

Differentiation continues indefinitely until we come to the level of the local variant. In many respects these local variants function similarly to religions without a literary tradition but at the same time they are continuously influenced and determined by the great tradition of their own religion. This is particularly clear in Christianity. The Roman Catholic church always attempted to preserve the unity of the church. Heresies often represented local variations (cf. the Cathars in northern Italy and southern France). The regional variants of religions often gave rise to the development of sects and denominations.

The integration of local traditions within great traditions is often a difficult and painful progress. Christianity, Islam, and other religions gave scope to the integration of local elements on various levels (e.g., veneration of saints that were transformations of local cults from an historical point of view). Christianity succeeded in suppressing some local customs (e.g., wakes, veneration of oak trees, sacrificing of horses) but had to accept other customs (e.g., celebration of Christmas at the winter solstice—the old Jule—celebration of Easter in the context of traditional pre-Christian customs).

As a rule the great tradition gradually supersedes local customs and beliefs that are considered to be superstition by the élites. The believers gradually identify more and more with the great tradition and the development of a world religion usually implies a rather homogeneous civilisation. Thus Hinduism, Christianity, and Islam developed relatively autonomous civilisations with their own traditions in art and science. Buddhism developed differently because it always co-existed with other religions.

We have already seen that the world religions extended over such vast areas that it was difficult for them to adapt themselves to local traditions in the same degree as religions without literary traditions. As a consequence these religions stress those aspects of human life that are considered to be universal. They preach universal ethics for all human beings, and they tend to stress the importance of the unity of the faithful regardless of cultural differences. These teachings should appeal to people of all cultures.

As a consequence the contents of the world religions are usually more abstract and general than those of the non-literate religions. In many cases we find a tendency to stress the ethical dimensions of a world religion to the detriment of cultic rules.

Because the religion has to be directed towards people of different cultures it becomes more individualistic. Every individual, regardless of his cultural background, should find answers to his fundamental questions in the religious teachings.

Thus the world religions tend to develop civilisations that transcend the specific cultures within those civilisations. New groupings arise, often associated with differences in status, wealth, and power, that can sometimes lead to the rise of many different religious organisations corresponding with the social hierarchy. Thus, for example, we see that in the United States most churches have a specific social status that is carefully considered by would-be participants.

The anthropological study of religion should consider very carefully the relations between traditions on different levels in time and space. In most introductions to world religions we read what the Muslim or the Christian believes, practises, etc. But the Muslim in Indonesia in the twentieth century and the Muslim in medieval Persia differ in many respects. At the same time they share a common set of beliefs and practices and their religions can be considered as each other's variants. Structural differences between variants have to be explained by historical and cultural conditions. Anthropological analysis of religion should aim both at the explanation of differences and the explanation of similarities.

The theoretical level of religion

When we study another religion we have to become familiar with its language. Key concepts in other religions (e.g., Tao in Chinese Taoism, Nirvāṇa in Buddhism, Inua in Inuit religion) are very complex notions that cannot be translated unequivocally into the terminology of our own language. Different interpretations of the same word may coexist and often the meaning of the word is subject to change in the course of time. The analyst distinguishes between his ability to understand the concept in terms of its own context and his capacity to translate the concept.

The religious concepts we examine are always part of a complex of religious conceptions and ideas. They may have an exactly defined place in a well-thought-out theological system, or they may be extremely vague. In all cases, however, the problem of translation arises. How do we describe concepts of another culture in terms of our own culture? We do not do this through the medium of an objective terminological apparatus, but by the aid of concepts that play a part in our own culture.

To translate the French word *ciel*, the most important possibilities are 'sky' and 'heaven.' In translating one considers the context of the word, how sky and heaven are used in English, etc. Finally, one chooses the word that most fitly renders *ciel* in that particular context. More difficult is the word *esprit*. The words 'spirit,' 'soul,' 'mind,' 'ghost,' and so on differ entirely in value and meaning, and careful consideration is necessary. We find in practice that one can use words, develop a feeling for language, translate, etc, without being able to give definitions of the words one uses.

In religion we have a good deal to do with terms which are fairly generally agreed to be pretty vague: God, spirit, soul, etc. A French dictionary will offer us the following possible translations of *âme*: soul, mind, spirit, life, conscience, feeling, ghost, person, essence, with additional special meanings such as bore (of a gun), sound-post (of a violin), core (of a bronze cast). These meanings certainly do not make clear what the place of the term *âme* has been in Christian anthropology in France. For that extensive research would be required. When the word is translated, a selection is made from a range of possible translations. The word *âme* does not have meaning as an independent and isolated unit, but in the context of many other related concepts. It has many associations and connotations, and in the process of translation some of these are eliminated while others are added. The translation of Lévi-Strauss' book *La pensée sauvage* into 'The Savage Mind' implied a fundamental change of the subject matter. It is only when the translator is completely familiar with different languages that he is fully aware of the transformations of meaning that are implied in the process of translation. The process of translation does not imply a substitution of one concept for another, but the transformation of one way of thinking into another way of thinking. Thus it is a process of communication.

Although many religious terms appear to be vague, the participants usually feel a clear distinction in the use of those terms. One may speak of a village of a hundred souls, but not of a village of a hundred spirits. At the same time it would be very difficult to fix the limits between the words soul, spirit, conscience, and so on. These concepts may play an important part in a man's personal religious life without his being able to give a clear conceptual definition of those concepts. We can see that the various meanings of *âme* given above are related and that their mutual connections can be described. The word *âme* obviously covers a fairly complex idea with many shades and connotations. It is only when one wishes to assign a well-defined meaning to the concept that one finds it troublesomely vague. The word simply has no unequivocal significance. In everyday languages the word can be used in many ways and its use does not raise any problems for the participants. Thus it is the problem of definition, not the use of these words, that constitutes the vagueness of the concept.

Concepts of the soul can be found in many cultures and usually they are very complex and apparently vague. On closer scrutiny they often appear to express complex ideas about the nature of human beings. The analysis of these concepts should not be directed towards the construction of definitions of these concepts but towards the rules that determine their use. As a rule the participants have only very vague notions about the meanings of these words just like the Christian who can often speak of the soul without having a very clear idea of its meaning. Sometimes philosophers and theologians speculate about the meanings of these concepts and then a new situation arises. The concept becomes a controversial issue and different interpretations of the word can be given at the same time. The anthropologist who examines the meaning of a concept then has to cover the whole range of conflicting and opposing interpretations a word has, while he should be aware at the same time that these rather abstract speculations often have little significance for the way the concept is used by the ordinary believer. Words like *karma*, *māyā*, *mokṣa*, *dharma* are interpreted in many ways in Indian religions, and the anthropologist should not give precedence to the philosopher's interpretations over those of the common believer. Both interpretations are sources of equal value for his understanding of the way a concept is used in religion. Different interpretations of a concept can coexist. The analysis of the theoretical level of religion usually aims at the construction of a coherent model of the beliefs of the participants. Usually, however, these beliefs do not constitute a coherent complex. Contradictory beliefs cannot only coexist in the same culture but even in the same person. Thus we find in many cultures mutually exclusive notions of the fate of deceased people. The participants may believe that they go to the realm of death while they are thought to reincarnate at the same time and sometimes even to haunt other people as bad spirits. Sometimes theologians attempt to harmonise contradictory beliefs, but as a rule many of them coexist in all religions and cause no apparent problems for the participants.

In hymns, theological treatises, etc, the merits of the gods are often extolled. They are described as generous, powerful, righteous. In mythology they often appear as jealous, selfish, deceitful. For the participants this does not raise any problems. Only when philosophical reflection develops, as in Greece and India, are explanations invented for the negative aspects of the great gods. The structure of the pantheon is usually determined by conflicting and competing interests. In Scandinavian religion Odin was the supreme god, but he was also the god of the nobility, while Thorr was considered to be a god of the farmers. Rivalry between the gods is evident in religious texts. In Indian religion Viṣṇu and Śiva both had large followings that exalted their own god and depreciated his rival. In Egyptian religion each town that rose to power tended to raise its own god to the supreme position in the pantheon.

The development and structure of the pantheon therefore have to be related to the social, political, and other interests of the participants.

While religious ideas can usually be organised in more or less coherent systems, myths require a different strategy of analysis. The most important strategies of mythological analysis have been developed in psychological and structural analysis. Psychological methods are rather unpopular in cultural anthropology because they tend to be ethnocentric. Structural anthropology dominates the field of mythical analysis, but it does not offer a consistent method. Thus we find strategies that attempt to reconstruct mythical cycles as ideal types or historical complexes (cf. Dumézil (1952), Ivanov and Toporov (1970), Lincoln (1981)). Structural analysis in the way it was developed by Lévi-Strauss attempts to explain the differences between different variants. Although the latter approach raises many methodological problems it seems more promising than the former, since it does not imply any value judgments concerning the truth or historicity of a variant.

Lévi-Strauss developed the general notion that myths express basic problems in human society. He tends to stress the importance of social problems, particularly problems of alliance. Although there is no need to assume that each myth has one particular meaning or message it seems evident that crucial problems in the order of human culture will be expressed in the structure of the myth and structural conflicts in myths will inform us about structural problems in society. It should be clear, however, that myths are in no way unequivocal expressions or reflections of the structure of society. They can present alternatives to the existing order and often provide negative proof for it.

Myths are tales, and tales do not constitute a consistent logical system in the way religious ideas do. Tales are often bizarre and absurd. They appeal to people because they discuss relevant problems in relevant ways. The anthropologist attempts to discover the rules that determine their organisation and the transformations between different myths in time and space. Myths provide a very interesting perspective on religion because they express the religious order at an unreflected level. The participants do not know why they tell myths in a certain way, although they do know very well how they should be told. It is up to the anthropologist to explain this.

Thus mythical analysis provides an important perspective on the unconscious structures of religion (cf. Oosten 1981 for a more extensive discussion of the problem of the relation between structure and meaning).

Norms and rules of behaviour also belong to the theoretical level of a religion. They express how people think they should behave and are therefore action-orientated. They can be of an ethical and of a ritual nature. The importance of this distinction should not be exaggerated however. Mary Douglas has done important research on the nature of ritual injunctions and she made it quite clear that ritual injunctions can express complex notions about the order of the world. Ritual injunctions mark important boundaries that have to be respected in religious behaviour.

Songs, proverbs, etc, all belong to the theoretical level of religion. They express different notions about the nature of the gods, wisdom and so on. The theoretical level of religion can usually be considered as a system of classification. Male-female, men-animals, right-left, life-death, and so on are ordering principles that determine the organisation of this system. Different domains in the theoretical level, however, can express different notions and sometimes internal contradictions can exist between them. Myths provide room for speculation: many things are possible that cannot be realised in daily life. Ritual injunctions, however, are directed towards religious behaviour and these rules have to take into account the practical conditions of life. Hymns will praise the gods, while myths often place them in quite another perspective.

As a rule, however, we should assume that the theoretical order represents a rather well organised complex. It is not created to confuse people, but to give significance to their lives. At the same time it has to account for conflicting perspectives of different social groups, men and women, nobility and commoners, etc., and the anthropologist should attempt to explain the internal contradictions by an examination of the relations between the theoretical level of a religion and other cultural orders. At the same time he should be aware that the religious system itself can contain contradictions that cannot be solved. The theologians of those religions sometimes try to eliminate these contradictions but in other cases they stress the importance of the paradox. Thus the dogma of Nicaea established the mutually exclusive natures of Christ. He was considered to be both man and god (*credo quia absurdum*).

The theological speculation of the religious élite is an important field of study but we should be aware of the fact that in many cases it has only a limited relevance for the belief of the majority of believers and its importance should therefore not be exaggerated.

The practice of the religion

Ritual practice involves both social and individual religious behaviour. Ritual can be defined as standardised religious behaviour. It can require a group of people, but it can also be practised by an individual e.g., in prayer. Standardised means that the behaviour is determined by certain rules.

While myth can be speculative and discuss alternatives to the existing order of the world, ritual has to take account of this order of the world. It is determined by the categories of time and space. While myth is almost completely verbal, ritual is almost completely action. In ritual words have less importance, and constant repetition of words is a common feature of ritual. The repetition of the words as an action takes precedence over the meaning for the participants who often are not even aware of the meaning of the words they utter.

Myths and ritual are often related. Sometimes a myth is recited in the context of ritual, in other cases the ritual is a re-enactment of a myth. Ritual can also inverse the myth. The Inuit blackened the faces of their sexual partners with soot at the ritual of partner exchange at the new-year's festival, while an important myth relates that Seqineq, the spirit of the sun, once blackened the face of her brother, the moon-spirit Aninga, with soot when he had an incestuous relation with her. Thus men marked women at the partner's exchange and a woman a man in an incestuous relation. It is not clear to what extent rituals constitute systematic complexes similar to those in mythology but this seems to be a fruitful field to explore.

Ritual is action and therefore it involves time, space, participants, and material means. It takes a certain time and it needs a space that is sometimes strictly separated from other places and considered as sacred. Places of worship, churches, temples, etc, often become sacred places and the participants need to perform certain rituals to enter these places if they are allowed to do so at all. Often the place of ritual is determined *ad hoc* and only becomes sacred for a limited period. Sometimes the sacred period is a symbolic representation of the creation and history of the world just as the sacred place is a microcosmic representation of the whole world. These dimensions of sacred place and time have been very much stressed by Eliade. Thus the time and place of a ritual become crucial and we should expect the process of ritual in time and the ordering of ritual in space to express general notions about time and space among the participants. If the West is considered as the region of death and East as the region of life a ritual will usually express these notions. Thus ritual gives us much information about the *Weltanschauung* of the participants and analysis should be directed towards the discovery of its ordering principles. Structures of time and space are not only expressed in ritual, but ritual itself is also directed towards the structure of time and space. Crucial transitions in the year will be accompanied by ritual. The end of the harvest, the beginning of the hunting season, the coming of rain are all periods that can be marked in ritual. Ritual is also related to the human cycles of life. Birth, initiation, marriage, death are all marked by ritual. These rituals often express a basic symbolism of life and death, and van Gennep's important study (1980) of initiation rituals has clearly demonstrated some of the organising principles of these religious practices.

Ritual always requires participants. When a ritual is focussed on specific people, e.g., because it makes an important transition in their lives as in marriage, these people will have a central position in that ritual. When ritual involves a whole society the organisation of a ritual will often involve all significant members of that society. The ordering of a ritual will often have to be explained in terms of the hierarchical and social organisation of a particular culture. Sometimes hierarchical relations will be expressed in the order of a ritual, sometimes they will be inverted (cf. the Saturnalia, Carnival, etc.). In both cases an explanation is required. Complex rituals often involve many symbols and just like myths they cannot be reduced to a single message or meaning. The great rain rituals in southern Africa are often also first fruit ceremonies, kingship rituals, etc. In functionalistic approaches the harmonising aspects of ritual were often unduly stressed. In practice, however, ritual also often expressed antagonism and hostility and could lead to serious quarrels. In Indian societies the Potlatch rituals also offered a ritual domain for competition that could induce bitter conflicts between individuals and groups.

Religious professionals usually play an important part in ritual. Ritual tends to become more and more complex and in many cases only religious specialists are thought to know how rituals should be performed. And these ritual specialists often manipulate the powers they acquire in and through these rituals.

Ritual usually requires sacred objects, which belong to certain groups and persons. The manipulation and exchange of these objects give us important information about the social structure of society. The nature of these objects gives us much information about the religious order. Victor Turner in particular has done very important research in this domain. He demonstrated (1974) how different objects were selected and shaped according to rules that expressed basic notions about the nature of the world. The objects can express notions about color symbolism, elongated versus round, hard versus soft, etc. An interesting approach was developed by Lévi-Strauss in *La Voie des Masques* (1975) to analyse ritual objects. He attempted to demonstrate that masks can be considered as elements in a system and although his results are not always very convincing he opened up a promising perspective.

Ritual requires material objects, individuals, and groups of people that will not always be present in equal measure. While a myth can always be told in the same way, ritual will often be executed in different ways and the ideal way of performing a ritual may never be realised. This constitutes a major problem in the analysis of rituals.

Ritual behaviour is usually very different from everyday behaviour. It is intended to be an alternative behaviour that relates man to another world. Thus we find moods of devotion, exaltation, joy, grief, etc., very strongly expressed in ritual. Huizinga (1958) and Jensen (1960) have linked ritual to play. It is a combination of seriousness and playfulness. The strong emotions that are expressed in rituals have only a limited relevance for everyday life. Sometimes religion seems to constitute an emotional outlet. Victor Turner has stressed the dialectical relationship between structure and nonstructure. Although man has to live in a structured world he longs to turn to a world where structure loses its meaning. He finds this world in ritual in the stage of 'liminality' where the order of the world is temporarily suspended. Structure can be explained as the need to organise human life, liminality as the need to escape that structure. In many ways Turner's notion is reminiscent of Mauss's notion of a pendulum movement between individualistic and social life (1905), but while Mauss stresses a sociological approach Turner often seems close to a psychological reductionism that attempts to find the meaning of ritual in the moods of the participants.

Although the moods and motivations of the participants are important for our understanding of ritual, it seems clear that the structure of ritual can only be explained by its relation to the structure of other cultural domains: notions about the relation between life and death, male-female, etc.

The word religion is usually reserved in our own culture for the great tradition of religion, and belief in witches, gnomes, etc., is usually excluded from it. Similar beliefs in other cultures are often included. In the same way many ritual practices like shaking hands (particularly right hands) and kissing are usually not considered to be religious although similar practices are often considered as religious in other cultures. It should be clear, however, that these practices often give much information about the conception of the world. Thus the shaking of hands has its structural position in a wider context of symbolism of the hands, itself part of an even wider complex of symbolism of the body in western culture.

Individual behaviour can be qualified as ritual behaviour to the extent that it conforms to cultural rules. For example, prayer is a ritual act connected with certain ritual actions like the bending of knees, the closing of eyes, etc.

In cases of social as well as of individual ritual behaviour, the research should focus on the rules that determine that behaviour.

While both the theoretical level and the practical level of religion express ways of ordering the world they use different means. The theoretical level is predominantly verbal. Words convey meaning and emotions to the participants. At the ritual level the participants can actively express the religious order in their behaviour, and performance of ritual itself has significance and conveys strong emotions to the participants. It is interesting to notice that the two levels are not always equally balanced. Thus we find much ritual and little mythology in some cultures, while we find little ritual and much mythology in other cultures. In our own culture the theoretical level is usually considered as more important than the practical level although our own culture is less devoid of ritual than most of its participants often assume.

Conclusions

The anthropological study of religion is a process of communication between different cultures. As our own society develops, our cultural perspective of other cultures will change. The participants in non-literate cultures have been transformed from savages into human beings in the perspective of western culture. The study of religion should be based on an awareness of the relativity of our own perspective and a basic respect for participants in other cultures.

In this chapter I have argued for a systematic approach to religion as a cultural order that gives significance to human beings and their world. This approach can be applied both to the theoretical level and to the practical level of religion. It does not imply a static approach to religion but accounts for variations in time and space. The anthropological study of religion should be directed towards the explanation of religious differences between different religious variants. As a rule these differences will have to be explained by relations between religion and other cultural orders. Since religion is at the same time a relatively autonomous domain that deals in its own way with fundamental human problems like life and death, these explanations will never be completely exhaustive. Both the internal structure of religion and the structure of its relations towards other cultural domains should be examined by the anthropologist.

Bibliography

Berger, P.L. *The Sacred Canopy*. New York: Anchor Books, 1969.

Boas, F. *The Central Eskimos*. 50th Annual Report of the bureau of ethnology to the secretary of the Smithonian Institution 1884–5. Washington, 1888.

Douglas, M. *Purity and Danger*. New York: Pelican Books, 1970.

— *Natural Symbols*. New York: Pantheon Books, 1970.

Dumézil, G. *Les dieux des Indo-Européens*. Paris: P.U.F., 1952.

— *Les dieux des Germains*. Paris: P.U.F., 1952.

Durkheim, E. *Les formes élémentaires de la vie religieuse*. Paris: P.U.F., 1968.
Eliade, M. *Images and Symbols: Studies in Religious Symbolism*. London: Harvil Press, 1962.
— *Shamanism*. New York: Pantheon Books, 1964.
— *Traité d'histoire des religions*. Paris: Payot, 1964.
Evans-Pritchard, E.E. *Theories of Primitive Religion*. Oxford: Oxford University Press, 1965.
Findeisen, H. *Schamanentum*. Stuttgart: Kohlhammerverlag, 1957.
Frazer, J.G. *The Golden Bough*. London: MacMillan, 1890.
Geertz, C. 'Religion as a Cultural System,' 1–46 in Michael Banton (ed.) *Anthropological Approaches to the Study of Religion*. London: Tavistock Publications, 1965.
Huizinga, J. *Homo Ludens*. Haarlem: Tjeenk Willink, 1958.
Hultkrantz, A. 'Die Religion der Amerikanischen Arktis,' in J. Paulson, A. Hultkrantz, K. Jettmar, (eds.) *Die Religionen Nordeurasiens und der Amerikanischen Arktis*. Stuttgart: Kohlhammer, 1962.
Ivanov, V. et Toporov 'Le mythe Indo-Européen du dieu de l'orage poursuivant le serpent: Reconstruction du schéma,' in *Echanges et communications mélanges offerts à Claude Lévi-Strauss* à l'occasion de son 60ème anniversaire réunis par Jean Pouillon et Pierre Maranda. The Hague-Paris: Mouton, 1970.
Jensen, A.E. *Mythos und Kult bei Naturvölkern*. Wiesbaden: Franz Steiner 1960.
Kretschmar, F. *Hundestammvater und Kerberos*. Stuttgart, 1980.
Kroeber, A. and C. Kluckhohn *Culture: A Critical Review of Concepts and Definitions*. Cambridge: Harvard University. Papers of the Peabody Museum of American Archaeology and Ethnology, vol. 47, 1952.
Kuper, A. 'Evans-Pritchard and the History of Anthropological Thought,' *Times Higher Education Supplement*, 30 October 1981.
Lantis, M. *The Religion of the Eskimos*. Forgotten Religions 5. New York, 1950.
Lévi-Strauss, C. *Le Pensée Sauvage*. Paris: Plon, 1962.
— *Mythologiques I–IV*. Paris: Plon, 1964–1971.
— *La voie des masques*. Genève: Albert Skira, 1975.
Lévy-Bruhl, L. *Mentalité primitive*. Paris: P.U.F., 1960.
— *L'âme primitive*. Paris: P.U.F., 1963.
Lincoln, B. *Priests, Warriors and Cattle. A study in the Ecology of Religions*. Los Angeles, London: University of California Press Berkeley, 1981.
Mauss, M. 'Essai sur les variations saisonnières des sociétés Eskimos (1904–5), in *Sociologie et Anthropologie*. Paris, 1966.
Oosten, J.G. 'The Examination of Religious Concepts in Religious Anthropology,' in Th.P. van Baaren and H.J.W. Drijvers (eds.) *Religion, Culture and Methodology*. The Hague-Paris: Mouton 1973.
— *The Theoretical Structure of the Religion of the Netsilik and Iglulik*. Meppel: Krips Repro, 1976.
— *Religieuze veranderingen in de wereldgodsdiensten*. ICA publication no. 27. Leiden, 1978.
— 'Meaning and Structure in the Structural Analysis of Myth,' in Gretchen A. Moyer,

David S. Moyer and P.E. de Josselin de Jong (eds) *The Nature of Structure*. ICA publication no. 45. Leiden, 1981.
Rasmussen, K. *Intellectual Culture of the Iglulik Eskimos*. Report of the fifth Thule Expedition, vol. VII, no. 1. Copenhagen, 1929.
— *The Netsilik Eskimos. Social life and spiritual culture*. Report of the fifth Thule Expedition, vol. VIII, nos 1 and 2. Copenhagen, 1931.
Spiro, M.E. 'Religion: Problems of Definition and Explanation,' 85–126, in M. Banton (ed) *Anthropological Approaches to the Study of Religion*. London: Tavistock, 1965.
Turner, V. *The Ritual Process*. London: Pelican Books, 1974.
Van Baaren, Th.P. *Menschen wie wir*. Gütersloh: Gerd Mohn, 1964.
Van de Leeuw, G. *Phänomenologie der Religion*. Tübingen: Mohr, 1933.
Van Gennep, A. *The Rites of Passage*. London: Routledge and Kegan Paul, 1980.
Waardenburg, J. *Reflections on the study of Religion*. The Hague: Mouton, 1978.
Weber, M. *Gesammelte Aufsatze zur Religionssoziologie* Tübingen: Mohr, 1922.
Wittgenstein, C. *Philosophical Investigations*. Oxford: Blackwell, 1963.
Yinger, J.M. *The Scientific Study of Religion*. London: Macmillan, 1970.

7

Cultural Anthropology and the many Functions of Religion

WOUTER E.A. VAN BEEK

Utrecht

Religion has many interpretations, many facts and a host of functions. In the two preceding papers its main function—even if the interpetation varied—was either a sociological or a structural one: religion gives a group cohesion and orders a universe. Yet human life is not always ordered, neither is respect for or obedience to the group everywhere paramount. The erratic individual often moves from the more or less straight and narrow path his culture has laid out for him, not only causing lots of trouble and strife, but paving the way for religious innovation and cultural change. American anthropology in several of its myriad facets, has given ample attention to this dialectic relation between an individual and his religion. The dialectic is quite clear: just as any individual is the product of his society *and* vice versa the society stems from individuals, any religion not only is imposed upon its participants, but to a large extent is moulded by these very personalities it has been instrumental in shaping. Of course this sounds like the age old chicken-and-egg problem; so to avoid any insoluble dilemma let me rephrase the question: what kind of function does religion perform for the individual participant?

Let us start with the first question. The experiment in survival called *homo sapiens* does not live just with his brains, but to a large extent with his glands too. Emotions, though heavily underplayed in religious theory, do form the main motor for most actions. Our general scientific disregard for the 'lower' emotions as explanatory factors is more expressive of our own culture and our academic subculture, than of the religion of our fellow men. Of course, the affluent West can afford to look for the elated feelings of religiosity, nicely ordered wordviews, and coherent belief systems. But in the great majority of societies studied by anthropologists survival is the key word. Harsh surroundings, a merciless physical environment, droughts and famines all take their toll. Hobbes's picture of 'brutish, nasty and short' is an inappropriate description of tribal life surely not to be invoked. On the other hand, Rousseau's noble savage is widely off the mark too. Any field anthropologist knows from his own experience the quiet harmony a rural village offers him. Most of us long to go back to the field, if only for that reason. But as visiting scientists we really have the best of two worlds, the security and—medical—technology of the West and the intensive social interaction of the face-to-face community.

Recently an anthropologist, after having broken his leg in remote Nepal, was flown out by helicopter. No doubt his Sherpa friends were better adapted to the mountains, less clumsy on the steep slopes to say the least, and would not slip as easily; still, they must solve their own problems in their own way, by their own means, and would never in their lifetime be able to send for a helicopter. (Oral communication).

What has this to do with his religion? Well, religion is an important facet of the cultural array of problem-solving devices, either for big calamities or for small nuisances. Wallace, one of the main proponents of this view on religion, cites a charming example:

A Cherokee burning himself, blows fresh water in four parts on the burn reciting: Water is cold, ice is cold, snow is cold, rime is cold. "Relief" I will be saying (Wallace 1966: 117).

Another case comes from our own field experience:

A Kapsiki suffering from headache whirls a discarded potsherd three times around his aching head, and throwing the potsherd away sighs: "Well, that is fixed" (Van Beek 1978: 378).

Religion and personality

Bigger problems call for stronger measures. Long before Lévi-Strauss focussed attention on the *efficacité symbolique* (1958), the role of religious therapy in healing the hodge-podge of so-called psychosomatic illnesses had been acknowledged (e.g., Gillin 1948). Following C.G. Jung's distinction between *anima* and *persona*, Wallace (1966) distinguished social personality (*persona*) and self image (±*anima*). The social identity of a person forces him in a mould in which several personality traits have to be suppressed. One's self image and one's public personality are never identical. In some cases the discrepancy between both can cause a serious clash. The self-image, the weaker of the two, suffers heavily and disillusionment or neurosis results. Now, religion can solve this problem by offering some strong, viable models for personality with which one may identify at least for a short time. Three points are stressed here by Wallace: *some* psychic problems are normal in any culture and, second, each culture has its own brand of problems as well as its own version of normality; definition of mental—or even somatic—illness is culture-relative. Third, some phases in life are more problem-prone than others. Of course religion is not a panacea for all problems, but it sometimes does quite a lot. In ritual people are liberated from the strains their social personality imposes on them, resulting in a healthy catharsis.

The discussion on this issue centers on the question of the shaman. Someone who enters trance easily or with the help of drugs and who in helping clients helps himself too—should he be considered 'psychotic,' 'abnormal' or whatever ethnocentric label western observers may want to attach? In the eyes of many observers the *shaman* shows himself an unstable neurotic person who needs his trance to stay well. In Wallace's terms: a shaman needs regular reidentification with the religious personality model, as his self-image is decidedly at odds with the rights and duties assumed from his social personality. No *artic hysteria* nor any pathological illness, but a relativistic personality conflict. In many respects moreover, shamans are as able farmers, merchants, hunters, or fishermen as any of their compatriots.

Silverman (1967) underlines that there is no reason why shamans should have the same personality traits in all cultures. So Wallace may be right, even if mental defects should not be disregarded so easily. Kennedy (1973) neatly sums up this discussion. Some anthropologists harbour the view that shamans are superbly endowed individuals who have the valuable capacity to put themselves to trance. Castaneda's Don Juan (Castaneda 1968) would have been a splendid example but for the small detail that this material seems to be a fake (de Mille 1980).

Religion, however, is not reserved for special individuals such as shamans; ordinary individuals, too, meet their needs by religion, so in other aspects of religion the expression of not specifically pathological personality traits should be discernible. As an example Spiro's work on the Ifaluk can serve; any society has to build in safety valves for individuals and the Ifaluk society has a lot of inbuilt stress with which the inhabitants have to cope.

Ifaluk is a small Micronesian Island where a few hundred people live at close quarters. All arable land is under cultivation and no population expansion is possible. Living hemmed in like this, Ifaluk have to have a device to get rid of their frustrations, aggression or any kind of negative feeling. Their solution is a supernatural scapegoat. *Alus*, spirits are the core of their belief system, and these *alus* are responsible for anything bad. People hate the spirits, venting agression on them in a way they could never do on their fellowmen. Thus living in disharmony with their supernatural world they can afford to live in harmony with their living kinsmen (Spiro 1952).

Religion and socialisation

One drawback of this elegant reasoning is that it is just *ad hoc* reasoning, and anthropology should not content itself with just explaining the *status quo*. In the 1950s and 1960s a score of researchers and theorists addressed themselves to the problem how an individual is situated in his culture. Most of these researches do not center on religion, as from a theoretical and practical point of view personality development and childhood training are more important. Still, in nearly all studies, religion does play a part. Early stimulus in this direction came from Kardiner and Linton (1945) who developed a scheme of factors influencing personality development, which stimulated some new approaches. Du Bois's Alor study (1944) is the best known of these. In this approach religion is interpreted as a projective system, in which all kinds of residual fears from early childhood may be sublimated on the one hand, and on the other hand training practices and concomitant sociopolitical organisation find a direct expression.

Theoretical and methodological systematisation has come from Whiting and Childe in whose view (1953) a culture consists of a *maintenance system* comprising the basic economic, political, and social organisation. This system is for a large part responsible for the child rearing system, which in its accord shapes 'modal personality'—the standard or desired personality in that particular culture. This personality is a major factor in shaping the projective systems, like art and religion. Whiting and associates set up a huge comparative framework in which half a dozen coordinated field studies were undertaken to be compared later (Whiting and Childe 1953), one of the biggest research endeavours anthropology has ever known. Religious processes feature prominently in the statistical worldwide comparisons that the research team has done. Using a well-known standard sample of all the world cultures, part of the so-called Human Relations Area Files (see Murdock 1969) they extensively checked their theoretical options in operationalised testable propositions. One example: Whiting's neo-Freudian theory postulates a correlation between late weaning and harsh male initiation ceremonies. The reasoning is as follows: Late weaning favors a long *post partum* sex taboo, which incites the husband to have plural wives. This implies virilocality (residence of the couple at the husband's place), resulting in a fixed core of patrilineally related men. The child has a strong mother-bond and will see the father as a rival. Control of insurgent sons can be effected by puberty rites, so this cultural Oedipus situation leads to harsh initiation rituals, to keep the sons in line.

This proposition has been tested with quite positive results. Other projective elements in religion put to the test were interpretations of illness, witchcraft beliefs and accusations, and danger or benevolence in the supernatural world (resp. Whiting and Childe 1953; Spiro and d'Andrade 1958; Lambert, Minturn, Triandis and Wolf 1958).

At the end of the 1960s these studies changed direction; maybe they had run their course. Anyway, Whiting and Childe's massive research program clearly showed that their strict developmental approach yielded only limited results. Thus, one of the major conclusions of the famous *Six Cultures* study (Whiting and Childe 1953) was that the differences in child rearing within one culture surpass the difference between the modal educational ways. So the theory correctly predicts correlations, but those are not overly important. Reliability and validity are high, relevance low. Moreover, other interpretations of the same phenomena are possible.

Religion and social organisation

The covariance of social and religious matters, does not need a personality development scheme as a mediating factor; those correlations can quite easily be explained by the direct dependency of religion on its sociocultural foundation. In fact, this is the leading hypothesis of most of the British anthropological studies of religion, as Jackson shows. The comparative approach, however, is quite feasible too. Young (1962, 1965) showed that the correlation between virilocality and harsh initiation rites can be explained straightaway by pointing at the ways in which 'male solidarity' is organised and has to perpetuate itself. Cohen (1964) using the same approach pointed at the duties and responsibilities of unilineal groups, which necessitate certain ways of initiating boys and girls. The belief system, another projective part of religion, shows considerable covariation with social organisation regardless of child rearing practices. Swanson (1960) showed in another cross-cultural survey how monotheism, polytheism, witchcraft beliefs, and belief in reincarnation were tied in with social variables like level of state formation, social classes, bride prices, and war.

However, the main tide of anthropology has not been in cross-cultural surveys, however fascinating they may be. Thorough and penetrating analyses of individual cases—always the stronghold of anthropology—yield more insight into religious processes and cultural covariation.

General views of religion

A trend towards a more philosophical but still individualistic way of looking at religion can be spotted in several countries. Tying in with the above mentioned theories La Barre, in a giant volume on prophetic movements (La Barre 1972), tries to unravel the 'origins of religion.' For La Barre a religion starts in a prophetic movement, as the source from which all religion springs lies deep within each and every one of us, to be tapped by someone more fully aware of it than most, a prophet, seer, or revelator. Religion, in his view, is essentially part of the deep, non-charted areas in human experience. Religion is the human way to explain our participation in the unknown. A new religion springs from dreams, dramatic individual experiences, which are interpreted by the dreamer and accepted by groups of people.

Van Baal, in a series of major works on the theory of religion, starts from an existential standpoint (Van Baal 1947, 1971, 1981). Man is a strange phenomenon; he has the unique capability of observing not only the external world around him, but also himself, even his own processes of observation. In this he is out-of-this-world, alien and definitely a stranger. However, at the same time he is very much part of this same universe, part and parcel of his world. Man is subject and object, both stranger and friend. He is a subject longing for participation, longing for a partner. Religion, being an ascriptive way of thinking, is a way to partnership with the universe and the expression of the human condition. Symbols are the means of communication with this universe, which in itself is a cultural creation, imposed upon man by his society.

This approach closely resembles Turner's use of the term *communitas* (1969). Turner discerns two trends in human culture, the first focussing on organisation, with fixed positions, roles, and slots making up the social *persona*, and the other viewing society as a homogeneous community of idiosyncratic individuals who, despite external differences, all share a common humanity. This latter he calls *communitas*: the tendency towards integral humanity. This trend is emphasized in ritual, like in the installation of chiefs, who during the installation ritual are imbued in *communitas* to impress their duties towards the common people upon them. Thus any religion results from a dialectic between individualism and group membership, in which the former has an ethical superiority over the latter, a point mentioned also by Schoffeleers (Schoffeleers and Meyers 1978).

Two other areas of anthropological interest in religion are prominent at the moment. One is the broad specter of conflict, protest, etc., the other the ecological approach to anthropology.

Religion and conflict

Each society has its own tensions and problems which may show in religion. One favorite—i.e., for anthropologists—expression of problems and conflicts is witchcraft. Rituals of rebellion (Gluckman 1954, Norbeck 1963) are another way of expressing inherent insoluble conflicts. In both cases the reasoning closely follows the psychological tracks indicated above: the ritual, beliefs or accusations serve as a safety valve, and perform a catharsis for the society, which by playing on inherent contradictions makes those tolerable, thus preserving the *status quo* of society. However, in the long run this kind of catharsis, can have a negative effect too, as Wallace showed in his Iroquois example:

> The Iroquois channeled aggressive tendencies by means of the so-called Condolence Ceremony, towards other tribes; the Ceremony eliminated intratribal warfare and thus made intertribal warfare possible. However, the retaliation invoked by the surrounding tribes at the end decimated the Iroquois and nearly obliterated them as a tribal unit (Wallace 1966: 205–286).

Conflict, tension or protests often are invoked whenever anthropologists treat new religious movements. The literature on these is very vast but surveys are available (Wilson 1973, La Barre 1972, Köbben 1959). Most authors relate the new movement to some external influence, which plays hazard with the traditional ways of life. Balandier (1955) considers the colonial situation the main factor, the religious movement being a reaction against it: the only way in which people can regain the initiative, the only vertical social mobility, the only escape out of the system. A protest against social inequality Köbben calls it, and

Van Baal coins the term 'erring acculturation' explaining cargo cults as reaction to a thoroughly misunderstood cultural change. However, not all evaluations are negative; Balandier argues that this kind of movement really does give some 'reprise d'initiative,' Redfield sees it as a creative moment in culture (Redfield 1968) and Wallace uses the most positive term of all: cultural revitalisation. When the old structures have crumbled and the old culture is irrevocably lost, a prophetic movement can be a vigorous and positive factor in readjusting people to the new surroundings. Goodenough (1960) even advises development agents to ride the prophetic movement in their community development projects! Not all anthropologists would dare to go that far!

A recent development in these studies is the use of neo-marxist terminology. The main factors of change are conceived in terms of mode of production, productive forces, and the articulation of production. This materialistic approach is counter-balancing the recent trend in anthropology (see Oosten) towards cognitive studies, quite a dichotomy one might say! Materialism states that the societal superstructure reflects the clash of interests in the infrastructure and shields real conflicts from detection. Power structures are hidden by the ideological representation, thus preserving these very powers intact. Works by Werbner (1977), van Binsbergen (1979) and Schoffeleers (1982) exemplify this trend. In a way Burridge's (1969) treatment of millenarian activities fits in too. In his view religion primarily is a set of ideas about power, the ordering and distribution of it: where power structures break down, a millenarian prophet can construct new ways of dealing with power, creating a new power order.

Religion and the ecosystem

The second topic is just as materialistic. Religious rituals have other functions besides therapy, group cohesion, or catharsis; they have an ecosystemic function too. Ritual especially may serve as an ecological instrument. In several ways this can be shown. First ritual can be instrumental in shaping group consensus. Divination as a way of decision making is one example. Decision making is an important part of any production system: fields have to be sown, gardens cleared, trees cut down. What specific fields, trees, or gardens are to be treated is indicated by divination, the authority of the supernatural world guaranteeing a quick and easy consensus. In many instances the fact of deciding is more important than what decision is taken. If Sheridan's ass could have consulted a diviner, it would never have starved. Vogt (1952) draws attention to this aspect, to explain the persistence of the water witching practice in the USA. Scientific information on water availability is couched in probability terms, the—objectively—slightly less dependable water witching answers in clear terms, thus giving the farmer confidence in his labour intensive well digging. Divination can help in other ways too. Moore (1957) points at the problems of a Naskapi caribou hunter, who has no way of knowing the next caribou migration route as this changes every year. His safest means is, according to Moore, to randomise his hunting sprees in order to avoid over-hunting of an area and scaring the caribou away. Divination does just that. The Naskapi shoulder blade divination precludes patterning; human thinking always repeats itself, the cracks in the shoulder blade form a truly random indication.

In Harris's well known analyses (see Bibliography) ritual plays an even more crucial role. His goal is to disprove the independence of religion, by showing how it is tied in with the general ecology of the group. So he jumps into any case in which the people's life seems to be governed by religion. Starting with the *ahiṃsā* (non-violence) rule in India, Harris (1966) shows that the taboo on slaughter of cattle in India does not represent a classic case of protein waste in a poor community, but in fact is a needed protection of the cow, i.e., of agriculture. Cattle are so important for Indian agriculture that the no-slaughter rule is eminently feasible. Besides, cattle do not compete with humans for food; cows are scavengers in India, a useful niche anywhere. A 'naturally selected ecosystem' Harris calls this case, and the same could be said of the other instances in which the independent influence of religion on the economy has been reported. These range from pig-hating Middle Eastern cultures to pig-loving Melanesian tribes, from wife-beating Yanomamö to man-eating Aztec (Harris 1974). In all these cases the seemingly irrelevant taboos, the strange customs and curious practices stem from the ecology and on close inspection fit into the ecosystem. Of course a lively discussion resulted from Harris's somewhat simplistic all-encompassing theory building. Douglas (1973), of course, has a very different opinion on the origin of the pig taboo (see Jackson's paper); on the Indian case Harner gives at least a more balanced interpretation (1967). Whenever Harris draws heavily on one ethnographer, he usually is at odds with him, as with Rappaport (Melanesia, Tsembaga Maring, 1968) and Chagnon (Yanomamö, 1969). Harris's treatment of the classic Aztec material, is heavily disputed by Sahlins (1976). In Harris's view environmental depletion, lack of protein and population regulation are among the crucial factors influencing culture and religion, while the whole complex of warfare serves as an important cultural mechanism to cope with these problems. Sahlins (1976) argues that a culture is a symbolic system of meaning and should be understood in that way. Geertz, in a fascinating series of essays (1973), tries to bridge the two approaches. At the moment the discussions are in full swing. The dichotomy between cognitive and materialistic approaches centers on Harris and will not be resolved easily.

Bibliography

Baal, J. van (1947), *Over wegen en drijfveren der religie. Een godsdienstpsychologische studie.* Amsterdam: North-Holland.

— (1971), *Symbols for communication; religion in anthropological theory.* Assen: Van Gorcum.

— (1981), *Man's quest for partnership. The anthropological foundation of ethics and religion.* Assen: Van Gorcum.

Balandier, G, (1955), *Sociologie actuelle de l'Afrique noire. Dynamiques des changements sociaux en Afrique Centrale.* Paris: Presses Universitaires de France.

Beek, W.E.A. van (1978), *Bierbrouwers in de bergen. De Kapsiki en Higi van Noord Kameroen en Noord-Oost Nigeria.* Utrecht: Mededelingen Inst. voor Culturele Antropologie 12.

Beek, W.E.A. van (1979), 'Traditional religion as a locus of change,' in *Official and Popular religion; analysis of a thema for religious studies*: 514–543. eds. Vrijhof and Waardenburg. Den Haag: Mouton.

Binsbergen, W.M.J. van (1979), *Religious change in Zambia*. Dissertation Amsterdam University.

Binsbergen, W.M.J. van and Schoffeleers, J.W.M. (1981), *The social science of african religion: theoretical and methodological explorations*. (in press).

Burridge, K. (1969), *New heaven, new earth*. Oxford: Clarendon.

Castaneda, H.J.M. (1962), *The teachings of Don Juan: A Yaqui way of knowledge*. Los Angeles: University of California Press.

Chagnon, N. (1968), *The fierce people*. New York: Holt, Rinehart and Winston.

Cohen, Y. (1964), *The transition from childhood to adolescence. Cross-culture studies of initiation ceremonies, legal systems and incest taboos*. Chicago: Aldine.

Douglas, M. (1973), *Natural symbols; explorations in cosmology*. Harmondsworth: Penguin.

Du Bois, C. (1944), *The People of Alor*. Minneapolis: University of Minnesota Press.

Geertz, C. (1973), *The interpretation of cultures*. New York: Basic Books.

Gillin, J. (1948), 'Magical fright', *Psychiatry* 11: 387–400.

Gluckman, M. (1954), *Rituals of rebellion in South-East Africa*. Manchester: Manchester University Press.

Goodenough, W.H. (1966), *Cooperation in change*. New York: John Wiley and Sons.

Harner, R. (1969), 'Remarks on India's sacred cattle,' *Current Anthropology*, 222–245.

Harris, M. (1966), 'The cultural ecology of India's sacred cattle,' *Current Anthropology* 7: 51–66.

— (1968), *The rise of anthropological theory*. London: Routledge and Kegan Paul.

— (1974), *Cows, pigs, wars and witches*. New York: Random House.

— (1978), *Cannibals and kings. The origins of culture*. New York: Random House.

— (1979), *Cultural Materialism. The struggle for a science of culture*. New York: Random House.

Kardiner, A. and Linton, R. (1945), *The psychological frontiers of society*. New York: Columbia University Press.

Kennedy, J.G. (1973), 'Cultural Psychiatry', in *Handbook of Social and Cultural Anthropology*. J.J. Honigmann (ed), 1119–1199. Chicago: Honigmann.

Köbben, A.J.D. (1959), '*Profetische bewegingen als uiting van sociaal protest.*' *Sociologisch jaarboek* 13: 5–88.

La Barre, W. (1972), *The ghost dance. Origins of religion*. London: Allen and Unwin.

Lambert, W.W., Minturn, L., Trandis, M. and Wolf, N. (1959), 'Some correlates of beliefs in the malevolence and benevolence of supernatural beings: a cross-cultural study', *Journal of Abnormal and Social Psychology* 58: 162–169.

Lévi-Strauss, C. (1958), *Anthropologie structurale*. Paris: Plon.

Mille, R. de (1980), *The Don Juan papers: further Castaneda controversies*. Californian Ross Erikson Publ.

Moore, O.K. (1957), 'Divination—a new perspective.' *American Anthropologist* 59: 69–74.
Murdock, G.P. (1969), *Ethnographic Atlas*. Pittsburgh: University of Pittsburgh press.

Norbeck, (1963), African rituals of conflict. *American Anthropologist* 65: 1254–1279.

Rappaport, R.A. (1967), *Pigs for the ancestors. Ritual in the ecology of a New Guinea people.* New Haven: Yale University Press.
Redfield, R. (1968), *The primitive world and its transformation.* Harmondsworth: Penguin.

Sahlins, M. (1976), *Culture and practical reason.* Chicago: University of Chicago Press.
Schoffeleers, M. and Meijers, D. (1978), *Nationalism and economic action. Critical questions on Durkheim and Weber.* Assen: Van Gorcum.
Silverman, D. (1967), 'Shamans and acute schizophrenia.' *American Anthropologist* 69: 21–31.
Spiro, M.E. (1952), 'Ghosts, Ifaluk, and teleological functionalism,' *American Anthropologist* 54: 497–503.
Spiro, M.E. (1966), 'Religion: problems of definition and explanation,' in: *Anthropological Approaches to the Study of Religion.* ed. M. Banton, ASA 3: 85–126. London: Tavistock.
Spiro, M.E. and d'Andrade, R.G. (1958), 'A cross-cultural study of some supernatural beliefs.' *American Anthropologist* 60: 456–466.
Swanson, G.E. (1960), *The birth of the gods: the origin of primitive beliefs.* Ann Arbor: University of Michigan Press.

Turner, V.W. (1969), *The ritual process, structure and anti-structure.* Chicago: Aldine.

Vogt, E.Z. (1952), 'Waterwitching: an interpretation of a ritual in a rural American community,' *Scientific Monthly* 75: 175–186.

Wallace, A.F.C. (1966), *Religion. An anthropological view.* New York: Random House.
Werbner, R.J. (1977), *Regional Cults*, ASA 26, London: Tavistock.
Whiting, J.W.M. & Child, I.L. (1953), *Child training and personality: a cross-cultural study.* New Haven: Yale University Press.
Wilson, B.R. (1973), *Magic and the millennium. A sociological study of religious movements of protest among tribal and third world peoples.* London: Heinemann.

Young, F.W. (1962), 'The function of male initiation ceremonies: a cross-cultural test of an alternative hypothesis,' *American Journal of Sociology* 67: 379–396.
—(1965), *A cross-cultural study of status dramatization.* Indianapolis: University of Indiana Press.

The Authors

Wouter van Beek was born in 1943. He studied Cultural Anthropology at the University of Utrecht, Netherlands, and is presently associate professor at the Department of Cultural Anthropology of that University.

His research areas are: anthropology of religion, theory of cultural anthropology, and linguistic anthropology. He has done anthropological research among the Kapsiki and Higi on the border of North Cameroon and North Eastern Nigeria, and among the Dogon of Mali. His recent publications include *'Bierbrouwers in de bergen: de Kapsiki en Higi van Noord-Kameroen en Noordoost Nigeria'* (1978), *'Spiegel van de mens; religie en anthropologie'* (1982) and *'Masked dancers of West-Africa, the Dogon'* (1982). He contributed to and edited some collections of essays: *'Explorations into the anthropology of religion'* (1975), *'Symbool en betekenis'* (1979). At present he is doing a rehaul of Dogon ethnography.

Bert L. Hardin was born in 1939. He studied in the U.S.A. and in West Germany, and is presently employed in the Department of Sociology at the University of Tübingen. His research areas are: history of sociology, sociology of beliefs, and new religious movements. His recent publications include: 'Some Social Factors Affecting the Rejection of New Belief Systems' in: Eileen Barker (ed), *New Religious Movements: A Perspective for Understanding Society*, Edwin Mellon Press, N.Y., 1981 (with G. Kehrer), and 'Entstehen und Entwicklung der Vereinigungskirche in der Bundesrepublik Deutschland', in: G. Kehrer (ed.), *Das Entstehen einer neuen Religion: Das Beispiel der Vereinigungskirche*, Kösel Verlag, Munich, 1981 (with W. Kuner). At present he has a grant from the Volkswagen Foundation to document social science research in Germany during the allied occupation—1945–1949, and he is also studying the anti-cult movement in the Federal Republic of Germany.

Günter Kehrer was born in 1939. He studied Sociology, Social History and Social Ethics at Frankfurt and Tübingen, and obtained his Ph.D. in 1965. He is presently Professor of the Sociology of Religion at Tübingen University. His main fields of research include new religious movements in the 19th and 20th centuries and problems of religious organizations. He has more than fifty publications including: *Das religiöse Bewusstsein des Industriearbeiters*, 1967, and *Religionssoziologie*, 1968. He is presently editor of and contributor to *Zur Religionsgeschichte der Bundesrepublik Deutschland* (Kösel-Verlag, Munich 1980), and his is also editor of and contributor to *Das Entstehen einer neuen Religion: Das Beispiel der Vereinigungskirche* (Kösel-Verlag, Munich, 1981).

Michael Hill was born in Sheffield, England, in 1943. He read Sociology at the London School of Economics, 1962–65 (Hobhouse Memorial Prize, 1965) and at Wadham and Nuffield Colleges, Oxford 1965–67. He lectured at the London School of Economics, 1967–75 and got a London Ph.D. in 1971. He has been Professor of Sociology at Victoria University of Wellington, New Zealand since 1976. His books include *A Sociology of Religion* and *The Religious Order* (both Heinemann, 1973); he was Editor of *A Sociological Yearbook of Religion in Britain* (SCM Press, 1970–75); and Associate Editor of the *British Journal of Sociology*, 1975. He has various articles in journals—including *Social Compass* and *New Society*—and is currently researching and writing on religion in New Zealand.

Anthony Jackson (1926) is Senior Lecturer in Social Anthropology at the University of Edinburgh. He was educated at the universities of Cambridge and Gothenberg. His major work, *Na-Khi Religion* (1979), concerns a tribal minority in China who developed a unique pictographic writing to record their rituals. He has also written several articles on religion and allied topics. He is currently engaged in research on the Faroes besides editing some publications on the topic of Way of Life.

Jarich G. Oosten was born in Enschede, The Netherlands in 1945. He studied History of Religions, Philosophy and Cultural Anthropology at Amsterdam and Groningen. He is at present Senior Lecturer at the Department of Cultural Anthropology, University of Leyden. His main research interests are Arctic religions (*The Theoretical Structure of the Religion of the Netsilik and lglulik*, 1976) and mythology (articles in various journals). He has recently completed a study of the social organisation of Indo-European mythology (*The War of the Gods*, i.p.).

Frank Whaling read History and Theology at Cambridge and later lived for four years in India. After completing his Doctorate in Comparative Religion at Harvard in 1973 he became the co-ordinator of the religious studies programmes and degrees at Edinburgh University. He is Chairman of the Scottish Working Party on Religions of the World in Education. He has written or edited *A Dialogue between Hinduism and Christianity*, *The Rise of the Religious Significance of Rāma*, *The Wesleys* in the *Classics of Western Spirituality*, *The World's Religious Traditions: Current Perspectives in Religious Studies*, *Religions of the World*, and *Contemporary Approaches to the Study of Religion: The Humanities*. Forthcoming are: *Comparative Religion*, *Christian Theology and World Religions*, and *Think Globally or Perish*. He has also written a number of articles on many facets of religious studies. He has been a visiting professor at Dartmouth College, the Peking Institute for Research into World Religions, and Calcutta University, as well as lecturing at various other places around the world.

David M. Wulff holds an M.A. in experimental psychology and a Ph.D. in personality psychology from the University of Michigan. He is Professor of Psychology at Wheaton College, Massachusetts. His main writing and research have been in the area of psychology of religion. Forthcoming is his comprehensive work *Psychology of Religion: An Historical Introduction*.

Index of Names of Scholars

(Both indexes compiled by Frank Whaling)

General Index